W9-BFU-065

CONTENTS

FOREWORD TO THIRD EDITION

Of the thirteen chapters in this book, the first two, dealing with the mammals, were written by Professor J. L. Harrison, the rest by myself.

Although no territory now bears the name 'Malaya', this term and 'Malayan' are retained in the title and elsewhere to indicate, in a purely geographical sense, the Malay Peninsula and the islands off its coasts, including Singapore. The fauna of Malaysian Borneo or East Malaysia is similar to that of Malaya but by no means identical, and the incidence of animals in Borneo is not included in this book.

Illustrations of mammals are from drawings previously published in Professor Harrison's book *Mammals of Singapore and Malaya*. Dr. B. D. Molesworth drew the birds and the insect drawings (except Figs. 93 - 96) are by Rd. Goesti Abdulkadir. The rest are by myself. The plates are a new feature prepared for this edition and carry acknowledgements to the photographers.

M.W.F. TWEEDIE
January, 1970

vii

INTRODUCTION

To write a comprehensive Natural History of Malaya would be a task for a team of zoologists with years at their disposal; the results of their work, if ever published, would fill a book-case. An adequate account only of all those more common and conspicuous animals that a naturalist in Malaya is likely to meet could probably not be encompassed in one volume. This little book is no more than an introduction to our enormous fauna; its purpose to provide the young reader, uninstructed in natural history, and visitors from overseas, with a brief outline of how this fauna is constituted.

Only a small proportion of our animals have English names, and these names are often neither widely known nor very precisely applied. They are, moreover, only in use among English-speaking people. The Latin or scientific names have the great advantage that they are used by writers and speakers of all languages, and that they are designed to identify positively the animals to which they are applied. These are the names found printed in italics throughout the text of this book.

They are based on a system invented by a Swedish naturalist, Carl Linnaeus, two hundred years ago. By this system each species or "kind" of animal is known by two names, a specific name which identifies it precisely and a generic name which defines its closest relationship with other species. A group of animals included under one generic name is called a genus (plural genera); the word species is the same in singular and plural. The genus is put first, the species second, just as "John Smith" is printed "Smith, John" in a directory.

To illustrate this system of nomenclature let us take a familiar animal like our common Grey-bellied Squirrel. Its scientific name is *Callosciurus caniceps*. The first name indicates its close relationship to the Red-bellied Squirrel, *Callosciurus notatus*, the

Black-banded Squirrel, *Callosciurus nigrovittatus* and others which are placed in this genus. The second name, *caniceps*, completes its identification. Zoological classification goes further than this, grouping genera into families, families into orders, orders into classes and classes into phyla. All squirrels (including genera other than *Callosciurus*) are regarded as forming a family, the Sciuridae. This family is included in the order Rodentia or rodents, which includes many other familiar animals such as rats, mice and porcupines. The rodents are, of course, mammals and so form a division of the class Mammalia, which is included in the phylum Chordata. This is a very large group of animals comprising the mammals, birds, reptiles, fish and some other smaller divisions.

The Malays have lived in this country far longer, and in much closer association with nature, than any English-speaking people. Not every species of animal has been named by them, of course, but there is a large number of well-established and precisely allocated Malay names of animals, and it is necessary for a naturalist in this country, whatever his own language may be, to be familiar with them. Many readers will probably know the animals better under these names than by their English ones. An alphabetical list of Malay names with English and scientific equivalents is provided. References by number to this list are given in the general index to enable the reader to discover the Malay name of an animal from its English or Latin one.

Zoological terminology has been used as little as possible, but the use of some words that may be unfamiliar, or that are used in an unfamiliar sense, could not be avoided. A glossary of these is also printed at the end of the book.

Remember that the word "animal" is used in this introduction and throughout the book in its correct sense of a member of the animal kingdom, that is any living thing that is not a plant or a bacillus or some other kind of microbe.

CHAPTER ONE

MAMMALS

IT has been pointed out in the introduction of this book that the word "animal", correctly used, indicates the whole range of living creatures which are described in its pages. What most of us think of as animals, four-legged beasts covered with hair, such as cats, dogs and horses, are correctly termed mammals, and it is with the Malayan representatives of this group that this and the next chapter will be concerned.

It is one thing to give a general idea of what a word means, another to define it precisely. The mammals can be fairly satisfactorily defined by saying that they are warm-blooded animals which suckle their young with milk and whose bodies are wholly or partly covered with hair. It follows from this that we ourselves are mammals. All the Malayan mammals, and almost all elsewhere, bear their young alive. The only exceptions to this rule are certain primitive Australian forms which lay eggs, the Platypus and the Spiny Anteaters.

The term "warm-blooded" implies more than it says. In the mammals and birds the blood and the whole interior of the body is kept not only warm, but at a constant temperature which, normally, does not vary with that of the animal's surroundings. The warm coat of hair of a mammal (and the feathers of a bird) play a large part in making this possible. In all other animals the body temperature varies with its surroundings; a lizard or an insect is warm inside on a hot day and cool (and usually sluggish and inactive) on a cold one. Really the higher animals create an artificial climate inside their bodies which is kept constant no matter what the weather outside is like. Man has carried this mastery of his environment still further; he uses clothes to cover his body, suiting their thickness to the climate, and builds houses which can be heated in a cold climate and cooled, or "air-conditioned", in a hot one.

The fact that mammals bear their young alive, and that the parents and children remain together for some time after the latter are born, is another indication that they are among the highest animals in the evolutionary scale, for the young mammals can learn the more difficult arts of life from their parents. This is also true to some extent of birds, but in the great majority of the other, "lower" animals, parents and young never meet, and the animal receives no instruction beyond that of inherited instinct and the lessons of its own experience. In the case of solitary mammals parental instruction and personal experience are the beginning and the end of education, but those which go in herds or family groups continue to learn from each other's experience. You may catch one member of a troop of monkeys in a trap, but if the rest saw what happened that trap would never catch another of them.

Here again man has gone very much further than any of the other mammals. Through the medium of speech and reading we learn throughout our lives, not only from our parents nor even only from those whom we meet, but from people who live far away or who have died long before we were born.

Although some mammals, such as the squirrels, are active in the day, most of them are nocturnal, sleeping and resting during the day as we do at night. For this reason they are much less well-known and familiar to most people than are such creatures as birds and butterflies, which are mainly animals of the daytime. Moreover many Malayan mammals, especially the larger ones, are only found in jungle. Big beasts like elephants and tigers are a dangerous nuisance in well-populated country, and creatures like deer yield a handsome profit to people who hunt and kill them for food. When these larger beasts stray from their home in the jungle they are quickly hunted and shot by the most formidable and ruthless animal of all. If all the jungle were destroyed they would soon become extinct, and it is most necessary, if we are to preserve our magnificent fauna intact, to set aside large areas as reserves where the forest must not be felled and the animals must not be hunted. National Park (Taman Negara) and the other game reserves are a fine start in the right direction, but there is still plenty of room in Malaya for more natural sanctuaries.

From the point of view of our relations with them it is convenient to divide the mammals into two groups. The big ones which we know well from books and pictures, but which we seldom see for the reason given above, form one of these. The other comprises the multitude of small mammals, squirrels, rats, bats and the like, which we often see but know very little about. The remainder of this chapter will give an account of those groups of mammals which include mainly big animals, almost all dwellers in the jungle.

Biggest of all the land animals is the **Elephant.** There are now only two kinds of elephant living in the world, the African and the Asiatic. Ours belong, of course, to the latter species, which is found wild in southern Asia from India eastward to Indo-China, Malaya and Sumatra. The wild elephants of Borneo are thought to be not native, but to be descended from domesticated animals which escaped.

Elephants are by no means rare in the Malayan jungles and their great footprints, and other signs of their passing, are familiar to everyone whose business takes him into the forests. They go in herds and family groups formed of females and young animals. The old males lead a solitary life, visiting the herds occasionally. They live entirely on a vegetable diet; as an elephant may weigh three or four tons, the enormous quantities of this kind of food required to sustain it can well be imagined. They are destructive to cultivation and will sometimes wantonly attack the flimsy bamboo houses of the country people, or any other artificial structure they may encounter. It is difficult to scare or drive them away from a district which they choose to invade except by shooting one or more of the herd, and one of the less happy duties of the game wardens is to do this from time to time.

The teeth of an elephant are very peculiar. Inside the mouth only a single large molar tooth is present at any one time in each jaw. These teeth have a complicated structure of hard ridges set in softer material, and they work like files, grinding up the animal's food. When it wears out, each tooth is replaced by the next one in the row, which grows forward and pushes the old one out. The front teeth or incisors of the upper jaw have grown out to form the long tusks, which are usually developed in the male, less often in the female. They are used by the males mainly for fighting, but also for digging up roots and tubers.

The term **Ungulates** or **Hoofed Animals** is often used to comprise a large number of fairly big mammals whose finger and toe nails have become greatly enlarged and thickened for walking on, and whose actual fingers and toes, or digits, are always reduced in number below the primitive total of five seen on the feet of a lizard or on our own feet and hands. They are all herbivores or feeders on leaves and grass. There are two very distinct groups of hoofed mammals, the odd-toed ones and the even-toed. The study of fossils has shown that the two groups, though similar in appearance, are by no means closely allied, and for this reason zoologists have largely abandoned the term ungulate. It is a convenient one, however, and we will retain it, remembering that it does not designate a natural group of mammals in the scientific sense.

The odd-toed ungulates have the weight-bearing axis of the feet along the middle digit, so that reduction of their number produces the well-known single toe or hoof found in the horse. Three kinds of odd-toed ungulates, primitive relatives of the horse, are (or were) found in Malaya.

The **Malayan Tapir** (cover) is a most curious animal. Its nose is produced into a short trunk which just overhangs the mouth and the adult is quite startlingly coloured, black on the front part and limbs, white on the hinder part of the body, the pattern being sharply defined. In a zoo or a museum the beast looks very conspicuous, but in the irregular light and shade of the jungle scene the bold pattern effectively breaks up its outline and so conceals it. One sees a black patch or a white one, neither having the characteristic shape of a quadruped animal or any particular form that will attract attention. This principle in camouflage, known as the "disruptive pattern", is often applied in war-time to conceal large objects like buildings and ships. It seems to stand the tapir in good stead, for it is wholly defenceless against the attack of such an animal as a tiger, and yet remains common. Curiously enough the baby tapir is quite differently coloured, dark brown all over with numerous tawny spots and streaks. This affords camouflage on a different principle, as it directly simulates the effect of the sun-dappled leaves of the jungle floor.

Tapirs are seldom seen, but their three-toed footprints are often encountered by rivers and on muddy jungle paths.

The other two odd-toed ungulates are rhinoceroses. The **Two-horned** or **Sumatran Rhinoceros** (Fig. 1) is an animal of hilly jungle. It is rare nowadays but still fairly well established in the wilder parts of the country. The **One-horned** or **Javan Rhinoceros** is not known to exist in Malaya now and is an animal on the verge of total extinction throughout its range.

Fig. 1.   Sumatran Rhinoceros.

The existence of rhinoceroses everywhere is threatened by the enormous value as medicine placed by Chinese people on the horn, blood and other parts of these animals. It is a purely superstitious belief without any basis in fact, but if it persists there will soon be no rhinoceroses left alive. The horn or horns on the nose of the rhinoceros are wholly different in structure from those of other mammals, for they are formed of matted or consolidated hair.

In the even-toed ungulates the weight-bearing axis of the foot is between the third and fourth digits, so that reduction of their number finally produces two toes, forming a double or "cloven" hoof. Pigs, cattle, goats and deer are included in this group of mammals.

The **Common Wild Pig** is the only one of our larger mammals that can really take care of itself without any protection from the game laws. It is common in jungle and thrives also in scrub and on the fringes of cultivation, where it may be a serious pest, but it is wary, active and prolific enough to maintain itself against the guns, traps and even poison which are used against it. Young wild pigs are striped brown and buff, but, just as in the Tapir, the pattern soon disappears as the animal grows up. There is no real distinction between the wild and domesticated pig in Malaya, and they often interbreed.

Another larger species is the **Bearded Pig** which is lighter in colour and has two bushy tufts of hair on the snout. It seems to roam about the country in large herds which keep to deep forest and therefore are not often seen.

Wild cattle are represented in Malaya by the **Sĕladang** or **Gaur** (Plate 1). This is a magnificent beast, dark brown, almost black, with white "stockings", a whitish forehead and a high crest along the back over the shoulders, at which point it may stand over six feet in height. The young calves are light brown or fawn in colour. Sĕladang are found in herds in most of the heavily forested areas in Malaya and can usually be seen by visitors to the National Park. The bulls fight heroic battles with each other for mastery of the herd, but, unless wounded, are quite innocent of the reputation for ferocity with which some sensationally-minded people have endowed them.

The **Serow** is a beast resembling a large goat, which is found singly in hilly country. Its particular haunts are the steep limestone hills of northern and central Malaya.

The **Deer** differ from cattle and goats in having antlers instead of horns. Horns, which are usually borne by both sexes, are simple continuously growing spikes made of the same material as hoofs and claws; antlers, which are almost always borne by the male only (the arctic Reindeer being the only exception) are usually branched projections of bone which are shed and re-grown at intervals. They are used almost solely for fighting between the males. Two kinds of true deer are found in Malaya, the larger being the **Sambar** or **Rusa,** a beast with a wide distribution in Asia. It is a big animal, about four feet high at the shoulder, and is found in jungle, singly or in parties of two or three. These deer sometimes do damage by nibbling the bark of rubber trees and are a favourite prey of poachers as they yield a large quantity of excellent meat, which is acceptable to all the creeds and races of people living in Malaya.

The **Barking Deer, Muntjac** or **Kijang,** is much smaller, about the size of a goat, and the antlers are short and branch only once, forming a simple fork. The English name is taken from the call, which is made by both sexes and sounds rather like the bark of a dog.

The **Mouse Deer** or **Chevrotains** are not really deer, and have the distinction of being the smallest of all the hoofed mammals. They have no horns or antlers, rather rounded bodies and tiny slender hooves. Two very similar species occur in Malaya, the **Kanchil** or **Pĕlandok** and the slightly larger **Napoh.** The Pĕlandok stands only about eight inches high and is quite common in wooded country, surviving even in the remnants of jungle round the reservoirs on Singapore Island. The Napoh is rather less common, but it is not easy to distinguish the two species from the sort of fleeting glimpse which is all one generally gets of these creatures in the wild. In Malay fairy stories the Pĕlandok plays the same role as the famous Brer Rabbit of the stories from North America. He is the little fellow who gets the better of the bigger and stronger animals by superior cunning. It is a feature of human nature to admire this sort of character, and wherever they are, men invent stories in which it is personified.

The next order of mammals which we shall consider is the flesh-eaters or **Carnivores,** which includes such creatures as cats, dogs, civets and bears. Our largest and most formidable carnivore is, of course, the **Tiger.** Its appearance is too well known to need description, and its presence in inhabited areas always causes alarm which is by no means unjustified, for it will not hesitate to kill domestic animals and will sometimes attack man himself. A tiger is an immensely powerful beast for its size (the body is seldom more than five feet long) and is quite capable of killing a buffalo; even attacks on elephants are recorded. Its principal food in Malaya is, however, undoubtedly the common and destructive wild pig, and in killing these it certainly does good service. Most tigers will avoid men if they can, but an occasional one discovers that they are good to eat and extremely easy to catch and kill, and then there is trouble.

The **Leopard** or **Panther** is smaller than the Tiger, the body not more than four feet long. Typically leopards are tawny marked with black spots, each formed of a group of smaller spots in a ring; the markings look rather as if someone had put his finger-tips together, inked them and dabbed them all over the animal's coat. A form also occurs in which the coat is so dark that the spots scarcely show; this is the so-called **Black Panther,** and in Malaya is more common than the spotted form. It should be understood that these are simply colour variations of the same species; a family of leopard kittens may include black and spotted individuals. Panthers are less numerous than tigers in Malaya, but frequent more open country. They prey on mammals from the size of a pig downwards, and birds, and are fond of taking domestic goats, dogs and chickens. Unlike tigers they readily climb trees.

The **Clouded Leopard** (Fig. 2) is a little smaller than the Panther and far less common, being probably confined to jungle country in and north of Pahang. It is very beautifully marked; the face and legs are striped and spotted as in other cats, but the body is pale brown with large oval and oblong dark blotches, the space between them forming a light-coloured network. The Clouded Leopard has the reputation of being much less fierce and courageous than the Panther.

Fig. 2. Clouded Leopard.

Four kinds of **wild cats** are found in this country, the only common one being the **Leopard Cat** (Fig. 3). It is as big as a domestic cat, light brown with a pattern of simple black spots. It is a notorious chicken thief, and the kittens, though very pretty and engaging to look at, are quite impossible to tame. Of

Fig. 3. Leopard Cat.

the other species the **Golden Cat** and **Flat-headed Cat** are plain brown, the former nearly as big as a Clouded Leopard. The **Marbled Cat** has a light and dark pattern in the form of irregular lines and blotches. All these jungle cats can be distinguished from a domestic cat that has run wild by the shape of the ears, which are round, whereas pussy's are distinctly pointed.

The bear and dog families are each represented by only one species. The **Malay Bear** or **Honey Bear** (Fig. 4) is the smallest existing kind of bear, but fully grown ones are powerful and formidable animals nevertheless. It is black with a white V- or ring-shaped mark on the chest; the front legs are bandy and the claws very long and strong. These bears eat a wide variety of food, including all kinds of insects and their larvae, and they are extremely fond of the contents of a bees' nest,

Fig. 4. Malay Bear.

honey, grubs and all. Baby Malay Bears make attractive pets and are frequently kept by soft-hearted people. It is a mistake to keep them as they become dangerous long before they reach full size, and the problem of disposing of them is not easy to solve.

The **Sěrigala** or **Malay Wild Dog** is the same animal that is known as the Dhole or Red Dog in India. When fully grown they stand about eighteen inches high and are uniform reddish-brown in colour. They run in packs, which are small in Malaya, usually consisting of family groups of half a dozen or so, and will hunt and kill quite large animals, such as sambar. The aborigines have a distinctive breed of dog about half the size of a wild dog. This is certainly not derived from the Sěrigala, but has an ancestry in common with that of other domestic dogs. Domestication of the dog dates well back into the Stone Age and it is still uncertain what wild animal or animals were its forebears.

A group of fairly small carnivores, well represented in Malaya, is the **Civets,** of which we have eleven species. The true civets of the genus *Viverra* include the **Malay Civet** or **Tangalung**. The body is about two feet long, coloured grey with closely set black spots. The markings on the throat are distinctive, three parallel black stripes on a white ground. The larger **Indian Civet** is similarly marked, but the spots tend to run together in vertical stripes.

The **Palm Civets** or **Musangs** differ from the true civets in being adapted for climbing and living largely in trees. The **Common Musang** (*Paradoxurus hermaphroditus*) is a very common animal and is included in this chapter (which sets out to tell of large, seldom-seen jungle animals) only because it is convenient to treat all the carnivores together. It is found in forest but often lives also in garden trees, especially those with epiphytic ferns growing on them, and even takes up its abode among the rafters of houses, where it may be a noisy and smelly nuisance. The musang is about two feet long, grey with about five black stripes running down the back, and the flanks spotted with black. It lives on a mixed diet of fruit and small animals like rats and lizards. The **Three-striped Musang** (Fig. 5) which is confined to forest is very like the House Musang, but has only three stripes down the back. The male has a black face.

The **Masked Musang** (Fig. 6) is larger and uniform reddish-brown with black and white markings on the face, which give it its name. All the musangs make engaging pets when young, but this species is unusual in continuing to be gentle and tame after

Fig. 5. Three-striped Musang.

Fig. 6. Masked Musang.

it grows up. Less common is the **Binturong** or **Bear Civet**. It is brown with some white on the face, long fur and tufts of hair on the ears. Its tail is prehensile, that is to say it can curl it round a branch and hold on, a great help in climbing. It is the largest of the musangs and also the least carnivorous in habits, feeding mainly on fruit.

Other civets found in Malaya include the **Linsang,** a very pretty little animal, which resembles a cat not only in appearance but also in being able to sheath its claws, which no other civet can do. It is buff with broad black stripes running across the body, and is distinctly rare. The **Otter Civet** lives in water and although not related to the true otters has come to resemble them by reason of its living a similar sort of life, a process known as convergent evolution. It is very like an otter in appearance, but can be distinguished by the short tail, which is only about six inches long. It is a very rare animal.

All the civets have a strong and characteristic smell which, at its worst, can be very offensive. It is produced by glands near the anus and probably serves the purpose of enabling the animal to mark out a district or territory of its own and to recognise the presence in it of an intruder or trespasser of the same species. The unpleasantness of the smell may also protect the civet against attack by predators. In some mammals, notably the American Skunk, this feature has been developed to form a weapon of quite horrible effectiveness.

Closely allied to the civets are the **Mongooses,** of which three species occur in Malaya, none of them very commonly. They are short-legged, brownish-grey animals with a sharp pointed muzzle and inconspicuous ears. They prey on any small animals they can catch and are celebrated on account of their readiness to attack and kill snakes, venomous or otherwise.

The **Weasel family** includes the smallest of the carnivores. They are elongated, short-legged creatures, wholly predatory in their habits. The **Malay Weasel,** the **Yellow-throated Marten** and three kinds of otters represent this group of mammals in Malaya. The first is about eight inches long with a six-inch tail, pale brown above, yellowish-white below. The marten is larger, as big as a house musang, brown with a broad yellow or almost white patch on the throat.

The **Otters** are distinguished from most other mammals by their habit of swimming and spending most of their time in the water. They feed on fish, frogs and other water animals, and are such swift and agile swimmers that they can catch fish by open pursuit in their own element. They can be tamed if caught young and make most attractive pets, but they must be fed on fish. In rivers, including their upper reaches, the **Small-clawed Otter** is common, so called because its claws do not project and are almost invisible. The **Indian** or **Smooth Otter** is also found in rivers but lives along the sea shore, too. Of the two species mentioned this is the larger, with the body up to two feet long. The cry of an otter is a shrill whistle, the sort of call one would expect from a bird rather than a mammal.

It is now a matter of quite general knowledge that the **Cetaceans,** the **Whales, Dolphins** and **Porpoises,** are mammals and not fish. A number occur in the seas surrounding our country, and they can be included in this chapter, for they are large beasts and most of them seldom seen.

The **Blue Whale** or **Sibbald's Rorqual** ranges the seas of the world, and a young one was stranded on the coast of Malacca in 1892. Its skeleton is now in the Raffles Museum. It is seldom realised how huge the great whales are. They are by far the biggest creatures that have ever lived on the earth; a mature blue whale weighs as much as thirty or forty elephants. This, and perhaps the **Sperm Whale,** are the only two big whales that swim in our seas.

Of the small cetaceans the **Common Dolphin** is by far the most abundant and is familiar to everyone who has sailed or travelled in our coastal waters. It grows to seven or eight feet, is grey in colour and the mouth has the form of a narrow beak. Dolphins usually swim in shoals, sometimes of several hundred individuals, and are wonderfully swift and active, and enjoy challenging the speed of fast, power-driven boats. The name dolphin is usually applied to the beaked, small cetaceans, the round-headed ones being called porpoises. Unfortunately, not all the established names follow this convenient division; the **Irawaddi Dolphin,** which is found in river estuaries in our area, is round-headed. Rather similar to it, but lacking the dorsal fin, is the **Finless Black Porpoise,** also a dweller in river mouths. Both these appear black in the sea, as does also the **Indian Pilot Whale,** a large porpoise of fifteen to sixteen feet with a wide range in the Indian Ocean. Shoals of these animals will sometimes deliberately and suicidally strand themselves on the shore, where they die slowly, groaning distressfully.

The cetaceans provide a very remarkable instance of adaptation to a completely marine existence of animals whose remote ancestors must certainly have been dwellers on the land. The normal mammalian covering of hair has almost disappeared, being represented only by a few bristles on the snout and jaws. The hind limbs have gone, but the characteristic mammalian arm and hand can be clearly made out in the skeleton of the flippers. The tail has the form of a fish's tail but is set horizontally, enabling the animal to rise quickly to the surface to breathe, and the nostrils or nostril (in some it is single) are on top of the head, an adaptation to the same end. All of them live on animal food: sperm whales and all the smaller cetaceans actively pursue their prey in the water; the other large whales live on plankton, straining it out of the water by means of a special sieve-like apparatus in their mouths.

Fig. 7.   Dugong.

Another mammal adapted to living entirely in the sea is the **Dugong** (Fig. 7). As in the cetaceans, the fore limbs have the form of flippers or paddles, the hind limbs have disappeared and the tail has the same resemblance to a horizontally disposed fish-tail. Here the likeness ends, and the Dugong is more recognisably a mammal than is a whale or a porpoise. It is not in any way related to the cetaceans, nor to the seals, which it also somewhat resembles in appearance. Unlike either of them it is herbivorous, feeding on seaweeds. It is a heavy, clumsy animal, about eight feet long, and lives in shallow water along the coasts and in estuaries. Once common, it has now become rare because it has been persecuted for its meat and hide.

(J.A. Hislop)

Plate 1.   Herd of Sĕladang

(J.L. Harrison)

Plate 2.   Pangolin

(*J.L. Harrison*)

Plate 3.   Young Pig-tailed Macaque

(J.L. Harrison)

Plate 4. Shrew-faced Ground Squirrel

CHAPTER TWO

MAMMALS (*Continued*)

MOST of the mammals left for consideration in this chapter are animals which we see fairly often, but in many cases have little precise knowledge of what they are. The majority of them are small because, as we have seen, big animals must keep out of the way of men if they are to survive. Of some of the groups of small mammals, such as the bats, rats and squirrels, we can only give an incomplete account as the Malayan species are rather numerous.

It has been pointed out that man is himself a mammal. The order to which we belong, from the point of view of zoological classification, is called the Primates, a word which implies that it comprises the first or highest of the animals. In it are included also the apes, monkeys, lemurs, lorisids and tree-shrews. Although no clear distinction is made in everyday speech between an ape and a monkey, these terms, correctly used, do designate two distinct groups of primates.

The **Apes** are our nearest relatives among the animals, and so few species live in the world today that we can spare the space to mention them all. They are the Gorilla and Chimpanzee of Africa, the Orangutan or Mias of Sumatra and Borneo and the gibbons of eastern Asia. Three of the gibbons are found in Malaya. The commonest one is the **White-handed Gibbon** or **Wak-wak** (Fig. 8), which is the species commonly kept as a pet, and which can be heard loudly and musically shouting in almost any fair-sized patch of forest. The **Dark-handed Gibbon** is about the same size but much less common. Both species vary in the colour of the fur from almost white to almost black, just as humans vary from blonde to brunette. A black gibbon is easy to identify because a wak-wak would have white hands and feet; the pale individuals of both species have hands and feet coloured much as the body (a little paler in the wak-wak), and so

Fig. 8. White-handed Gibbon.

are hard to distinguish. Our third gibbon is the much larger black **Siamang**; it has a pouch of skin under its chin which is blown up when the animal makes its very powerful booming call. Siamangs are by no means rare in hilly jungle.

All the gibbons are wonderfully agile climbers and swing among the branches by their long arms. In the wild they seldom come down to the ground, where they can only run awkwardly, holding up their arms to balance themselves.

Monkeys are distinguished from apes by their lower intelligence and by possessing a tail. Five species are found in Malaya. By far the commonest is the **Long-tailed Macaque** (pronounced "makak") or **Kĕra,** the bold and familiar greyish-brown monkey of the Singapore Botanic Gardens and the Lake Gardens at Kuala Lumpur. In such places these monkeys are an attraction to visitors but a nuisance to the authorities, as rare plants have to be expensively enclosed to protect them from the animals' destructive hands. The kĕra is found everywhere in the lowlands, even in mangrove swamp, where they can be seen hunting crabs on the mud. In fact one of the names that has been given to this monkey is "crab-eating macaque", but it is not generally descriptive of the animal's habits and is best discarded.

The **Pig-tailed Macaque** or **Berok** (Plate 3) is larger and reddish-brown, and the tail is short and curly. It is common but does not frequent inhabited areas so openly as the kĕra does. It is kept as a domestic animal by the country Malays and trained to gather fruit, particularly coconuts, working with a collar attached to a long cord. A big bĕrok is a formidable and dangerous animal; in the wild he is quite ready to dispute the path with a man and domesticated ones should be treated with great caution. Both kinds of macaque will eat almost anything, fruit, leaves, insects, birds' eggs and their nestlings, nothing comes amiss. It follows from this that they are easy to feed in captivity, but they are not to be recommended as pets. The běrok grows dangerously large and a tame kěra is almost always destructive and untrustworthy. They frequently escape or are released by people who no longer want them. Such monkeys have no fear of man and may be a serious nuisance; there are instances of their entering houses and attacking children.

Fig. 9. Dusky Leaf Monkey.

The other three kinds of monkeys are **Leaf Monkeys** or **Langurs.** They differ from the macaques in having longer tails, longer hair and in eating only leaves. The hair on the head is particularly long and often stands up, looking like a cap. The commonest species is the **Banded Leaf Monkey,** which is grey or black with the inside of the limbs white. The **Dusky Leaf Monkey** (Fig. 9) lacks this feature and is further distinguished by having conspicuous white skin round its eyes and mouth. The **Silvered Leaf Monkey** has the hairs of its grey fur tipped with white. The last is a very local animal and confined in Malaya to the west coast between Province Wellesley and Malacca. The leaf monkeys seldom descend to the ground, and they are not easy to keep in captivity owing to the difficulty of providing them with suitable food. Although their tails are so long they seem to put them to no use at all; none of our monkeys use their tails in climbing, as the Binturong does.

Only one kind of lorisid occurs in Malaya, the **Slow Loris** or **Kongkang** (Fig. 10). This is a quaint-looking little animal about

Fig. 10. Slow Loris.

the size of a small cat with thick fawn-coloured hair, a very short tail and large eyes; it looks rather like a child's teddy bear come to life. Its movements are extremely slow and deliberate, it never jumps and will not let go of one branch until it has a firm grip on another. It feeds on fruit, eggs and small creatures like lizards and insects, which it catches by an unexpectedly quick grab with one of its hands. As its large eyes suggest, it is nocturnal in its habits. In captivity they can be fed on fruit and insects, but remember that they do not like being picked up by a hand under the body, and will bite if so handled. A pet loris must be allowed to walk onto your hand or arm.

Fig. 11. Flying Lemur.

True lemurs are found only in Madagascar; the so-called **Flying Lemur** or **Cobego** (Fig. 11) is not a lemur, it is not even a primate. Its relationship with the other mammals is, in fact, very obscure, and it is generally included in a separate order of its own, the Dermoptera or "skin-wings". It is about a foot in length with fairly long legs and a medium-length tail, all of which are enclosed in a membrane of skin which stretches from the fore feet to the hind feet and thence to the tip of the tail. Body and membrane are covered with soft fur, brown in the adult male, greyish in the female and young. The animal is almost helpless on the ground but entirely at home in the trees, where it either hangs from the underside of a branch, looking like a large dead leaf, or flattens itself against the trunk of a tree and simulates a patch of lichen. If it is threatened by an enemy or wishes to go to another tree it dives into the air and spreads its legs so that the membrane acts as a parachute, enabling it to perform a controlled glide. At the end of the glide, it lands on the trunk at which it aimed, at a point well below the level at which it took off, and climbs to a safe height again. It has no power to propel itself in the air or rise above its point of take-off, as a bat or a bird does, and so cannot really be said to fly. It feeds entirely on leaves and is extremely difficult to keep alive in captivity.

There are quite a number of these gliding animals in Malaya. We shall soon be describing the flying squirrels and later on flying lizards and even snakes and frogs. They are clearly creatures adapted to live in dense, continuous forest where an animal endowed with this limited power of flight can travel indefinitely without ever descending to the ground. Their presence is evidence that this type of vegetation has persisted in our part of the world for an immense period of time.

Very different in appearance and habits from the other primates are the **Tree Shrews**, which look so like squirrels that most people will fail to distinguish them. In the tree shrews the snout is long and pointed and the teeth numerous and needle sharp, wholly different from the chisel-like "rodent" teeth of a squirrel. Other points of distinction are the presence in the tree shrews of an oblique buff stripe on the shoulder and the fact that no hairs project on the under-side of the tail, so that it looks flat below. Two kinds occur in Malaya, the **Greater** and the **Lesser Tree Shrew,** which are respectively about eight and six inches long with a similar length of tail; the latter is shown at Fig. 12. In spite of their name they spend much of their time on the ground, and they feed on fruit and insects.

Fig. 12. Lesser Tree Shrew.

Allied to them is the rare and curious little **Pen-tailed Shrew.** This animal is about four inches long, greyish-brown with large eyes and ears. The tail is much longer than the body, naked in its nearer half and covered towards the tip with long white hairs which project on each side, so that the whole tail looks rather like a feather or an old-fashioned quill pen. Unlike the tree shrews the pen-tailed shrew is nocturnal and lives in trees, and it is very seldom seen.

The tree shrews were formerly included in the Insectivora, but are now regarded as very primitive primates, representatives of the early type of mammal from which the lemurs, monkeys, apes and ourselves, are descended.

The **Insectivores,** so called because they are mainly insect-eating mammals, include the shrews and tree shrews, the mole, and the moon rat, which is really a very large shrew. The **House Shrew** or **Musk Shrew** is a little creature five or six inches long, often mistaken for a rat. Its short tail, long pointed snout and strong musky smell distinguish it and, if it is closely examined, its numerous tiny needle-like teeth will finally settle its identity. It is found only in human dwellings and is not really a Malayan animal but has been brought here from India in ships, and has spread in this way as far east as Japan. Apart from its smell, which may be offensive to some people, it is not in any way objectionable: it does not invade our houses to steal our food, as rats do, but lives by hunting cockroaches. Its smell makes it distasteful to predatory animals: cats will often kill house shrews but will never eat them.

The **Short-tailed Shrew** is an obscure little forest animal, not unlike the house shrew in size and shape but brown and with a tail barely half an inch long; little is known of its habits. A number of similar but smaller shrews are also found in forest. The **Moon Rat**, biggest of all the shrews, is a foot long and is a most strange-looking creature. It is covered with long, coarse hair, black on the body, with large white patches on the face, white feet and the tail half black and half white; the nose is long and pink. It is found by forest streams and feeds on fish, which it catches at night. It has a particularly foul smell and its rather conspicuous coloration may serve as a warning that here is an animal which nothing can eat and which is best left alone. The **Malay Mole** is only known from the Cameron Highlands but presumably occurs elsewhere at high altitudes. It looks like a rather large shrew, velvety black, with the enormous spade-like front feet with which these animals burrow so fast that they almost swim through the earth.

The **Bats** are at the same time the most numerous and least well known of our mammals. Of a total of nearly two hundred mammals recorded from Malaya over one third are bats, and it is most probable that there are species yet to be discovered. They are the only mammals that really fly, and their wings consist of a thin double layer of skin stretching from the shoulders over the arms and fingers, down to the ankles and usually including the tail. The thumb is not included in the wing but is used for clinging and climbing, being armed with a claw for this purpose. When at rest bats almost always hang upside down by the claws of the hind feet. All of them fly at night and most of the smaller ones feed on insects, which they catch in flight. They have not good eyesight (but are not blind) and the insectivorous bats locate their prey, and avoid obstacles in flight, by a most extraordinary method which depends ultimately on their sense of hearing. While it is flying the bat is constantly sending out very high-pitched sounds, of the order of 50,000 vibrations a second, and so far beyond the limits of our sense of hearing. It makes short bursts of these sounds and listens for the echo from nearby objects, and is able in this way to locate them very exactly. The method is similar to the device known as Radar, which uses electromagnetic waves in the same way, and so it has come to be called "bat-radar". As a matter of fact it is even closer to the Sonar method of detecting submarines, in which sound waves are sent out from the bottom of a ship and the echo recorded.

During the day most bats shelter in caves, hollow trees, roof spaces in houses and similar places. In some of the caves in limestone hills in Malaya thousands of bats have roosted day after day for thousands of years, and the floors are deeply covered with guano which the rice cultivators eagerly dig out to fertilise their fields. The young are usually born one at a time and are carried about by the mother, clinging to her fur.

Bats are classified in two distinct groups, the **Fruit Bats** and the **Insect-eating Bats.** Both in maximum and in average size the former are the larger. Largest of all the bats are the **Flying Foxes,** the bigger and commoner species, *Pteropus vampyrus*, having a wing span of four or five feet. They can frequently be seen in the evening flying with slow wing beats, like those of a crow, from their roosting to their feeding grounds, probably an orchard, where they will scramble for fruit and quarrel noisily through the night. They roost in trees in the open. The **Common short-nosed Fruit Bat** is the species that so often resorts to the eaves and roof spaces of houses for shelter. They are rather a nuisance because they make a mess on the floor below, and they sometimes fly about the room at night, bewildered by the light and causing alarm to nervous ladies. The fur of this bat is brown, the wings dark brown with the skin over the finger bones paler. The wings span about nine inches.

The species of fruit bats number about a dozen, all the rest being members of the insectivorous group. These are far too numerous to allow any review of the species to be made here. One of the largest is the **Hairless Bat** (*Cheiromeles torquatus*), an unpleasant looking creature, about six inches long, quite black, almost entirely naked and with a peculiar and rather offensive smell. It has a pouch on each side of the body in which it is believed to carry its young. The **False Vampires,** which rather resemble certain American bats called vampires, are known to take small birds as prey, and the **Horseshoe Bats** have peculiar structures of skin growing on their faces which makes them, by our standards, fantastically ugly. Smallest of all are some species of the genus *Tylonycteris*, with the body an inch and a half long. One of these, the **Bamboo Bat** (*T. robustula*) roosts in the day inside hollow bamboos. To enable them to crawl in and out of the narrow slits in the partly broken bamboos the whole animal, including the skull, is flattened to a remarkable degree.

Before we leave the insect-eating mammals we must mention the **Pangolin** or **Scaly Anteater** (Plate 2). It is not related to any other Malayan mammal and to look at it one would suppose it to be some kind of lizard, for the whole visible part of its body is covered with overlapping scales. Closer inspection shows that it has hair on the belly and between the scales, which are themselves composed of consolidated hair as is a rhinoceros' horn. When alarmed it rolls into a ball with the head in the centre or crouches, with the head between the fore legs, and digs down into the ground with its claws. It cannot bite as it has no teeth, and the mouth can only be opened a little way. The tongue is long and thin and is used to lick up the ants and termites on which the animal solely feeds. The front claws are very large and strong and are used in burrowing and tearing down the hard earth of termites' nests, never, apparently, as weapons. They do, however, make the animal capable of fighting its way out of any ordinary box in which it is confined. Although it lives in a burrow it is quite a good climber, and the young is carried about clinging to its mother, often riding on her tail.

All the rest of the mammals that we shall describe belong to the order called **Rodents**, a word meaning "gnawing animals", which are clearly characterised by the arrangement of the teeth. The two front teeth (incisors) in each jaw are shaped like chisels, are hard in front and softer at the back and continue to grow throughout the animal's life. The upper and lower teeth meet and wear against each other, the back wearing faster so that a sharp edge is maintained. Between these teeth and the molars or grinding teeth in the cheek is a gap, the eye teeth or canines being absent. The front teeth are designed for chiselling away hard substances, which are then ground up between the molars. The rodents are a very large and successful group of animals and include almost all the mammals, apart from his own species, which are to be accounted serious enemies of man.

They can be said to have taken two main lines of evolution: the ground-dwelling forms—the rats and porcupines—which are active at night; and the tree-dwelling rodents, typified by the squirrels, which are active in the day. There are a few exceptions to this grouping, such as tree rats and ground squirrels.

Fig. 13.   Common Porcupine.

There are three species of porcupine in Malaya. The **Common Porcupine** (Fig. 13) is a thick-set animal, about two feet long, with the back and hinder parts covered by long hollow sharp-pointed spikes called quills, which are really greatly enlarged hairs. Normally these lie along the body, but when the porcupine is alarmed they are erected and stand out in all directions, a very effective defence. The tail is only about two inches long and is quite hidden by the quills. This is a fairly common animal, probably most abundant in limestone hill country, where it shelters in the caves; elsewhere it lives in burrows. In cultivated country it may be a pest of such crops as pineapples. Porcupines live mainly on a vegetable diet but are very fond of gnawing bones. Even the tusks of an elephant which has died in the jungle are soon destroyed by them, a remarkable instance of the efficiency of rodent teeth.

The smaller **Brush-tailed Porcupine** is fairly common in forest. It is about a foot and a half long and the quills are quite short; the tail projects well beyond them and is tipped with a brush of curiously flattened hairs. The **Long-tailed Porcupine** is quite small, the size of a large rat, and has short spines and a fairly long tail which also has a brush of hairs, but they are not flattened.

The **Bamboo Rat** is rather over a foot long with a six-inch tail and ginger yellow fur. The incisor teeth are yellow and very large, so that the animal can never really close its mouth. It lives in burrows in the forest where bamboo is growing and probably feeds mainly on the young bamboo shoots, but will eat sweet potatoes in captivity.

We come now to the true rats. It will be convenient to divide them, according to their habitat, into house rats, field and garden rats and forest rats. The former are to be regarded always as pests and may be a serious or even dangerous nuisance, the field rats are sometimes pests of agriculture, the forest rats have little or no contact with man and are harmless.

The **Norway Rat** occurs only as an introduced animal in sea-port towns such as Singapore, Port Swettenham, and Penang. This is the so-called "Brown Rat" of Europe, but as we have many kinds of brown-coloured rats in Malaya the name is not suitable for use here. Norway rat is derived from the scientific name, *Rattus norvegicus*. The name perpetuates a scientific error, for the animal has no particular connection with that country. It is about eight inches long and can be distinguished from all other house rats by its tail which has the under-surface rather paler than the upper.

The **Malaysian House Rat,** which is about six inches long, is the only one of the rather numerous forms of *Rattus rattus* to be found in Malayan houses. This is the rat which is common on ships, whence the name Ship Rat, while a black form, common in Europe has given the name Black Rat to the whole species, although most forms are brown. The house form is distinguished from the others by its dull brownish-grey belly. Another rat which occurs commonly in houses, but also in scrub and grass land, is the **Little Burmese Rat,** which is three or four inches long without the tail, and a third, the **House Mouse,** usually less than three inches. These three house pests are similar in colour and can be distinguished only by size.

Two others allied to *Rattus rattus*[1] are classed as field rats. The **Malaysian Field Rat** or **Ricefield Rat** lives in *lalang* grass and ricefields and has the belly silvery grey. The **Malaysian Wood Rat** is found in gardens and rubber and oil palm estates, and becomes a pest in the latter; in this form the belly is white. The third field rat is the **Lesser Bandicoot Rat** which is found in Malaya only in the north west, in Kedah and Perlis and on Penang Island. It lives in ricefields and is rather like a large house rat, up to ten inches long, with the tail only three quarters the length of the body. It makes very extensive burrows.

Fig. 14. Long-tailed Giant Rat.

Of the forest rats we can only give a brief account. **Müller's Giant Rat** is common in lowland forest; it is eight to ten inches long with a buff or yellowish belly and black tail. The **Long-tailed Giant Rat** (Fig. 14) is about the same size but the tail is very long, about fifteen inches, and white below and at the tip. The fur is bright brown above, pure white below. In similar country are to be found the **Spiny Rats,** which have stiff hairs mixed with the fur of the back, and fairly short tails which are white underneath. The spines are not easily seen, but are felt if the fur is stroked from tail to head. There are several species of which the **Rajah Spiny Rat,** about seven inches long, and **Whitehead's Rat,** about five inches long, are typical.

In the mountain forest these lowland species are replaced by others. **Bower's Giant Rat** is one of these; it is grey on the back, white below and at the tip of the tail, and is unusual in being

[1] The three forms of the *Rattus rattus* group are: Malaysian House Rat, *R. r. diardii;* Malaysian Field Rat, *R. r. argentiventer;* Malaysian Wood Rat, *R. r. jalorensis.*

always perfectly tame, even when freshly caught.

The forest rats we have described are all ground dwellers. There is also a number of species of tree rats. One of the commonest is the **Dark-tailed Tree Rat,** four or five inches long, brown with a creamy white belly, black tail and spines in its fur like the spiny rats. The **Pencil-tailed Tree Mouse** is a little fellow about three inches long, brown above, white below, with a black tail having a pointed brush of hair at its tip. It lives inside the stems of bamboos, gnawing a hole to the outside and often making holes through several of the partitions or "nodes," and so making itself a house with several rooms. When your eye is trained to notice the outside hole it is easy to catch the mice by plugging this up and then cutting out the section of stem with them inside it. But although they are pretty they do not make good pets as they sleep all day and quarrel among themselves.

The **Squirrels** are animals of the day and so frequently seen. They are found in Malaya in great variety, many are handsomely and distinctively coloured, and their active and graceful movements among the trees are delightful to see. Watching squirrels can, in fact, be combined with bird watching as described in the next chapter. Although we cannot give a complete account of the Malayan squirrels we consider there is a good case for devoting rather more space to them than to the other small mammals; they will, accordingly, occupy the rest of this chapter.

The most familiar of them are the medium-sized tree squirrels of the genus *Callosciurus*, some of which are very frequently seen in gardens and estates and among coconut palms. In central and northern Malaya the **Grey-bellied Squirrel** is the common garden species. It is brown above and grey below without any other markings, and often draws attention to itself by its loud alarm call, "*tak, tak, tak,*" each "*tak*" accompanied by a jerk of the whole body. This species is not found south of Malacca, and in Johore and Singapore its place is taken by the **Common Red-bellied Squirrel,** which has the belly reddish with a black and buff stripe along each side between the lower red and upper brown colour. It is not confined to the south and at the level of Kuala Lumpur is about as common as the grey-bellied species. In forest a third species, the **Black-banded Squirrel**, is found. It has the same stripe on the sides, buff above and black below, as the last one, but the belly is grey, not red. The **Mountain Red-bellied Squirrel,** which is seen in the hill stations above about 3,500 feet, is brown above and red below, but without the particoloured lateral stripe. To avoid confusion let us repeat the characters of these four in tabular form:

A.   Grey-bellied squirrels.
   1.   No black-and-buff stripe along the sides; lowland garden squirrel of north and central Malaya. **Grey-bellied Squirrel** (*Callosciurus caniceps*).
   2.   A black-and-buff stripe along each side; inhabits lowland forest. **Black-banded Squirrel** (*C. nigrovittatus*).
B.   Red-bellied squirrels.
   3.   A black-and-buff stripe along each side; lowland garden squirrel most common in south Malaya. **Common Red-bellied Squirrel** (*C. notatus*).
   4.   No black-and-buff lateral stripe; found only in the mountains. **Mountain Red-bellied Squirrel** (*C. erythraeus*).

Three more species of *Callosciurus* must be mentioned. The very beautiful **White-striped** or **Prevost's Squirrel** is rather larger than the ones described above and has the back and tail glossy black, the belly and legs bright chestnut red, and between the two a broad pure white stripe from the nose to the base of the tail. It is mainly a forest animal, but occurs also in oil palm and coconut plantations, sometimes commonly enough to earn the dislike of the planters, for it feeds on the fruit of both. The **Slender Little Squirrel** (*Callosciurus tenuis*) is small, the body only four or five inches long, and looks rather like a young grey-bellied squirrel, but is buff rather than grey below and the tail is more slender and thinly haired. It can be confused with the Lesser Tree Shrew, but has the typical blunt squirrel's head. It is seen in forest, scrub and cultivated areas, but not in gardens. In hill stations this squirrel is replaced by the **Striped Little Squirrel** (*C. mcclellandi*), of very much the same size and shape, but with a series of yellowish stripes separated by black lines down the back.

We come now to the **Giant Squirrels** (genus *Ratufa*) of which there are two. They are very large, body and tail together well over two feet, and live high in the trees in forest country, leaping twenty feet or more from tree to tree and rarely descending to the ground. The **White-thighed Giant Squirrel** is usually yellowish-white in colour though it may be darker, but it always has a pale band on the outside of the thigh and is pale on the under side of the tail. The **Black Giant Squirrel** is always black above and orange or buff below without any paler markings.

The **Flying Squirrels** have been mentioned when we described the flying lemur. Their gliding apparatus is of the same kind, but ends posteriorly near the base of the tail, not at its tip; also the membrane is spread more widely in front by being attached to a sideways projection from the wrist, which is really one of the wrist bones elongated like an extra finger. They fall sharply into two groups, the giant flying squirrels and the smaller kinds.

The **Giant Flying Squirrels** are as large as the giant squirrels (*Ratufa*) and, like them, inhabit the tree tops or jungle canopy. When in "flight" they are among the most spectacular of all our animals, and in steep, hilly country, have been observed to cover a distance of 400 to 500 yards in a single glide. Their tails are longer than the body and bushy like that of an ordinary squirrel. The **Black Giant Flying Squirrel** is almost black all over, the belly a little paler. The **Red Giant Flying Squirrel** is bright reddish-brown above and orange coloured below, and the third species, the **Spotted Giant Flying Squirrel**, is similar, but the fur is spotted and flecked with white. All three are rather rare and seldom seen and are said to be largely nocturnal; they are, however, sometimes active in the daytime.

Fig. 15. Dark-tailed Flying Squirrel.

The smaller flying squirrels number about half a dozen species. None of them is common and they are active only at night, and very little is known of them. They all have the hairs of the tail projecting only sideways, so that it is flattened like a feather, and no doubt assists the flying membrane in giving support in the air. They feed on soft fruits and leaves and are said to make gentle and confiding pets. One of the species, the **Dark-tailed Flying Squirrel,** is shown at Fig. 15.

All the squirrels so far described are arboreal, that is to say they live above the ground in the trees. There remain a few species of ground squirrels.

Fig. 16. Striped Ground Squirrel.

The **Striped Ground Squirrel** (Fig. 16) is of medium size with a short tail, brown above, pale buff below. Along the back there are three parallel black stripes. This squirrel is confined to forest, but is not rare. Its call is a tremolo whistle with a falling note; it has been described as very like that with which a referee ends a football match. The **Red-cheeked Squirrel** is found in the mountains. It is olive brown above, grey, flecked with white, below, and the underside of the tail is chestnut brown. A reddish patch on each cheek gives it its name. The **Shrew-faced Ground Squirrel** (Plate 4) is a curious little animal which differs from all other squirrels in living on a diet of insects. Its snout is long, like a shrew's, and its teeth, although recognisably rodent's teeth, are modified for its peculiar diet. It is brown above, buff or white below, and would be difficult to distinguish from a tree shrew were it not for its short bushy tail, very different from the rather long sparsely haired tails of those animals. The habits of the tree shrews and of this squirrel are really very similar.

CHAPTER THREE

BIRDS

ONLY the most unobservant and insensitive of people can fail to appreciate the beauty and charm of birds, but to derive the full pleasure from observing them one must learn a little about them, what kind of animals they are and the species one can expect to see in various types of country.

The birds are a very clearly defined group; there is never any doubt whether an animal is a bird or not. They resemble the mammals in being warm-blooded, that is to say their body temperature is kept at a constant level, usually considerably higher than that of their surroundings. It is this fact that enables the mammals and birds to maintain a higher level of nervous and mental activity than any other animals. All birds have a covering of feathers, reproduce by laying eggs with a hard or brittle shell and lack teeth in the jaws. The two last features are shared by some reptiles, but no other animals possess feathers or anything at all closely resembling them.

Birds have been derived, in the course of evolution, from reptiles. Any one who doubts this should consult an encyclopaedia for an account of the fossil bird called *Archaeopteryx*. This creature lived about a hundred and forty million years ago, and a more perfect and convincing link between the reptiles and birds could hardly be imagined. It had wings and was covered with feathers (marvellously preserved in the fine-grained stone of a German slate quarry) but had the toothed jaws and long flexible tail of a lizard.

The vast majority of birds can fly and they excel all other animals in their mastery of the air. Their often brilliant plumage and surprising gift of song, and the wonderfully ingenious nests which they construct in which to brood and cherish their eggs and young, have excited the admiration of humanity from earliest times. More naturalists now concern themselves with the study of birds than with any other animals, and in all civilised countries laws are enforced to protect birds from wanton destruction, and rare species from extinction.

The **classification of birds** is based mainly on anatomical characters difficult for the naturalist who is not a specialist in ornithology to appreciate. The "highest" group, from the evolutionary point of view, are the so-called Passerine birds, of which the sparrow is a typical member, and from whose name in Latin, *Passer*, the word is derived. In Malaya, and in fact throughout the world, nearly half of the birds belong to this group. Those of the other half are classified into a number of orders of equal rank with the Passerine order, but, of course, containing far fewer species; these will be grouped together here as "non-passerine" birds. From this convenient, if rather unscientific, arrangement three categories can be separated: (1), sea birds, water birds and Waders (all non-passerines); (2), non-passerine birds of the land; (3), the Passerine birds. On this division into three this and the next two chapters will be based.

Only a fraction of the total number of species found in Malaya can be mentioned in the space available here, but it is of interest to note that the most recent authoritative work on the subject records 603 species of birds as resident and breeding in this country, as casual visitors, or as visiting the country regularly on migration.

In cold and temperate regions the **breeding season** of birds is practically always the spring, when the upsurge of life after the winter provides an abundance of food for the nestlings. In Malaya the seasons are very much less marked and are determined by relatively wet and dry periods rather than by hot and cold ones. It might be expected either that breeding would be continuous throughout the year or that it would be correlated in some way with the rainy and drier periods. This is not, however, the case. Although nests may be found in this country at any time of the year there is a well marked breeding season which starts, in southern Malaya, in January, continues at full intensity for the first quarter of the year, is less intense during the second quarter and dies away about July. Towards the north there is a tendency for birds to breed later, starting about April or May. This fact shows clearly that breeding is not correlated with the main rainy season, as this is earlier (August to November) in the north than in the south (October to January).

The great majority of birds follow this breeding rhythm more or less closely. There are some, like the Sparrow, which breed all the year round, but they have a peak period in the early months of the year. The herons, and perhaps some of the other water birds, have their nesting season later in the year, and the larger birds of prey nest rather before the main breeding season.

Many species of birds, including a good proportion of those found in Malaya, have the habit of **migration.** A migratory bird is one which performs yearly journeys between two different regions of the world, breeding in one region and passing the remainder of the year in the other. Most migrants of the northern hemisphere fly to temperate or even arctic latitudes in the spring to nest. They spend the spring and summer there brooding and rearing their eggs and young, and then, in the late summer or autumn, fly south again to the tropics to escape the severity of the winter. Most of our Waders are migrants, many of our Warblers, and a good proportion of birds in other groups as well.

A great deal of experimental work has been done to discover how migratory birds navigate or find their way. One method, which is practised on a very large scale, involves capturing the birds, marking them with rings on their legs, releasing them, and then advertising widely for the recovery of such birds, with information about the date and location. As in some cases young birds, unaccompanied by their parents, fly over a route and reach a goal which they have never seen before, it is clear that some mysterious instinctive sense of direction is involved, and as long journeys over the sea are sometimes made, this cannot in all cases be an inherited memory of the geographical features of the route. It has been suggested that the birds are sensitive to the earth's magnetic field, and so navigate by compass, or that they can appreciate forces created by the rotation of the earth and interpret these forces to guide them in their flight.

When critically examined, however, neither these nor any of the other theories that have been proposed are satisfactory, and it must be admitted that the problem of how birds find their way on migration is still unsolved.

At one time the **collecting of birds and their eggs** made a very important and necessary contribution to our knowledge of them. Except in some remote and unexplored regions this time is now past, and no good purpose is served by killing birds or robbing their nests in our country; in most cases it is a breach of the law to do so.

On the other hand much useful knowledge and infinite pleasure can be gained from **watching birds,** recording their breeding and occurrence in different parts of the country and studying the complicated and fascinating patterns of their behaviour. To gain the most from the ever increasingly popular hobby of bird watching you need a small amount of equipment and a great store of patience. No comprehensive book on Malayan birds is available at the present time (1970) but *Common Birds of the Malay Peninsula* by M. W. F. Tweedie (Longman) provides for the identification of most of the frequently seen species. A rather greater number is dealt with by G. C. Madoc in his *Introduction to Malayan birds,* published by the Malayan Nature Society.

While useful observation can be done without them, field-glasses are almost a necessity. Very powerful glasses are not desirable; they are heavy and it is difficult to pick the bird out with them. A magnification of 6 or 8 diameters is best, combined with a wide field. Use a note-book to record details of plumage etc., of unknown birds; your memory is not to be trusted, and when you come to look the bird up in the book the feature which will decide its identity is just the one you have forgotten. There are correct names for the parts of the body and plumage areas of a bird. Learn these from a diagram in some standard book about birds, and write your notes accordingly. Wear dark coloured clothing, and when you have a bird under observation let all your movements, including those of your field-glasses, be in slow motion.

Birds are everywhere, in jungle, on the sea shore, padi fields, cultivated and kampong country and even in the towns, and all are well worth watching. The jungle in the mountains is particularly rewarding. Often along a path at a hill station you find yourself suddenly surrounded by numbers of small birds of various kinds, where a minute before there were none. These "bird waves" are of frequent occurrence in the hills and are the result of companies of insect-eating birds banding together and working through an area of jungle. An insect accidentally disturbed by a single searching bird is likely to fly away and escape, but if a numerous company of them is present it may well alight within sight of a bird other than the one which disturbed it and so be captured. This is a remarkable and unusual instance of co-operative effort by different species of animals.

Do not forget your glasses and note-book when going on a sea voyage. Rare vagrant and migratory birds may be seen, and we have much to learn about the seasonal distribution of our commoner sea birds.

The remainder of this chapter will be devoted to an account of the commoner and more interesting Malayan Sea Birds, Water Birds and Waders.

Gannets and Frigate Birds. These are birds of the open sea, living entirely on fish and nesting on small islands. The **Brown Booby**[1] is our only common gannet, and may be seen fairly frequently at sea in the Malacca Strait. It nests in large numbers on Pulau Perak west of Penang. It is a large, rather clumsy-looking bird, sooty brown above and on the throat and chest, the rest of the underparts white. Like other gannets it dives into the sea in order to catch fish swimming under the surface. It makes its nest on the ground or on a cliff ledge and will defend it fiercely against intruders, human or otherwise.

The frigate birds are magnificent masters of flight with long sharply curved wings and deeply forked tail. They are always black with a varying amount of white on the underparts. The smallest of them, the **Lesser Frigate Bird** is seen around the islands off the East Coast, especially Pulau Tioman, and less commonly in the Malacca Strait. The span of its wings is rather over six feet and the adults have only a little white on the underparts, on the breast in the female, further back in the male. Frigate birds normally nest in colonies in trees or bushes on islands, but no records of their nesting are known from our area.

Where frigate birds and gannets live together, as at Christmas Island, the former seldom catch fish for themselves, but live by robbing the gannets or boobies. If one of the latter is seen by a

1 The English names of the Malayan birds are now standardised. Their Latin names will therefore not be used in this book.

hungry frigate flying heavily to the shore, its crop laden with fish, the robber swoops upon it repeatedly, like a fighter aeroplane, until the harassed booby disgorges its fish, and the frigate, with marvellous sleight of wing, catches the prize before it falls into the water. Where there are no boobies to rob they pick food up from the surface and are known to capture flying fishes in flight.

Herons and Bitterns. Long legs and neck and a sharp dagger-like bill are distinguishing features of this group of birds. They frequent the sea coast or inland swampy country, and most of them feed on fish or frogs. The **Little Green Heron** is dark greenish-grey above, lighter grey beneath, and is most often seen in mangrove swamps. The **Reef Egret** is larger and its plumage may be either dark grey or pure white. This remarkable dimorphism, as it is called, is not seasonal and does not depend on the age or sex of the bird. Intermediate piebald forms are occasionally seen. The dark grey phase is the commoner one. The Reef Egret frequents rocky coasts and feeds mainly on coral reefs when the tide is far out.

Fig. 17.   Cattle Egret.

The **Cattle Egret** (Fig. 17) is probably our most familiar heron, as it is often seen in populated districts where cattle are allowed to graze. Flocks of these beautiful white birds accompany the herds of cows or buffalos in order to capture the insects which they disturb as they trample the grass. They are specially numerous in the northern rice-fields, but are found throughout the country, even in Singapore. In the breeding season the head and neck become orange and ornamental plumes of this colour develop on the breast and back. Birds in breeding plumage are sometimes seen in Malaya, but nests have not been recorded in this country. The Cattle Egret and the white phase of the Reef Egret are very similar in appearance, but the latter is nearly always seen singly, the other in flocks. Also each bird keeps rather strictly to the type of habitat described; a white heron on the sea shore is almost certainly a reef egret, in the rice-fields or grassy country a cattle egret.

The **Large Egret**, although much less common, does breed in our area, there being heronries, of which it is the principal tenant, on Pulau Ketam near Port Swettenham and off Port Weld in Perak. The bird is larger than the Cattle Egret and pure white in colour.

Bitterns are very like herons, but the plumage is brown instead of white or grey, and they are secretive birds, hiding away in swamps and reed-beds. Only one is common, the **Cinnamon Bittern,** which is chestnut brown above and pale buff below. It inhabits rice fields and fresh-water swamps and makes a nest of reeds; the two or three eggs are chalky white. Among dry and withered vegetation its coloration is very effective in concealing it, and it will take advantage of this by "freezing" motionless if disturbed, often with the bill pointing to the sky, so as to align it with the reeds.

Ducks. These are essentially birds of the temperate regions and very few kinds are found in Malaya. The only one that is at all common is the **Lesser Whistling Duck,** a small duck, dark brown above, grey and chestnut below with the wings black with a chestnut patch. It is found in rice fields and swampy country on both sides of the main range but is commoner in the north and on the east coast. The **Cotton Teal** is much less common than the Whistling Duck. It is a handsome bird, the drake mainly green above with the sides of the head and the under-parts white, the female duller coloured with the under-parts washed with brown. Both these species inhabit the same sort of country but have very different breeding habits; the Whistling Duck makes its nest on the ground, the Cotton Teal nests in hollow trees and occasionally in buildings. The only other resident species of duck is the rare **White-winged Wood Duck**.

The **Rails and Coots** are birds of swampy country, expert swimmers, poor and reluctant fliers. Only the naturalist who is prepared to brave the mud and buffalo-leeches of swamps and rice fields is likely to see the more uncommon species.

Fig. 18. White-breasted Water Hen.

The **White-breasted Water Hen** (Fig. 18) is the commonest of them; it is, indeed, by far the most common of Malayan waterfowl. Unlike the other rails it often leaves the swamps and is seen in gardens or on the roadside. It is a long-legged, short-tailed dumpy bird, which will usually run in preference to flying, and is coloured slaty grey above, white below, with some chestnut under the tail. The nest is usually built in thick vegetation near the water and sometimes in reeds actually over water.

The **Moorhen** is black with some white markings on the wings and under the tail, and a bright red "shield" above the bill. Its habits are similar to those of the last species, but it is much more local in its distribution. It is most frequently seen on the mining pools round Kuala Lumpur.

One other species of rail is fairly common, the **Slaty-breasted Rail.** Its head and neck are chestnut, the rest of the upper parts greyish brown barred with white and the underparts ashy grey on the breast and white on the belly. It lives in swampy areas or anywhere where there are pools and ditches with thick vegetation. It is very shy and secretive and so appears more rare than it really is.

The **Purple Swamphen** is far from common and included here only on account of its striking beauty. It is greenish-brown above and bright blue to blue-green below, the legs and bill red. It is found in thick reedy swamps in the lowlands of the north-western states.

The term "**Waders**" is a convenient one often used to include such birds as plovers, snipe, sandpipers, curlews, etc. About forty species have been recorded from Malaya, but very few of them are resident and breed here. The great majority are winter visitors which breed far to the north, some even in the arctic regions. For this reason the visitor to Malaya from

Europe or northern Asia will recognise old friends among the migrant waders, Redshank, Curlew and Golden Plover, though almost all the other birds will be unfamiliar. The waders are, in fact, pre-eminent among the migratory birds, and some of them fly thousands of miles to and from their breeding grounds every year. There is still a lot to be learned about our visiting waders. The occurrence of some of them rests on single or very scanty records and species not known to visit Malaya will probably be discovered when the hobby of bird watching becomes more general here. They are, however, subjects for the enthusiast and the expert. Most of them are shy and spend their time on wide sand and mud flats, where they are difficult to approach and their surroundings not very attractive, particularly on a hot day. Also the species are often separated by obscure characters, difficult to appreciate in the field. The waders are the despair of the faint-hearted and the beginner, but favourites of the experienced ornithologist, a welcome challenge to his endurance and knowledge.

Breeding habits throughout the group are rather uniform. The nest, if a nest is made at all, is on the ground; often the eggs are simply laid in a hollow scraped in sand or shingle. They are pear-shaped, beautifully and variously marked and coloured to match their surroundings, and large for the size of the bird. Three or four are usually laid and arranged with their small ends inwards, so as to occupy the least possible space. When the young hatch they are covered with down and are able to run almost immediately. This ability is shared by a few other groups of birds including the ducks and rails and, among land birds, by the pheasants and their allies.

Only three waders are known to breed in Malaya. One of these, the **Red-wattled Lapwing**, is a beautiful bird, white underneath, brown on the back with the wings and tail strikingly marked with black and white; the head and neck black and the base of the beak crimson. It is local in its distribution but fairly common on the east coast in open country. Its habit of swooping and tumbling about above the observer and its clear, plaintive cry, show it to be a close relative of the common European Lapwing, although its plumage is so very distinct. Nests have been found near Kuantan in Pahang.

The **Malay Sand Plover** is more widespread and occurs on sandy beaches all round our coasts. It is a small plover, white below and brown above, and the male has some black markings on the head and neck. It is not easy to distinguish from such species as the Ringed Plover, Kentish Plover and certain other sand plovers which are winter visitors. The nest is a depression in the sand on the shore, a little above high tide-mark.

The **Painted Snipe** is a peculiar bird whose name is misleading, for it is not really a snipe and bears only a superficial resemblance to one. It is white below, the throat and upper breast brown, the back patched and barred with olive, black and buff. This "painted" colouring and the presence of a white eye-stripe make it easy to recognise. The beak is long and slightly curved. Its flight is also very different from that of a snipe, being straight and rather laboured; it is definitely not a sporting bird. It is local in distribution but fairly widely spread, and frequents and nests in marshy places. This is one of the few birds in which the normal breeding behaviour is reversed; the female courts the male bird, and then leaves him to brood and hatch the eggs.

It is difficult to make a selection among the visiting waders. The **Common Sandpiper** is probably the most familiar of them as it frequents river banks as well as the swamps and mud-flats to which most of them betake themselves. It is a little bird with slender bill and legs, grey above and white below, with a white bar on the wing, conspicuous in flight. It is very commonly seen along streams and rivers from the coast far up into the mountains, even as high as Cameron Highlands. The sandpipers generally arrive about August and leave about March, but occasional birds are seen in the summer months and probably a few stay throughout the year, though there is no reason to suppose that they breed here.

The **Wood Sandpiper** is another small wader, dark brown mottled with white above, with a conspicuous white patch above the tail. Unlike the Common Sandpiper it is often seen in flocks and haunts marshy land near the coast.

Of the mud-flat waders the **Curlew** is one of the most conspicuous. It is shy and unapproachable, but large enough to be recognised, with field-glasses, at a considerable distance.

Its size, long legs and very long curved bill are distinctive. Smaller, commoner and with a shorter bill is the **Whimbrel.** A further feature distinguishing it from the Curlew is the presence on the head of distinct brown and white stripes; in the larger bird the head is white merely streaked with brown. The **Redshank** (Fig. 19) is another common bird on the mud. It is grey above, white below, with a white band on the wing, conspicuous in flight. When on the ground the long bright red legs are its best recognitional feature. August or September to March is the season these birds spend with us; they nest far to the north, in the tundra of Manchuria and Siberia.

Of the migrant plover the **Eastern Golden Plover** (Fig. 20) is certainly the most often seen. The upper parts are black mottled with yellow and buff. In winter plumage, when they are with us, the underparts are white, but birds with some of the black characteristic of the breeding plumage, are sometimes seen just after arrival or before departure. These plover frequent the shore like the other waders, but often flocks of them visit open spaces inland, such as race courses, golf courses and even "padangs' and football fields in the towns.

Strangest of the plovers and by no means uncommon is the **Pratincole.** The pratincoles are plovers which have adopted the way of life, and something of the appearance, of swallows and swifts, in fact they are sometimes called Swallow Plovers. Instead of seeking their food on the ground or in the mud as all the other waders do, they hawk their insect prey on the wing. This is a very handsome bird, brown above, white above the tail, buff and white below with a black horse-shoe mark on the throat and breast, its two ends reaching the eyes. It is known to nest in Thailand and may extend as a breeding bird into northern Malaya, though this has not been established.

Snipe visit Malaya in the winter in large numbers and are warmly welcomed by sportsmen. Three species are found, by far the most common being the **Pintail Snipe** (Fig. 21). The other two are **Swinhoe's Snipe** and the **Common Snipe,** and it is always worth examining a "bag" of snipe to see if either of the rarer species is present. The best way of determining their identity is to examine the tail. In the Pintail this has about seven narrow stiff pin-like feathers on each side of the ten normal feathers in the centre. In the Fantail the tail consists of fourteen feathers, all rounded and normally shaped. Swinhoe's Snipe is less easy to distinguish from the Pintail; the tail consists of 20 or 22 feathers of which the outer six or seven are narrow and stiff, but not so much so as to be pin-like.

19.

20.

21.

Figs. 19 to 21. Waders: 19. Redshank; 20. Golden Plover; 21. Pintail Snipe.

The snipe begin to arrive in August and are most numerous in October. Almost any open space that is wet and muddy attracts them and rice fields provide them with their most extensive habitat in Malaya. They are by far the best sporting birds we have, for pursuit of them calls for a lot of energetic walking as well as great skill with a gun.

The **Gulls** and **Terns,** so very familiar and abundant on temperate coasts, are not well represented in our waters. The only gull known to occur is the **Black-headed Gull**, which is a rare winter visitor. A number of terns have a similar status and four species are resident. The **Black-naped Tern** (Fig. 22) is

Fig. 22.   Black-naped Tern.

white and pale grey with a black band encircling the back and sides of the head. It inhabits and breeds on rocky islets all round the coast. The **Bridled Tern** and the **Roseate Tern** have similar habits but a more restricted distribution. The former is black above and on the head and white below, the latter grey and white with the head black, bill and legs red, and, in the breeding season, a rosy flush on the underparts. The **Chinese Little Tern** is much smaller and mainly white with a little black on the crown, a very graceful, dainty little bird. It does not inhabit islands, as the others do, but lives along the coasts. It is known to breed on the east coast and up some of the larger rivers.

CHAPTER FOUR

BIRDS (*Continued*)

IN this chapter is given a short summary of the commoner Malayan land birds which do not belong to the Passerine order.

Birds of Prey. This order of birds includes eagles, vultures, hawks, kites, etc. They have powerful flight, very keen vision and are further equipped for a predatory mode of life by strong claws and a sharp hooked beak. Although most of them prey on birds and other animals, some have become degenerate in their habits and feed by scavenging. Such are the vultures, which depend for their food on the carcasses of large animals, and the Brahminy Kite, which picks up garbage of various kinds from the water around harbours and fishing villages. It should be remembered that owls, though armed with beak and claws similar to those of the true birds of prey, belong to a wholly distinct order of birds.

Our largest common bird of prey is the **White-bellied Sea Eagle** (Plate 5). The adult is grey above with the head, neck and under-parts pure white. It is seldom seen far from the coast and is attached to small jungle-covered islands. The nest is always built in the high branches of a tall tree and is constructed of sticks and small branches. It is used year after year and constantly added to, so that it may grow into a great pile of dead sticks, six feet high and over four feet across. It is often built in well populated areas, such as the residential districts of Singapore, but tall trees growing in mangrove swamp are favourite sites. Two eggs are laid, chalky white without markings. These eagles obtain all their food from the sea, capturing fish and sea-snakes in the water and crabs on the shore.

The **Changeable Hawk Eagle** is hardly smaller than the Sea Eagle and is the commonest large bird of prey found inland. It is so named because it assumes two distinct colour forms, just as does the Reef Egret. The eagle appears in a dark phase, with the whole plumage sooty brown, and a pale one in which the underparts are white or light brown streaked with black and the back and wings somewhat darker brown. Here again the two distinct phases are not connected in any way with season, age or sex. The **Crested Serpent Eagle** (Fig. 23) is hardly less common than the Hawk Eagle and of about the same size. When flying it can be distinguished, if it is low enough, by the presence of a broad

23.   24.

Figs. 23. and 24. Birds of Prey: 23. Serpent Eagle; 24. Whitebacked Vulture.

white band near the base of the tail. It also has a prominent crest of feathers on the head. Unlike the Sea Eagle these two birds seek their prey on land and cannot be said to be harmless, for they are notorious chicken thieves.

In the mountains one may see the **Black Eagle,** which is as big as the Sea Eagle, and quite black except for the barred tail. It lives entirely in forested country and little is known of its habits.

The **Honey Buzzard** is a brown eagle-like bird, resident in small numbers, which are reinforced in winter, about October to March, by migrant birds from the north. These belong to a distinct subspecies or race, the Siberian Honey Buzzard, but the two forms cannot be distinguished in the field. Their diet consists largely of wild bees and their larvae and honey; the bird attacks the great combs of the Giant Honey Bee, tearing them to pieces, and seems to be protected in some way from the stings. But this immunity does not extend to onlookers, and the fury of the bees is likely to fall upon any living thing in the vicinity. If you see a honey buzzard attacking a bees' nest, never approach to get a better view; turn, rather, and hasten in the other direction.

Commonest of all our birds of prey, at any rate in populated coastal areas, is the **Brahminy Kite.** This is a handsome bird when adult, the head and chest white, the remaining plumage bright rufous chestnut. As mentioned above it prefers scavenging to hunting and it is commonest around harbours and fishing villages, where it can get its fill of garbage and fish-offal. The nests are most often situated in mangrove swamp, usually thirty to forty feet from the ground but sometimes lower. Two eggs are laid, white, sparsely marked with reddish brown.

Of the smaller hawks the **Japanese Sparrow-hawk** is a common winter visitor. It is dull brown above, pinkish-brown, faintly barred with white below. As its name implies it feeds on small birds. The **Black-winged Kite** is a very handsome hawk, pale grey above and white below with a black patch on the wing. It is most often seen in rice-field country, flying high over the padi in search of rats. The Malay cultivators call it Lang Tikus (Rat Hawk) and recognise it as a friend.

Perhaps the most attractive of all our birds of prey is the little **Falconet.** It is prettily coloured, black above and chestnut below, with the forehead, chin and throat white and is only a little larger than a sparrow. It likes open country with scattered trees and may be seen in the residential areas of towns. Though it occasionally takes small birds its usual prey is large insects like grasshoppers and carpenter bees. Its nesting habits are quite unusual for a hawk, for it breeds in holes in trees; like those of most hole-breeding birds its eggs are unspotted white.

Vultures are confined in Malaya to the northern states, bordering on Thailand. These birds depend for their food on the dead bodies of relatively large animals. They spend their time circling at a great height above the ground and continually watching for dead or dying animals. When it is remembered that they often fly at such a height as to be invisible to the

(Loke Wan Tho)

Plate 5.   White-bellied Sea Eagle

(*F.G.H. Allen*)

Plate 6.   Long-tailed Tailor Bird

Plate 7.   Racquet-tailed Drongo

(*F.G.H. Allen*)

Plate 8.   Pied Fantail Flycatcher

human eye, the extraordinary quality of their eyesight is realised. They do not frequent thickly forested country where the ground, where all large animals die, is quite concealed under a covering of trees. In open populated country absence of vultures denotes a prosperous, efficiently governed peasantry with healthy cattle. During the disorder of the Japanese occupation of Malaya the **White-backed Vulture** extended its range as far south as Malacca, but it soon retreated after the liberation. This is the vulture shown at Fig. 24.

Game Birds. In temperate countries the pheasants and partridges and their allies have received this name on account of their pre-eminent position among sporting birds; birds, that is to say, which provide sport for those whose pleasure it is to hunt and shoot them. It does not fit the Malayan members of the order very well, as only one of them, the Jungle Fowl, can legitimately be regarded as a sporting bird.

The **Red Jungle Fowl** is chiefly interesting as the ancestor of all the various breeds of domestic fowl, which was almost certainly first domesticated in some part of south-east Asia The ordinary kampong chicken is not far removed from the wild type, which is hardly surprising in view of the frequency with which these birds are visited by their jungle relatives. The Jungle Cock is very handsome, with flaming reddish-orange back, dark brown wings and black tail and underparts. Jungle fowl are found most often in dry lowland jungle and scrub, and come out into clearings to feed in the evening and early morning. The nest is made on the ground and about six creamy white eggs are laid, which can easily be hatched under a domestic hen.

None of the Malayan pheasants and partridges are common birds, and they are seen extremely seldom. The specimens preserved in museums have almost all been obtained by the skilled trapping methods of jungle people. Finest of all of them is the **Great Argus Pheasant,** which has the feathers of the wings and tail elongated and intricately patterned with eye-like markings. As in all pheasants this display plumage is developed only in the male. The bird lives in hilly jungle and is by no means rare, as its loud musical call, the "kuang" which has given it its Malay name, is often heard; but very few people have ever seen a wild argus pheasant. The males make small clearings in the jungle for their displays, areas of bare earth from which every twig and leaf is cleared away.

The **Peacock Pheasants** and **Fireback Pheasants** are also shy uncommon jungle birds. Least rare of them, perhaps, is the **Crested Fireback** which is black with a flame-coloured patch on the back.

Fig. 25. Peacock.

Peafowl (Fig. 25), which are really a kind of pheasant, occur in Malaya and on the coastal flats of Trengganu and Pahang are quite common. There is no need to describe a peacock. Domestication has made its spectacular beauty perhaps a little too familiar; it would be esteemed more highly if the bird were rare and seldom seen.

The **Blue-breasted Quail** (Fig. 26) is a round little bird about the size of a sparrow. It is brown above and the male has the underparts steel blue and chestnut. It frequents grassy country and is often seen in the "rough" on golf courses. The nest is made in lalang or other long grass and the eggs are olive, finely speckled with black.

The **Common Button Quail** is classified apart from the true game birds and differs from them in lacking a fourth (hind) toe. It is no less common than the Blue-breasted Quail and looks rather similar, but the male lacks the blue and chestnut underparts. In nearly all birds in which the sexes differ the male wears bright plumage, in which he struts and displays before the female, whose dull colour serves to conceal her when she is brooding the eggs. In the present species this domestic duty is performed entirely by the male bird (as it is in the case of the Painted Snipe) and the female is larger and brighter than her spouse, displaying a black throat and breast. Moreover it is she who does the courting and she is even said to punish him if she finds him neglecting the nest; a hen-pecked husband indeed.

Quite a number of **Pigeons** and **Doves** are found in Malaya. Largest are the **Imperial Pigeons,** of which perhaps the most often seen is a hill bird, the **Mountain Imperial Pigeon.** It is maroon brown with the head, neck and underparts pinkish grey; its note is a deep booming coo. The **Green Imperial Pigeon,** bronzy green where the last is brown, is a bird of the coastal mangrove, locally distributed in the western states.

Fig. 26.
Blue-breasted Quail.

The **Pied Imperial Pigeon** is also seen in mangrove, but is far more common on jungle covered islands both in the Malacca Strait and in the South China Sea. It is a beautiful bird, ivory-white with some black in the wings and tail.

The **Green Pigeons** are smaller; of several species of them the **Pink-necked Green Pigeon** or **Punai** is by far the most common. It is a pretty bird, the male green with the head and throat grey and an orange patch on the breast; both sexes have a yellow bar on the wing which distinguishes them from the allied species. Its swift flight and habit of flying in flocks over definite routes make this little pigeon a favourite quarry of sportsmen. Like that of almost all pigeons its nest is a simple platform of sticks on which two white eggs are laid.

Two species of doves are very common and familiar birds. Both are earthy brown above and pinkish brown below; the **Spotted-necked Dove** (Fig. 27) has a black and white checkered patch on the neck while the **Zebra Dove** is smaller, lacks the checkered neck and is faintly barred with black underneath. Both of these charming little birds are frequently seen in gardens, often in pairs, and are very tame. Their call is a low musical "coo." Tame, hardy and attractive, they pay a sad price for possessing these qualities, for all too often one sees them imprisoned in little cages.

Fig. 27.   Spotted-necked Dove.

Fig. 28.   Long-tailed Parakeet.

The **Little Cuckoo-Dove** is chestnut above, cinnamon brown below, and has a rather long tail. It is a mountain bird and may be seen in the hill stations, often in small parties.

Three kinds of **Parrots** occur in Malaya, but only one is often seen. This is the **Long-tailed Parakeet** (Fig. 28), which is green with the head rose-pink except on the crown; the centre tail feathers are long and narrow. The birds fly swiftly in flocks, screaming unmusically; this and the long needle-like tail feathers distinguish them in flight from green pigeons. They nest in holes high up in trees.

In the minds of visitors from Europe **Cuckoos** are associated with a single characteristic call and with the practice of placing their eggs in other birds' nests, for only one kind of cuckoo occurs there. In Malaya we have over thirty species of these birds, not all of which have this parasitic habit. One of the

Fig. 29.   Lesser Coucal.

commonest is the **Lesser Coucal** (Fig. 29). It is a fairly large, clumsy-looking bird with a long tail, the head, neck and underparts black, the back and wings chestnut. Its call sounds like "boot-boot-boot". It is found in rough open country where lalang and low bushes are the dominant vegetation. It makes its own nest, usually well concealed in the tall grass, and lays two white eggs.

Raffles' Malkoha is one of a group of cuckoos with long tails and red or green bills. This species is chestnut above, chestnut and grey below, the tail black or brown with a white tip. The beak and a patch of skin round the eye are bright green. This is a common bird in lowland jungle and is usually seen climbing and scrambling about among the branches. The malkohas make their own nests and lay two white eggs.

Of the parasitic cuckoos the **Plaintive Cuckoo** is possibly the most common. It is bronzy brown above, pale buff below, with the head and neck grey, but is much more often heard than seen. Its usual song is a dismal, tuneless series of about seven descending notes, the first ones the longest, but sometimes it calls in phrases of three notes in an ascending scale, "keep-the-sweet, keep-the-sweet". It lays its eggs in the nests of various small birds, among which tailor birds and ioras have been recorded.

The **Owls** are predatory birds resembling the true birds of prey in their armament of beak and claws, but the two groups are really quite distinct. The flat, disc-like face, very large eyes and soft fluffy plumage, which provides for noiseless flight, are characteristic of the owls. All the commoner Malayan species have the plumage some shade of brown above, lighter below, and intricately streaked and barred with lighter and darker colour. Some have curious tufts of feathers on each side of the head, looking rather like ears or horns.

The **Malay Fish Owl** is a large bird with long ear-tufts and strongly barred brown and buff plumage. It is common in the lowlands, especially in rice-field country. It makes no attempt to build a nest but breeds in hollow trees, old nests of other birds and similar sites; the eggs, like those of all owls, are pure white and almost round.

Fig. 30.   Collared Scops Owl.

The **Hawk Owl** is a common bird in the lowlands. It likes wooded country but is by no means confined to jungle and is most often encountered in rubber estates. It is of medium size and dark brown above with no ear-tufts. Being a nocturnal bird it is not often seen, but its call, a deep, single "pook," is very frequently heard, especially on moonlight nights. Smaller still is the **Collared Scops Owl** (Fig. 30), which is brown with a pale buff collar and has long ear-tufts. It is a frequent visitor to gardens and sometimes comes into houses, where it may be dazzled to helplessness by the lights.

The **Nightjars** are curious birds with intricately marked brown plumage, rather like an owl's, and a wide, gaping beak. They are nocturnal and live by hawking insects on the wing, just as the swifts and swallows do by day. The most common of them is a very familiar bird, though few people would be able to describe its appearance. Driving along the road at night one frequently sees a red eye reflected in the headlights' beam, and

Fig. 31. Long-tailed Nightjar.

as the car approaches, a bird hastily rises from the road, though sometimes not hastily enough to save its life. Arriving home one may be irritated and rendered sleepless by a monotonous "chock, chock, chock," repeated anything from three or four to as many hundred times. Both the red eye and the voice belong to the **Long-tailed Nightjar** (Fig. 31), which frequents gardens and rubber estates all over the lowlands. It nests on the open ground in such places, and when it is brooding its eggs, its brown mottled plumage makes it very hard to see. The two eggs are pinkish mottled with brown and grey and are concealed by their colour almost as effectively as the bird.

Allied to the nightjars, but not to the swallows and martins, which they resemble in appearance, are the **Swifts.** They are birds which spend almost the whole of their active lives on the wing, hawking flying insects which are their sole food, and their sharp curved wings and bullet-like body are obvious adaptations for swift and sustained flight. Commonest of them is the **House Swift** (Fig. 32), which is black with white on the throat and on the hind part of the back. This is the bird that builds clusters of mud nests under arches and on buildings. They seem to have a preference for large buildings like clubs and hotels, and there must be few people in Malaya who are not familiar with their shrill, chattering cry, loudest in the evening, and even heard at night if they are disturbed. The **Crested Tree Swift** is a common bird in wooded country and rubber estates. It is black above, grey and white below, with a crest on the head which, when raised, readily identifies the bird. The male has a chestnut patch on the side of the face, the female a green one. The nest is most peculiar, like half a miniature saucer, an inch or so wide

Fig. 32. House Swift.

and a quarter of an inch deep, stuck to the side of a small branch; it is made of the bird's dried and hardened saliva. This tiny nest is hardly big enough even for the single egg which is laid, and of course the bird cannot sit on it; when brooding the egg or young it perches on the branch and covers its charge with the puffed out breast feathers. Largest of the swifts is the **Spinetail Swift,** so called because its tail feathers are naked at their tips. It is most often seen on mountain tops, where it often flies close past the observer with an alarming hiss, like a projectile. It is the fastest of all birds and its speed has been estimated at 200 miles an hour.

The **Swiftlets,** of the genus *Collocalia*, are in some nearby countries (but not in Malaya) of some economic importance. They are little sooty brown birds with fluttering flight, rather different from the swift cleaving of the air that characterises their larger relatives, though they feed in the same way. They nest in colonies, usually in caves, but sometimes in buildings, and the nests are made either of moss or other material cemented with the bird's saliva, or solely of the hardened saliva. About half a dozen species occur in our area; although they are almost impossible to recognise in the field, their discrimination is of importance as each species makes a certain type of nest, and the pure saliva nests are collected for making the costly Chinese delicacy, bird's nest soup. In Sarawak and Sabah a considerable revenue is derived from the farming of the nests to the local inhabitants, and the birds are protected and enabled to maintain their numbers by imposing a close season, during which nests may not be collected. In Malaya they are exploited on a small scale in one place only, Tioman Island off the coast of Pahang.

The **Trogons** are among that, unfortunately, rather numerous company of Malayan birds which are beautifully and brilliantly coloured, but inhabit thick jungle and are seldom seen. The males usually have the head and underparts black and bright red, the pattern varying in the different species.

The **Kingfishers** are birds of brilliant plumage with long, dagger-like beaks. Two kinds are common, one of them, the **White-breasted Kingfisher** (Fig. 34), a familiar garden bird. The back and wings are bright blue, the throat and breast white, the head and the rest of the underparts chocolate brown and the beak and feet red. Most kingfishers frequent the vicinity of water and feed on small fish, but this one seems to live mostly on large insects such as grasshoppers, though it is sometimes seen diving rather clumsily for fish and frogs. Its cry is as familiar as its appearance, a loud, laughing screech. Like all kingfishers it breeds in holes, which it usually excavates in a bank by a road or stream, and its eggs are round and glossy white. The **White-collared Kingfisher** is very common on the coast, especially in mangrove. It has none of the red and brown colouring of the last species, but is greenish-blue with the underparts and a collar round the neck white, and the beak and legs black. It has a very noisy laughing cry which has been rendered "kree-chah, kree-chah". Its breeding habits are peculiar, for it usually excavates its nesting burrow in an inhabited termites' nest in a tree.

A variety of small kingfishers is found in jungle and along streams, all beautiful, brilliant birds, and in the coastal mangrove one may sometimes see the largest of all of them, the

Stork-billed Kingfisher, which is blue above, brownish-yellow below, with a very large bright red bill.

The **Bee-Eaters** are a distinctive group of birds, easily recognised. They are slender with pointed wings, rather long, curved bill and the two common Malayan species have the central tail feathers prolonged. The **Blue-throated Bee-Eater** (Fig. 33) has the head and upper back brown, the throat blue

33. 34.

Figs. 33 and 34. 33. Blue-throated Bee-Eater; 34. White-breasted Kingfisher.

and the rest of the plumage mainly green. This bird is common in open country in the lowlands where it can be seen sitting on telegraph wires or the bare branches of trees and flying swiftly out to catch the large insects on which it feeds. Bees, dragon-flies and butterflies are the usual prey. The nesting habits resemble those of kingfishers except that the bee-eaters nest in colonies; burrows are dug in sandy soil to a depth of several feet and the eggs are round and glossy white. The other common species, the **Blue-tailed Bee-Eater** is a winter visitor and does not breed in Malaya. It differs from the last in having the head green and the throat and breast chestnut, with some yellow under the chin. It is common from September to April and in some places seems to take the place of the Blue-throated Bee-Eater, which departs on migration. The two species have very similar habits.

The **Hornbills** are among the strangest looking birds in the world. They are all fairly large, the plumage black and white and the bill huge and often surmounted by a projection called the "casque". Their nesting habits are no less strange than their appearance. The female enters a hole in a tree, which is then plastered up with a kind of cement, leaving only a small aperture

Fig. 35.   Rhinoceros Hornbill.

through which the male devotedly feeds her with fruit and berries throughout the period of incubation and rearing of the young birds. She is able at any time to break her way out, and no doubt would do so if threatened with starvation. The only observation that has been made of the duration of a female hornbill's "imprisonment" in Malaya records the period as eighty-seven days. The flight of hornbills is laboured and direct, and the wing-beats of some species make a loud noise that has been likened to a locomotive labouring up a hill. The purpose of the casque on the bill is rather obscure, but it has been recorded that the males fight formal duels during the courting season, diving at each other and colliding head-on in mid air.

The **Southern Pied Hornbill** is the commonest species and one of the smallest. It is black and white with the beak and casque ivory white. Much larger and more spectacular, and by no means rare, is the **Rhinoceros Hornbill** (Fig. 35), in which the casque is turned up in a point in front and ornamented with red and yellow.

The **Barbets,** which are allied to the woodpeckers, are fairly small green birds with the head and throat usually coloured red, blue and yellow. The beak is broad and powerful and, like the woodpeckers, these birds bore a hole in a tree to nest in. They all have a repetitive call and that of the **Coppersmith Barbet** (Fig. 36) is a sort of "tonk, tonk, tonk," like the beat of a hammer

36.   37.

Figs. 36 and 37. 36. Coppersmith Barbet; 37. Common Golden-backed Woodpecker.

on metal. This species is common in the north and extends south about as far as Perak.

Between twenty and thirty species of **Woodpeckers** are found in Malaya. A woodpecker can always be recognised by the way it clings to vertical tree trunks and branches, sitting back on its stiff tail feathers, and by its strong, dagger-like beak. Most of the species, especially the males, are brilliantly coloured and frequently have a crest or tuft of red on the head. The **Common Golden-backed Woodpecker** (Fig. 37), is one of the most common species and also one of the most beautiful. The upper back is golden yellow, behind which and over the tail it is bright red; the underparts are white marked with black and the male has a crimson crest on the head. This bird is often seen in gardens in the lowlands running up the trunks of coconut palms, tapping the bark in search of insects. The nesting hole is usually excavated in the trunk of a dead palm tree.

The woodpeckers range in size from the **Great Slaty Woodpecker,** which is a little larger than a crow, down to the tiny finch-sized **Piculets,** which bore their nesting holes in the stems of bamboos.

CHAPTER FIVE

BIRDS (*Continued*)

THE birds of the order Passeriformes, often called the Passerine or Perching Birds, will form the subject of this, the last of our bird chapters. The order is not easy to define simply and precisely, and the term "perching birds" is rather misleading as many non-passerines habitually perch in trees, and there are Passerines which live mainly on the ground. All Passerine birds (but some non-passerines as well) have four toes, three of which point forwards, and the gifts of song and of complicated nest-building are most highly developed in this order.

As was pointed out in the introductory part of chapter 3, nearly half of our birds belong to this order. It is subdivided into a large number of families, and these are the headings under which the birds are grouped in this chapter.

The **Pittas** are ground-dwelling birds of retiring habits, mainly confined to jungle and not often seen. They have short wings and tail and rather long legs, and are only mentioned here because they are birds of unusually brilliant plumage. The **Blue-winged Pitta** is a migratory species and for the most part a winter visitor to Malaya; on its migration flights it is rather frequently killed at the lanterns of lighthouses. Its back and wings are green and bright blue, the head brown marked with black, the underparts pale brown on the breast and bright red under the tail. There is a number of species of resident pittas, mostly rather uncommon jungle birds.

The resemblance of the **Swallows** to the non-passerine Swifts has already been pointed out. Our commonest species is the **Pacific Swallow,** which breeds in south-east Asia. It is black, glossed with blue above, rusty brown on the head, throat and breast, and the rest of the underparts are pale smoky brown. It nests in caves and on sea cliffs and also under bridges and in houses. The nest is made largely of dried mud, which the bird collects in puddles, and lined with grass and feathers. The **Barn Swallow** (Fig. 38) is a winter visitor and often very numerous during its stay with us, occurring in large flocks. It is very like the resident bird, but has the underparts white and the tail more deeply forked.

Fig. 38. Barn Swallow.

The **Cuckoo-Shrikes** and **Minivets** are included in one family, though they differ greatly in appearance. Of the former the **Pied Triller** (Fig. 39) is a common lowland bird, often seen in gardens. The male is black above, marked with white on the head, wings and tail, and white, washed with grey,

Fig. 39. Pied Triller.

below. The female has a similar pattern in brown and pale buff. It is usually seen in pairs and has a curious mewing, complaining call. The **Mountain Minivet** is one of the most beautiful and striking of our small hill birds. The male is scarlet below, black and scarlet above, and the female has the same pattern in yellow and black. They often take part in the "bird waves" mentioned early in chapter 3.

The **Drongos** or **King-Crows** are medium sized birds, usually glossy black, with powerful beaks and an aggressive disposition, especially towards intruders to the vicinity of their nests. Other birds, including birds of prey, are summarily driven off and they will sometimes attack human trespassers as well. The commonest species is the **Greater Racquet-tailed**

Drongo (Fig. 40 and Plate 7), which has the outer pair of tail feathers greatly elongated with the shafts naked except for a rounded "raquet" at the tip. When the bird is in flight the shafts are invisible, and it has the appearance of being closely pursued by two large bees. This drongo is common in the lowlands in wooded areas, even those of small extent such as survive on Singapore Island.

The **Orioles** are birds of bright coloured plumage, usually yellow and black. The **Black-naped Oriole** (Fig. 41) (often miscalled Golden Oriole) is a rather local lowland bird, but very common on Singapore Island. Its plumage is mainly saffron-yellow with some black on the nape, wings and tail, and its song a melodious flute-like whistle, "*pou-ee-you.*" Adequately described by its name is the **Black-and-crimson Oriole**; it is a mountain bird, not really uncommon but seldom seen because it frequents the tree tops.

Fig. 40. Greater
Racquet-tailed Drongo.

Crows are not numerous in Malaya. The only common indigenous species is the **Large-billed Crow,** which is entirely black. It is most often seen around fishing villages, where it competes for offal with the Braminy Kites. The **House-Crow** was introduced to the neighbourhood of Klang in Selangor about 1895 to combat a plague of caterpillars in the coffee plantations. We have reason to be thankful that this ill-considered action did not result in a plague of house-crows throughout the country. The birds established themselves in Klang, where they are still to be seen, but did not spread much beyond the limits of the town. A small colony was found to be established, after the war, in the Tanjong Pagar area of Singapore, but this too has not spread, and nothing is known of its origin. This is an unusual sequel to the introduction of an exotic animal; normally it will either multiply and probably become a nuisance, or quickly disappear. The House-Crow is easily distinguished by the grey, unglossy appearance of the neck and fore part of the body.

Fig. 41. Black-naped Oriole.

It has been said that the **Babblers** are simply an assemblage of those genera of Passerine birds about whose affinities the systematists are still unable to decide. This may or may not be so, but they certainly form a very miscellaneous group. Almost all of the numerous lowland species are obscurely coloured and secretive in their habits, but the family includes several rather conspicuous hill birds.

Fig. 42. Silver-eared Mesia.

The **Silver-eared Mesia** (Fig. 42) is an attractive bird with a black head and a large silvery patch behind the eye. The throat and breast are orange yellow and the rest of the plumage is grey and olive with some patches of crimson on the wings and at the base of the tail. In the female the crimson is replaced by orange. This is a tame and familiar hill station bird, usually seen in small flocks. Also found commonly in the mountains is the **Long-tailed Sibia.** It is dull slaty grey with a white spot on the wing and a very long tail, the feathers of which are progressively longer towards the middle, so that the tail appears stepped or graduated along its edges. It is often seen in small parties, climbing about in trees and bushes in search of insects. The little **Golden-headed Babbler** is a frequent participant in the mountain bird waves. It is olive above, yellow below, with a patch of orange on the crown.

43.   44.

Figs. 43. and 44. 43. Common Iora; 44. Common Tailor Bird.

The **Common Iora** (Fig. 43) is often seen in gardens, especially in coastal districts where casuarina trees are plentiful. The male is mainly yellow with a black tail and the wing black with white bars. Included in the same family as the Iora are the **Leaf-Birds,** all small birds with bright grass-green plumage and, in the males, a black throat. They are birds of the jungle, inhabiting the thick foliage of the high trees, and so are seldom seen, though really very numerous.

A number of species of **Bulbuls** is found in Malaya, and one of them, the **Yellow-vented Bulbul** (Fig. 45), is possibly our most common garden bird. It is brown above and white below with a patch of bright lemon yellow under the tail, and the head is striped with black and white. It is no songster, but its galloping, bubbling cry is very cheerful and attractive. It is a bird of the lowlands seldom seen far from human habitations, but has followed man into the mountains where he has made hill stations, like those at Fraser's Hill and Cameron Highlands. This is interesting as it shows that the sort of surroundings provided by gardens and roadsides are of more importance to this bird than is the climate. It builds its deep, cup-shaped nest in bushes and hedges and lays two eggs, white thickly speckled all over with brown and grey.

45.   46.

Figs. 45 and 46.   45. Yellow-vented Bulbul; 46. Magpie Robin.

In the northern states near the border of Thailand, the very handsome **Red-whiskered Bulbul** is common.   Its head carries a black crest and there is a large patch of crimson under the tail and a small one under each eye. It is a popular cage bird, and escaped birds are sometimes seen in the more southern states, and may even have established themselves and nested here and there.

The **Magpie Robin** or **Straits Robin** (Fig. 46) is the most familiar Malayan representative of the thrush family, and is almost as common in gardens as the Yellow-vented Bulbul. Like that species it is a lowland bird which has followed man up into the hill stations. It is black above and on the head and upper breast, the remaining underparts, a patch on the wing, and the outer tail feathers being white. The Pied Cuckoo-Shrike is sometimes confused with it, but that species has no black on the underparts and the head is marked with white. The Magpie Robin is a vigorous songster with a great variety of loud, clear whistling notes, and the males, quarrelling with each other, sometimes make a harsh, scolding noise. The nest is seldom far from the ground, banks and hollow stumps being frequently chosen as sites for it. It is a fairly large, shallow cup and the eggs, usually three, are greenish, thickly marked with brown and purple.

The **White-rumped Shama** is usually considered to be the finest Malayan song bird. Unlike the Magpie Robin, however, it is seldom seen near houses and gardens and must be sought in uncultivated country, along jungle paths and streams or at the edge of rubber estates. It is a handsome bird, black above with a white patch over the tail, which is long, and black and chestnut below. The nest and eggs are very much like those of the Magpie Robin. The **Forktails** are beautiful birds with mainly black and white plumage and deeply bifurcated tails. They are entirely confined to the rocky, torrential streams of the hills, and there are two common species whose range is determined by altitude. Below 3,000 feet and in the foot-hills the **Chestnut-naped Forktail** is found; higher up in the mountains its place is taken by the **Slaty-backed Forktail,** which can often be seen along the rivers and streams at Cameron Highlands.

The **Warblers** are all small, slender, brown or greenish coloured birds, many of them migrants which breed in temperate regions and visit the tropics in winter; about half of those on the Malayan list are winter visitors. Of the resident species the **Fantail Warbler** is one of the commonest. It is a small brown bird, streaked with black and buff, and is found everywhere in the lowlands where there is open grass-land and "lalang." The nest is hidden deep in the long grass and is very difficult to find. The most interesting of our warblers are the **Tailor Birds,** of which several species are found. They are dull coloured little birds and not easy to distinguish from each other, but can be recognised collectively by a conspicuous chestnut or rusty red patch on the top of the head. They are named on account of their peculiar nesting habits. Usually a single large living leaf is curled round and the edges are joined by a remarkable technique resembling sewing or rivetting. Holes are pierced, opposite each other, near the edges to be joined, and spider's web or vegetable fibre is pushed through each pair of holes and teased out on each side to form securing knots. Sometimes two or even three leaves are stitched together in this way, and the nest is built in the resultant pouch. It is usually close to the ground, and nests are sometimes found in gardens made in the leaves of cannas. The **Common Tailor Bird** is shown at Fig. 44 and Plate 6.

About thirty kinds of **Flycatchers** occur in Malaya. They are all insect eating birds, mostly small, and they catch their prey in a characteristic manner, fluttering out from a chosen perch to capture insects on the wing and immediately returning to it. In many of them the sexes are very different in appearance, the male being brightly coloured, often largely blue, the female dull brown or grey. The commonest lowland species is the **Pied Fantail Flycatcher** (Fig. 47 and Plate 8), which is brown above, white and buff below,

Fig. 47. Pied Fantail Flycatcher.

with a white streak over the eye and a black bar on the chest. Its restless movements, combined with posturing and spreading the tail, have earned for it the Malay name of Murai Gila (Mad Robin). The **Paradise Flycatcher** is mainly a jungle bird. The male is remarkable in having two plumage phases, a case of dimorphism, like that of the Reef Egret (p. 36), but here confined to one sex. The head and neck are black and there is a conspicuous crest on the crown; in one phase the male resembles the female in being chestnut above and grey and white below, in the other he is silvery white above and below. In both phases of the male the tail has the central feathers ribbon-like and three times the length of the body. He is, in fact, especially in the white phase, a spectacularly beautiful bird.

In the mountains two flycatchers are common. The **Little Pied Flycatcher** is a charming little bird, tame and easy to approach. The male is black above with a white streak over the eye, a white wing-bar and white below; the female is grey and brown. This is another frequent participator in bird waves. The **Niltava** is often seen on jungle paths in the mountains. It is larger than most flycatchers and the male appears shining dark blue all over, the female rusty brown with some light blue on the head and neck.

The **Wagtails** and **Pipits** are classified in one family. The former will be familiar to visitors from Europe as breeding birds, but they only come to Malaya as migrant winter visitors. The **Grey Wagtail** is common from August to March, especially along the hill roads and streams. It is grey and yellow with black and white on the wings and on the long tail, and it has the quick running gait and dipping flight of this very distinct genus of birds. **Richard's Pipit** is a common bird of open, dry grass-lands, its plumage is brown streaked with black above, light speckled with darker brown below. Like the wagtails the pipits do not hop but progress in short, rapid runs. It nests in the grass and its plumage makes the brooding bird very difficult to see.

The **Starlings** and **Mynas** form an attractive group of birds, most of which seem to prefer the open type of country, which results from habitation and cultivation by man, to the natural forest, and for this reason they are conspicuous and familiar. They have the habit of associating in flocks or smaller parties outside their breeding season. The **Philippine Glossy Starling** is often seen in large flocks in the towns, or singly and in pairs around high buildings, which provide it with nesting sites. Both sexes are dark, glossy green all over with a conspicuous red eye. The **Hill Myna** is larger and black with a white patch on the wings; a pair of large fleshy wattles on the nape and a patch of bare skin below the eye are yellow. This is the least "domesticated" of our starlings, and likes open country with dead trees. It feeds on fruit and seldom comes down to the ground. It is often kept as a cage bird and is an accomplished mimic, both of other birds' songs and of the human voice.

The other Malayan Mynas are mainly ground-living birds. The **Jungle Myna** is an indigenous species, brownish-grey above, paler below, and has a white patch on each wing and a white border on the tail. It has the habit of associating, just as egrets do, with buffalos and cattle feeding in long grass. It is often seen perched on the backs of the beasts and may do them some service by picking off ticks, but its main object is to catch the insects which they disturb as they trample the grass. The **Common Myna** (Fig. 48) is a newcomer and has only spread into Malaya from the north during the last thirty years or so. It is similar to the Jungle Myna, but more robust, and can be distinguished by the presence of a patch of bare yellow skin just behind the eye. This bird undoubtedly prefers to live

Fig. 48. Common Myna.

in close association with man, and its spread has been brought about by the development of more or less continuous habitation and cultivation from continental Asia down into the Malay Peninsula. It is bold and confiding and can often be seen walking about on lawns and open spaces in the towns, with an air of considering that it has quite as much right to be there as anyone else. It breeds in any hole in a tree or building that will afford space and shelter for its nest fifteen to twenty feet from the ground.

The **Chinese Crested Myna** has been introduced into Penang but has not spread beyond the island. Except for the white patches in the wings and a narrow white border to the tail it appears almost wholly black. Another, the **Javanese Myna,** exists as an introduced species on Singapore Island. It is not easy to distinguish from the Buffalo Myna, but is more grey and uniformly coloured than that species.

The eggs of the Glossy Starling and the Hill Myna are blue spotted with brown; those of the others are unspotted blue.

The **Sunbirds,** with which are classified the **Spider-Hunters,** bear a slight superficial resemblance to the humming birds of the Americas. Both groups consist of very small birds with long, slender beaks and often displaying bright, metallic colours in the plumage, and both feed to a large extent on the nectar of flowers. There the resemblance ends, for their anatomy shows them to be by no means closely related, and their flight is very different. No sunbird ever hovers with vibrating wings as the humming birds do. The males are distinctively and often brightly coloured, but the females are usually greenish above and yellow below, and almost impossible to identify in the field. All the species have a long, tubular tongue for extracting nectar from flowers, and all make pouch-shaped nests hanging from twigs, or in any other situation which will give this kind of support.

In coastal regions and on Singapore Island the commonest species is the **Yellow-breasted Sunbird** (Fig. 49), of which the male is olive above, yellow below, with the forehead, throat and upper breast metallic blue-black. This is the sunbird that so often hangs its nest from creepers on houses, or on telephone wires. The nest follows an invariable pattern, having an elongate, pear-shaped form with an untidy looking "tail" of vegetable scraps hanging from the bottom and a neat little eave over-hanging the entrance hole in the side. Two eggs are laid, greenish-white with brown spots and lines. In gardens inland the **Brown-throated Sunbird** is the species most often seen. The male is metallic green and violet above with the wings mainly brown, the chin and throat brown with a narrow metallic violet border, the rest of the underparts yellow. This Sunbird is particularly fond of coconut palms and cannas. It spends much of its time in the tops of the palms, feeding on the nectar of the flowers and on the insects which attend them; to obtain the nectar from cannas it pierces the flowers at the base with its beak.

Of the more brilliant species the **Yellow-backed Sunbird** is the least uncommon, especially in Singapore and Penang. The front half of the bird, above and below, is bright crimson, the lower back yellow, the wings brown, the tail metallic violet and the hinder underparts grey. In the mountains the **Black-throated Sunbird** is both common and extremely tame. Except for the yellow and grey underparts almost all the plumage is deep metallic violet and crimson. It is fond of visiting cultivated flowers and comes frequently into gardens, and will even enter verandahs to take tribute of the nectar of potted plants.

The **Spider-Hunters** look like large sunbirds, with the beak even more long and slender, but neither sex ever has bright metallic colours in the plumage, both being usually olive, streaked with brown above and yellow below. The **Little Spider-Hunter** (Fig. 50) is common in the lowlands. Its nest is a

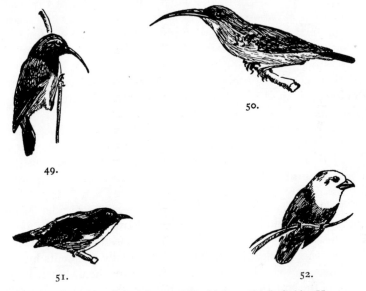

49.

50.

51.

52.

Figs. 49 to 52.   49. Yellow-breasted Sunbird; 50. Little Spider-Hunter; 51. Scarlet-backed Flower-Pecker; 52. White-headed Munia.

remarkable structure, a sort of trough or tube of leaves, moss and vegetable fibre, attached to the underside of a large horizontal leaf, most often a banana leaf. The nesting material is attached to the leaf by a sewing technique very like that of the tailor birds; numerous holes are pierced in the leaf and spider's web, teased into a knot on the outside and threaded through them, is anchored in the fabric of the nest below. In the mountains a larger species, the **Streaked Spider-Hunter,** is a common bird. It is coloured like the other spider-hunters, but has orange feet.

The **Flower-Peckers** are all tiny, brightly coloured birds, differing from the sunbirds in having the beak short. Most of them have more or less red, orange or yellow in the plumage, but no metallic coloration, and the females resemble the males, the bright colours being present but less well developed. They spend almost the whole of their time among the foliage of trees and bushes, and the nests are small, pouch-shaped structures, built hanging from twigs and well concealed among leaves. The **Scarlet-backed Flower-Pecker** (Fig. 51) is bright scarlet above, white below, with the wings, tail and sides of the head black. It is common in the lowlands, especially near the coast, and prefers open country to forest. It is said to be fond of eating the berries of the parasitic plants of the mistletoe family, so assisting in spreading their seeds from one tree to another. Another common species is the **Orange-bellied Flower-Pecker,** which is grey with the back and belly orange in the male, greenish-yellow in the female.

The **White-Eyes** are small greenish birds which live among trees and bushes, climbing actively about in search of insects. All of them have a conspicuous ring of white round the eye. The **Oriental White-Eye** is found fairly commonly in small parties, mainly in the coastal mangrove.

The last family of Passerine birds we shall consider is the one which includes the **Sparrows, Munias** and **Weaver-Finches.** The common sparrow of Malaya is the **Tree-Sparrow.** The name is misleading as the bird habitually frequents human dwellings and is seldom seen far away from them, but it is the result of the situation in Europe, where another species, *Passer domesticus*, the House-Sparrow, has become virtually parasitic on man, and the local race of our sparrow, *Passer montanus*, is a bird of open, sparsely wooded country. To avoid confusion the same English name is applied to the Asiatic race of this species, although it does not describe its habits here. There is no need to describe the sparrow or its habits. He must be a bird lover indeed who does not regard as a nuisance its practice of building its nest and conducting its untidy domestic arrangements on or even in our houses.

The **Java Sparrow** is a conspicuously coloured bird, pale grey above, pinkish-white below, with black and white head, black tail and pink beak and legs. It is not a native of Malaya, but of Java and Sumatra, but as it is very easily tamed, and survives in the smallest of cages, it is carried about in captivity and establishes itself wherever numbers of birds are released or escape, and can find sufficient food. It was much more common before the war than it is now, probably because in these days very much less rice is fed to chickens and thrown wastefully about than in those far-off days of plenty.

The **Munias** or **Rice-Birds** are little sparrow-like birds which almost always fly in flocks, and in some parts of Asia are serious pests in the fields of ripening rice. All have the thick, conical beak characteristic of this family, an instrument well designed for crushing the seeds on which they feed. The most unmistakable, and one of the commonest, of them is the **White-headed Munia** (Fig. 52), sometimes called the Cigar Bird from its resemblance to a partly smoked cigar. It is chestnut in colour with the head and neck white. Other common munias are the **Striated Munia,** which is mainly dark brown with a white patch above the tail, and the **Spotted Munia,** chestnut above, the head darker, and grey finely barred with dark brown below. All these birds make a rather untidy nest, like a ball of grass, and lay pure white eggs.

In appearance the **Baya Weaver** is not remarkable, being mainly brown streaked with darker brown and black above, and pale brown below. In breeding plumage the male is bright yellow on the crown. Its nest, however, is a really marvellous structure. It is usually built in colonies in trees in open country, and frequently the trees chosen are infested with fierce Kĕrengga ants (the Weaving Ant), so that a climb to the nests will be an uncomfortable adventure. The nest is made of fine strips of grass, closely and evenly woven to form a flask-shaped structure hanging from a branch, its lowest part rounded to contain the eggs. From near the bottom, and to one side, a downwardly-directed tube-like entrance is made, so that the bird goes upwards, sideways and then very briefly downwards to get into its nest; the edges of the tube are finished off with a lace-like fringe, and lumps of mud are built into the lower part of the nest to keep it steady when the wind blows strongly.

The male and female work together in building the nest, and

the material is prepared by the birds cutting a notch in a blade of grass and tearing off a narrow strip above it; grass stems and complete blades are not used. At first both birds collect material, but when the nest is half built the female stays in it and works with grass strips brought to her by the male. After the young birds hatch holes are made in the sides of the nest through which they are fed, presumably to save the parent birds the trouble of performing the rather strenuous acrobatic feat of entering the nest every time they bring food.

It is a curious fact that there are always more males than females in weaver bird colonies. The instinct to weave nests is so strong in these birds that the "batchelors" start to make nests on their own. Such nests are built up to the point where the female usually takes over the work of construction, but get no further than this, and the resulting incomplete nests are an almost invariable feature of these colonies.

CHAPTER SIX

REPTILES

PERHAPS the most important, if not the most obvious, difference between the birds and mammals and the reptiles is the fact that the latter are "cold-blooded". That is to say their internal body temperature, instead of being kept at a constant an dfairly high level, varies with that of the surroundings. Changes in temperature therefore have a profound effect on reptiles; in warm weather they become active but cold makes them sluggish. They are not found in very cold countries and are scarce in temperate climates, where they invariably hibernate during the cold months of winter. It is in the tropics that reptiles are abundant and varied, and Malaya forms no exception to this rule.

By definition reptiles are vertebrate animals which breathe air during the whole of their lives and usually have a covering of scales, never of hair or feathers as mammals and birds have. Most of them are land animals, but quite a number inhabit fresh water and two groups, the marine turtles and the sea-snakes, are entirely marine. The majority reproduce by laying eggs, but some are viviparous, bearing their young alive.

Classification of reptiles. Four of the five[1] main groups of reptiles now living are well represented in Malaya. They are:

The **Turtles and Tortoises,** in which the body is encased in a bony shell.

The **Crocodiles,** large aquatic reptiles, too well known to need definition.

The **Lizards,** in which four limbs are normally present, though they may be reduced in burrowing forms and are absent in one rare Malayan species; external ears, appearing like holes or depressions in the head are generally present.

The **Snakes,** in which the limbs and external ears are absent.

[1] The fifth, known as the Rhynchocephalia, has only one surviving member, the Tuatera of New Zealand. In past ages many other groups of reptiles flourished, including the well-known Dinosaurs and the flying Pterodactyls.

Turtles and Tortoises.

Marine Turtles. These are distinguished by the fact that they live in the sea and by their limbs being entirely converted into paddles for swimming. Four species are known in the seas surrounding Malaya. The commonest is the **Green Turtle** (*Chelone mydas*) whose flesh is used for food, though in our region the eggs are commercially more important. The shell is smooth, brown or olive above with lighter markings and yellow below. It grows to between three and four feet in length.

These turtles spend the whole of their time at sea except when they come ashore to breed. This they do at night on clean sandy shores such as are found on the east coast and the islands lying off it. Only the females come ashore, dragging themselves up until they are well above high water mark. There each turtle excavates a crater-like depression with its front flippers and then, turning round, a shaft a foot or more in depth with its hind ones. In this the eggs are laid, often more than a hundred at a time. When laying is completed the hole is filled up and smoothed over so that the nests are hard to find unless they are marked with a stick as soon as the turtle leaves.

Certain islands off the coast of Sarawak are particularly favoured by the turtles and the gathering of the eggs is under government control. The annual yield of eggs from these islands is over a million. They are round, rather like a ping-pong ball, and have a parchment-like skin. They are best boiled for eating but do not set hard like a fowl's egg, the albumen or white remaining quite liquid.

When the baby turtles hatch from such eggs as are left they make for the sea, but very few survive to come to maturity. On land many fail from exhaustion and they may be attacked by birds and crabs; in the sea sharks and other predatory fishes are waiting for them.

The diet of the Green Turtle is almost entirely vegetarian, consisting of seaweeds and other marine plants.

Hawksbill Turtle (*Eretmochelys imbricata*). This species is not so abundant as the Green Turtle, but is of some economic importance, though for quite a different reason. The thin translucent horny plates which cover the dorsal surface of the shell furnish the so-called tortoise-shell of commerce. The plates are removed, after the animal is killed, by immersion in hot water. Heating of the plates renders them plastic and they can be welded together, so that the form of the articles manufactured is not limited by the thickness of a single plate. Sometimes the plates are removed by heat from the living animal, which is returned to the sea in the belief that it will grow new ones. There is no foundation for this belief and the practice is a cruel one which should be stopped whenever it is met with.

The Hawksbill feeds mainly on crabs and prawns, which it crushes with the hooked jaws which give it its name.

The **Leathery Turtle** (*Dermochelys coriacea* Plate 9) is by far the largest of the turtles and is, in fact, the largest living Chelonian (a term comprising turtles and tortoises). It may measure nearly eight feet in length and weigh over half a ton. It is recognised by the seven longitudinal ridges on the shell, which differs from that of all other turtles in consisting not of a few symmetrically arranged shields but of a great number of closely set small bones covered with smooth leathery skin.

The Leathery Turtle has always been considered to be rare. but in 1952 it was discovered that large numbers of them come ashore every year to lay their eggs on the coast of Trengganu, north of Dungun. The breeding habits are similar to those of the Green Turtle, but the eggs are larger, as big as billiard balls. The tracks made by these turtles in the sand, as they laboriously make their way up and down the shore, are easily recognisable, as their width, representing the span of the front flippers, is about seven feet.

The **Loggerhead Turtle** (*Caretta caretta*) is occasionally taken in Malayan waters. The large head and greater number of large dorsal shields on each side of the central row (usually 6 to 9 as against 4) distinguish it from the Green Turtle.

Of the **Freshwater Turtles or Mud Turtles** the **Malayan Mud Turtle** (*Trionyx cartilagineus*) is the only common species. The shell is flattened and covered with soft skin instead of the symmetrically arranged shields found in most tortoises and turtles; it is olive in colour, unmarked in the adult but usually some yellow-bordered black spots are present in the young. The snout ends in a fleshy proboscis and the feet are webbed for swimming. The shell may exceed two feet in length.

Mud turtles live in swamps and slowly flowing rivers, feeding on fish and frogs, which they catch by hunting or by lying in wait, buried in mud but for the head. The neck is long and the head can be shot out with great speed to deliver a vicious bite. Large ones are dangerous and should be handled with great caution by grasping the edges of the shell just in front of the hind limbs; they can reach anywhere forward of this with their jaws.

The flesh is eaten by some of the country people.

Three species of **Land Tortoises** and eleven of **Water Tortoises** or **Terrapins** are known in Malaya.

The former live in hilly jungle and can be recognised by their strangely club-shaped hind feet and by the fact that there is no trace of a web between any of the fingers or toes. Only one species, the **Burmese Brown Tortoise** (*Testudo emys*) is at all common.

Of the Terrapins the following are the most frequently met with:

Malayan Box Tortoise (*Cuora amboinensis*). This species is easily recognised because the lower surface of the shell has the front and back portions moveable along a transverse "hinge", so that the shell can be completely closed. The shell is very convex, brown or black above and yellow beneath with large black spots, or black with the margins of the shields yellow; the head is brown with yellow markings. The Box Tortoise is common in ponds and rice-fields; it can be kept in captivity and fed on fruit and vegetables, and is particularly fond of bananas.

Spiny Hill Tortoise (*Geomyda spinosa*). The young are remarkable in having the whole margin of the shell serrated like the edge of a saw, but the sharp teeth become reduced with age and confined to the front and back margins. The shell is dark brown above and on the under surface each shield is marked with brown and yellow radiating streaks. The head and limbs are brown marked with bright red spots. This tortoise is found both in hilly and lowland jungle and is quite common in Singapore in the wooded country round the reservoirs.

Black Pond Tortoise (*Siebenrockiella crassicollis*). The shell is black above and black, or yellow marked with black, below.

(M.W.F. Tweedie)

Plate 9.   Leathery Turtle

(M.W.F. Tweedie)

Plate 10. Paradise Tree-snake

(M.W.F. Tweedie)

Plate 11. Wagler's Pit-viper

Plate 12.   Kuhl's Flying Gecko

(*M.W.F. Tweedie*)

The head is black with yellow markings, which include a spot surrounding the eye, one on each temple and others on the jaws. It lives in ponds, swamps and streams and is carnivorous, feeding on frogs and snails; it seems to be most frequent in the northern states.

The **River Tortoise** (*Batagur baska*) is a fairly large aquatic tortoise with a prominent up-turned snout. It is entirely herbivorous and lives in the mouths of the larger rivers, ascending to the higher reaches to bury its eggs in sand-banks. Its breeding behaviour is similar to that of the Green Turtle and its eggs are held in even higher esteem.

Crocodiles. These are large aquatic reptiles and the Estuarine Crocodile, which is a member of the Malayan fauna, grows to a greater size than any other reptile now living. Two species are found in Malaya, and a third, the Siamese Crocodile (*Crocodilus siamensis*) may extend into the northern part of Malaya.

Estuarine Crocodile (*Crocodilus porosus*). This is the common crocodile of the tropical Asiatic river mouths and mangrove swamps. It grows to an enormous size; the two largest individuals recorded were 33 and 29 feet long, the former from Bengal, the latter from the Philippines. The Bengal specimen is said to have measured 13 feet 8 inches round the middle. They are, however, mature before they reach half this size, and crocodiles have been hunted so long and so relentlessly that large ones, exceeding twenty feet are now very rare.

As its name implies this crocodile is chiefly an inhabitant of the muddy deltas and swamps of the larger river mouths. It does not ascend into the upper reaches of the rivers but often travels overland in the lowlands and takes up its abode in lakes and deserted mining holes. It also ventures into the sea, swimming along the coast from one river mouth to another.

Large crocodiles are dangerous and one of ten feet in length is quite ready to attack a man and capable of overcoming him. Victims are usually taken when wading, but people walking at the water's edge may have their legs swept from under them by a stroke of the reptile's tail and be dragged under the surface in its jaws. Animals coming to drink are often attacked and when dragging large prey into the water the crocodile twists or rolls over and over, making it impossible for the victim to get a foothold to enable it to resist. It has been stated that the body of a large victim is sometimes hidden under an overhanging bank until decomposition renders it easier to tear to pieces for swallowing, but this has never been proved, and a large crocodile can certainly dismember and devour a body without keeping it in this way. They do not, of course, depend entirely on such dramatic methods to obtain food, but subsist largely on fish, water birds, turtles, etc., and the young eat crustaceans and insects.

The breeding habits are interesting. When the female is due to lay her eggs, she seeks a damp and secluded situation on the land and there makes a dome-shaped nest of leaves or reeds in which the eggs are enclosed. There they are kept damp and protected from the heat of the sun, though the warmth of the decomposing vegetable matter probably aids incubation. The mother crocodile digs wallows near the nest in one of which she remains to guard the eggs until they hatch. The eggs have a hard white shell and measure about three by two inches; as many as sixty may be laid in a nest. Baby crocodiles can be kept in captivity; they like to spend most of their time in water and can be fed on scraps of meat or fish. They do not become tame, however, and are always liable to bite.

Both crocodiles and marine turtles are in danger of extermination by hunting to provide frivolous luxuries: fancy leather from the former and soup for banquets from the turtles. Civilised people should refrain from buying or using either.

Malayan Gharial (*Tomistoma schlegeli*). This crocodile is easily distinguished by its long slender snout and numerous small teeth. It is found only in fresh water and lives in the inland swamps and rivers. Although it grows to about fifteen feet it is not dangerous and appears to feed on fish, its slender jaws and numerous sharp teeth being clearly adapted for seizing them. The Malayan Gharial resembles the Indian Gharial (*Gavialis*) in appearance, but is not really closely related to it. No confusion need arise as the two are found in quite different parts of the world, *Tomistoma* being confined to the Malay Peninsula, Borneo and Sumatra.

Lizards. A large number of species of lizards inhabits Malaya, and no attempt can be made to describe or mention more than a representative few. If two rare species, which need not be mentioned here, are excluded, they can be classified as follows:

I. Top of the head covered with small, irregularly arranged or granular scales.

(1) The body covered with small granular scales; either there are no moveable eyelids or the pupil of the eye is like a vertical slit or (more commonly) both these characters are present; body flattened from above, legs short, tail not very long or flexible. **Geckos**

(2) The back with usually larger, often overlapping scales; eyelids moveable and pupil round; legs and tail long, the latter flexible; mostly tree dwellers. **Agamids**

(3) The back with granular, never overlapping, scales; tongue long and forked like that of a snake; large ground-dwelling lizards. **Monitors**

II. Top of the head covered with symmetrically arranged shields; legs always short, sometimes rudimentary. **Skinks**

Geckos. The most familiar of the lizards, in fact by far the most familiar of our reptiles, are the little house geckos or chichaks, which run up the walls of our rooms and astonish newcomers to the tropics by their extraordinary capacity for walking upside-down on the ceiling. If a chichak's feet are examined the toes are seen to be expanded, the expansions being divided into a number of little overlapping flaps of skin (Fig. 53).

When examined with a microscope these are seen to be covered with exceedingly small, closely set hairs, making their surfaces rather like velvet. It is the clinging action of these hairs, making close contact with minute irregularities, that enables the chichak to run vertically, or even upside-down, on quite smooth surfaces. The flaps of skin do not, as has been supposed in the past, act as suckers; a moment's thought will show that on a porous surface like the plaster of a ceiling a sucker would be ineffective. On rough surfaces the claws are, of course, used as well.

Another interesting thing about the house geckos is that they are among the few animals which gain advantage from the presence of civilised man without becoming his enemy. Generally, when houses and fields take the place of jungle, most of the animals retreat and a few, like the rat and some insects, remain and multiply at the expense of our crops or other products. But the chichaks, which are not very common in jungle, find our houses quite as comfortable as a hollow tree, far freer from their deadly enemies, the snakes, and, most important of all, are provided with an abundant food supply by the insects which are attracted to artificial light. Cases of this kind are rather rare; an obvious parallel is seen in the way houses provide nesting sites for cliff-dwelling birds like swifts and swallows.

Although many lizards can do this, none are more ready to part with their tails than the geckos. This manœuvre is obviously useful if the lizard is seized from behind by a pursuing enemy, and the continued twitching of the severed tail serves to engage the attention of the pursuer while the gecko makes its escape. A new tail grows, but differs in appearance from the old one, so that it is easy to see whether a gecko has ever parted with its tail; a surprising number will be found to have made the sacrifice.

Like other lizards and snakes geckos shed the outer layer of their skin from time to time.

The **Common House Gecko** (*Hemidactylus frenatus*) is the most abundant of the chichaks. Two other species are also common; the **Flat-tailed Gecko** (*Hemidactylus platyurus*) has the body and tail more flattened and the toes partly webbed, and the **Four-clawed Gecko** (*Gehyra mutilata*) is similarly flattened and differs from *Hemidactylus* in having the inner toe on all its feet without a claw. The **Tokay** (*Gekko gecko*), which also inhabits houses, is rather uncommon in Malaya. It is much larger than the chichaks, growing to a foot in length, and even more vociferous. Its call consists of a preliminary cackle followed by a loud "tok-kaa" repeated several times. It is blue-grey above spotted with yellow or brick red. The Tokay feeds not only on insects but on other lizards and even mice and birds; its jaws are powerful and can give quite a severe bite if it is carelessly handled. A house gecko intermediate in size between the chichaks and the Tokay is the **Spotted Gecko** (*Gekko monarchus*); it is marked with black spots on a pale ground and grows to about eight inches, and is not uncommon.

Of great interest are the **Flying Geckos**, of which **Kuhl's**

Flying Gecko (*Ptychozoon kuhli*, Fig. 54 and Plate 12) is the most frequent. They have the feet broadly webbed, the tail with a scalloped frill of skin on each side and the body and head with lateral expansions of thicker skin which are curled underneath the animal except when it takes to "flight." When it launches itself

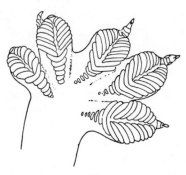

53.

Figs. 53 and 54. Geckos: 53. Four-clawed Gecko, underside of fore-foot; 54. Kuhl's Flying Gecko, the hinder part of the tail has been lost and has grown again without the scalloped edges.

54.

into the air the flaps on the head and body are forced out by air pressure and, together with the webbed feet and frilled tail, buoy the lizard up so that it goes into a controlled glide like that of a flying squirrel.

All the geckos lay round white eggs with a brittle shell like a bird's egg. Those of the chichaks are like white peas and are laid, usually two at a time, in crevices and behind pictures and pieces of furniture; they remain about two months before hatching. They are all nocturnal animals and like to find a dark cranny into which to retreat during the day; chichaks greatly prefer old houses to new ones.

Next to claim our attention are the so-called **Agamid Lizards.** Most of these are long-legged, long-tailed arboreal lizards, though one Malayan species burrows in sandy ground. A portrait of a typical arboreal Agamid, *Gonocephalus belli*, is shown as the frontispiece of this book.

Our commonest Agamid is the **Green Crested Lizard** (*Calotes cristatellus*, Fig. 55). It is often wrongly called the Chameleon; it is not a chameleon, these being a group of peculiar lizards almost confined to Africa and Madagascar and not found in Malaya. Another most unsuitable name by which it is sometimes known is "bloodsucker"; it does not and cannot suck blood. This is the slender, bright green, long-legged lizard, with a serrated crest on its back, often seen scrambling about in trees and bushes. Its power of changing colour is almost as startling as that of the chameleons with which it is confused. If it is grasped or in any way seriously alarmed it turns dark brown, almost black, in a few seconds. Other colour changes are recorded and apparently reflect the lizard's mood rather than its surroundings; for instance in the breeding season the lips, cheeks and throat of males become red or crimson. When courting the male inflates the pouch under his throat and advances towards the female, solemnly raising and lowering his head and at the same time opening and shutting his mouth.

There is a superstition that the bite of this lizard is poisonous; this is entirely without foundation, no venomous reptiles other than snakes occur in Malaya. The eggs are long and spindle-shaped, covered with parchment-like skin and are buried a few inches deep in the ground.

The most remarkable of the Agamids are undoubtedly the **Flying Lizards** (genus *Draco*). In these the last five to seven ribs, instead of curving round and enclosing the chest in the normal manner, are prolonged outside the body and support a membrane of skin. These ribs are hinged to the backbone horizontally, so that the whole apparatus can be folded back against the sides of the body or extended when required for "flight".

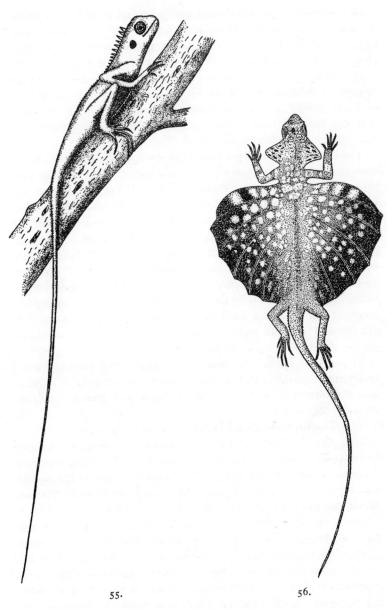

Figs. 55 and 56.   Agamid Lizards: 55. Green Crested Lizard; 56. Flying Lizard
(*Draco volans*), in attitude of flight.

Of course these lizards do not really fly, but glide from a point on one tree to one at a lower level on another. Like the flying squirrels and lemur and the flying gecko described in this chapter they are a product of the dense tropical forests, where great tracts of country can be crossed by passing from one tree to another without ever descending to the ground. The evolution of these highly specialised arboreal animals provides evidence that the tropical rain forests must have been continuously in existence for an enormous period of time.

The **Common Flying Lizard** (*Draco volans*, Fig. 56), is often seen in gardens and estates and by the roadside. When running up the trunk of a tree the "wings" are folded out of sight and it looks like an ordinary lizard; its mottled brown coloration makes it remarkably inconspicuous against a background of bark. It is not easy to persuade one to fly to order, it is more likely to run up the tree and seek safety in its branches, but occasionally one is lucky enough to see one in action by chance. Both sexes have a pouch under the throat, yellow in the male, bluish-green in the female, and a lateral flap on each side of it. These are much larger in the male are used in the courtship display, when they are inflated and the pouch pushed backwards and forwards by means of a bone which extends into it.

Flying lizards seldom voluntarily come to the ground except to lay their eggs, which are oval, usually three or four in number and are buried in leaf-mould at the base of a tree. They feed entirely on insects.

The **Granular-scaled Lizard** (*Liolepis belliana*) is exceptional among the Agamids in being a ground dweller. It inhabits burrows in sandy places near the coast and is largely a vegetable feeder. It has the long legs and tail characteristic of the family, but the body is flattened from above and the dorsal scales are small and granular. When alarmed it makes for its burrow with amazing speed, raising its tail and running well up on its hind legs. It grows to over a foot in length and has a pattern of yellow black-edged spots or stripes on the back and black and red bars on the flanks. *Liolepis* is found on both sides of the northern and central parts of Malaya and is especially abundant in the flat sandy country near the coast in Kelantan and Trengganu.

The **Monitors** include the largest of the lizards, the biggest species of all being the **Komodo Monitor,** which lives only in the region of Komodo Island and West Flores in the Lesser Sunda Islands. These great lizards are very bulky but probably do not exceed ten feet in length, despite exaggerated reports to the contrary.

Their large size and the long, forked tongue, which can be protruded from the mouth, distinguishes the monitors from other Malayan lizards. The commonest and largest Malayan species is the **Common Water Monitor** (*Varanus salvator*), which is said to attain eight feet in length; its tail, however, is proportionately much longer than that of the Komodo Monitor, so that our species is far less bulky. It is nevertheless a big animal and quite formidable, defending itself mainly by lashing with its tail, with which it can deal a very powerful blow, and hissing in an alarming manner. Monitors feed on such birds and other small animals as they can catch, and are enemies of domestic poultry. They are great destroyers of turtles' eggs, digging for them on the sandy shores, and are probably the chief foe against which the mother crocodile guards her nest. They also feed on crabs and insects and are very fond of eating carrion. They can run fast and are expert swimmers, especially *V. salvator*, which can remain below the surface for a long time and has been encountered swimming far out to sea.

The eggs are deposited in holes or hollow trees beside rivers. The young of the common species are handsomely marked with transverse rows of yellow spots on a black ground, but the spots become obscure with age and adults are usually blackish with indistinct yellow markings.

Several other monitors occur in Malaya; in all of them the nostril is either nearer to the eye than to end of the snout or about half way between the two. The Common Water Monitor has the nostril much nearer to the end of the snout than to the eye. The skins of monitors are the main source of the ornamental leather known as lizard skin.

The **Skinks,** although they do not invade our houses as the geckos do, must be familiar to all observant people in this country. The commonest species is the **Sun Lizard** (*Mabuya multifasciata*), which is often seen sunning itself on a path or slipping actively away into the grass or bushes. The scales on its head, like those of all skinks, are large and symmetrically arranged; the body is bronzy brown above with a metallic lustre, there is a patch of orange on each flank and the under parts are greenish or yellowish white. If a specimen is closely examined each scale is seen to have three (sometimes five) longitudinal keels or ridges.

Among the **Supple Skinks** (*Lygosoma*) there are some species in which the legs are vestigial, being reduced to little functionless tags, and the body is elongated like a snake's. Such forms are burrowers and two are common at Cameron Highlands and other localities in the mountains. One of these (*L. larutense*) is olive with oblique white stripes on the neck, and the other (*L. miodactylum*) is glossy black. Wholly legless skinks, appearing like snakes, are known from other countries.

Some of the skinks lay eggs, others, including the Sun Lizard, bear their young alive. All, so far as is known, feed on insects, the burrowing forms on termites, insect larvae, etc.

CHAPTER SEVEN

REPTILES AND AMPHIBIANS

Snakes. Study of their anatomy makes it clear that snakes have been evolved from lizard-like, limbed ancestors, having passed through stages like those leading to the legless and almost legless skinks. In some primitive snakes such as the pythons vestiges of the hind limbs are present, but no snake is known in which any trace of the fore limbs exists. All snakes (except a few which are blind) have transparent immovable eyelids and none have any external ear-opening. The right and left jaws, both upper and lower, can move independently of each other, as they are not firmly joined in front, and the tongue can be protruded or withdrawn into a sheath, like that of the monitor lizards. The poison apparatus of the venomous snakes consists of a pair of enlarged teeth in the upper jaw which are hollow or deeply grooved and connected by ducts, or tubes, to glands which secrete the venom. Although it may be deadly to large animals it is not much use as a weapon of defence as its action is slow; its real purpose is probably to paralyse a struggling prey and make it easier to swallow. Apart from the poison fangs the teeth of snakes are simple, backwardly directed hooks. The prey is swallowed whole, generally head first, by alternate backward and forward movements of the jaws, all four of which can move independently of each other, as pointed out above.

Like lizards, snakes slough off their skins from time to time, but the skin usually peels off entire like a stocking. The cast skins may sometimes be found in thick grass or herbage. The colour and pattern of a snake are always brighter just after the skin is cast, and they are also almost invariably brighter in young than in adult snakes; in some species they change profoundly as the reptile grows up, so that the young and adult are entirely different in appearance.

For the sake of convenience we will divide the snakes into poisonous and non-poisonous groups and give some account of the latter first. They are far more numerous, numbering nearly a hundred species, and only a few can be mentioned.

Non-poisonous Snakes. Two species of pythons are found in Malaya and the larger, the **Reticulated Python** (*Python reticulatus*) has the distinction of being the largest snake now living. The tropical American Anaconda is stouter, but not sufficiently so to compensate for its lesser maximum length. Pythons are known to grow to about thirty feet, and one of this length would weigh as much as 250 pounds; the normal length of an adult is about twenty feet. The Reticulated Python is handsomely marked with a pattern of black yellow-edged lines forming a network on a brown background; the scales are beautifully iridescent, especially just after the skin is cast. Vestiges of hind limbs are present in the skeleton and are visible externally in the form of a claw-like spur on each side of the vent.

These pythons feed mainly on birds and mammals, and even big ones prefer fairly small prey such as monkeys or, near habitations, cats and dogs. It follows from this that a python is most unlikely to attack a man with a view to eating him. They kill their prey by coiling the body round it and squeezing it to death. The power of constriction is very great but is often exaggerated; the bones are not crushed, the victim merely being squeezed until it can no longer breathe. Young pythons do good service by destroying rats. Pythons lay their eggs in hollow trees or similar places, usually thirty to fifty or sixty in number. Unlike those of most snakes they are not abandoned as soon as laid, but the mother python coils round them, guarding and brooding them until they hatch. Her maternal instincts do not, however, extend to the young snakes, which are left to look after themselves. When newly hatched they are about two feet long.

The **Short Python** (*Python curtus*) is much smaller, not exceeding nine feet; the body is extremely thick in contrast to the small head and short, pointed tail. It is brown or brick red with lighter markings on the back and sides.

Perhaps the commonest, and certainly the most frequently encountered, Malayan snake is the **House Snake** (*Lycodon* *aulicus*). These little snakes often enter houses, probably in search of geckos, on which they feed. The colour is dark brown and some of the scales have white edges, which form an irregular pattern of fine wavy white lines. The snout is rather flattened and there is a white cross-band on the neck which may be spotted with brown. Its appearance is very distinct from that of any other Malayan snake (certainly from any of the poisonous ones) and it is quite harmless.

Another pretty, inoffensive snake often seen in gardens is the **Striped Kukri Snake** (*Oligodon octolineatus*). It is yellow or buff in colour with pairs of longitudinal black stripes running the length of the body and tail. The two uppermost black stripes enclose a bright red one along the middle of the back; underneath it is pink. It is so named because some of the teeth, which are extremely minute, are shaped rather like a Gurkha Kukri.

The **Red-tailed Pipe Snake** (*Cylindrophis rufus*) is also common. It is iridescent black, barred with white underneath, and the underside of the tail is bright red. When molested it raises the tail, the effect being as if a luridly coloured head were being raised in defiance. On account of this habit it is sometimes called the 'two-headed snake'.

Among the larger ground snakes are the **Racers** (genus *Elaphe*), of which the **Common Malayan Racer** (*Elaphe flavolineata*) is quite often seen. It grows to over six feet in length and is black above, paler below, with some black blotches low down on each side of the fore part of the body, and a black mark below, and another behind, each eye. It is often confused with the Malayan Cobra, but this snake is everywhere black except for some white marks under the throat. The **Striped Racer** (*E. taeniura*) is the pale coloured snake which is found in the dark bat-haunted caves in limestone hills, as at Batu Caves near Kuala Lumpur. These snakes feed entirely on bats which fall, sick or injured, from the roof of the cave.

Larger still are the **Rat Snakes**. The **Keeled Rat Snake** (*Zaocys carinatus*) is dark olive brown with a checkered black and yellow pattern on the tail. It grows to over twelve feet and is very fast and active. These snakes are certainly useful in destroying rats, as their name implies, but prey on other animals as well.

The **Common Blind Snake** (*Typhlops braminus*) is a burrowing snake, often found under logs and stones or in the course of digging, and is easily mistaken for a black earthworm. It is very small, six inches or less, and the eyes are quite concealed under the scales, which are themselves so small as to be visible only by close examination. There are several other species of blind snakes and they all live underground and feed on insects.

Many snakes are inhabitants of the trees and are expert climbers. The **Paradise Tree-snake** (*Chrysopelea paradisi*, Fig. 57 and Plate 10), is typical of them. It is a beautiful creature, black with a bright green spot on each scale, so that the body is marked with a regular pattern of green spots; in addition there is a row of four-petalled red spots along the back and the underside is yellowish green. Its powers of climbing are remarkable. It can crawl straight up the vertical trunk of a large, rough-barked tree, an extraordinary feat for a limbless animal. It is, of course, perfectly at home among the twigs and branches and can leap considerable distances. It even has the power of falling in a controlled glide like that of the flying lizards; it does this not by spreading a membrane of any kind but by hollowing the under side of the body so that a cushion of air is trapped below it.

The **Grass-green Whip-snake** (*Dryophis prasinus*, Fig. 59), is easily recognised by its long pointed snout and extremely slender body, nowhere thicker than a man's finger in a five foot specimen. The eyes of the whip-snakes are curious, the pupil being horizontally elongated.

The **Yellow-ringed Cat-snake** or **Mangrove Snake** (*Boiga dendrophila*, Fig. 58), is one of the largest of the tree-snakes, and grows to seven feet. It is a handsome creature, black with narrow yellow cross-bands which may or may not meet over the back. It is found in lowland forest and mangrove swamp and is easily tamed. Snake charmers often keep mangrove snakes and sometimes wrongly call them kraits. The cat-snakes (Genus *Boiga*) are so called because the pupil of the eye is vertically narrowed like a cat's. Several species occur in addition to the present one, but all are less common. They feed on birds and lizards.

All snakes can swim and some of them are entirely aquatic. The **Dog-faced Water-snake** (*Cerberus rhynchops*) is one of the commonest of these. It is a drab coloured reptile, brownish grey with indistinct darker markings and each scale has a strong longitudinal ridge on it. These snakes are often abundant in swampy country both near the sea and inland. They feed on fish and frogs and can be taken on a baited hook.

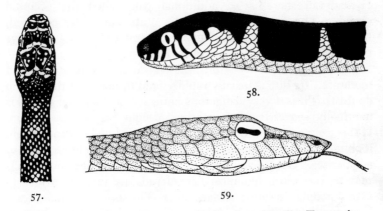

Figs. 57 to 59. Head and fore part of body of: 57. Paradise Tree-snake; 58. Yellow-ringed Cat-snake; 59. Grass-green Whip-snake.

Poisonous snakes. Far fewer kinds of poisonous than of harmless snakes are found in Malaya. The twenty species of sea snakes are all venomous; of those that live on the land sixteen of a total of over a hundred species are poisonous and none of these is very abundant. One seldom hears or reads of cases of snake-bite in Malaya, and very seldom of fatal cases. The Malayan poisonous snakes fall into three distinct groups, one comprising the cobras, kraits and coral snakes, another the vipers and a third the sea snakes.

The **King Cobra** or **Hamadryad** (*Naja hannah*) is the world's largest poisonous snake; adults are usually about fourteen feet long and the largest one ever recorded was over eighteen feet. The colour is olive with or without darker cross-bands, and the throat is yellow or orange, a feature which becomes conspicuous when the snake rears up and spreads its hood. The appearance is very like that of the large rat-snakes and it is not easy to distinguish them at a glance, but if the snake is killed examination of the scales on top of the head will immediately decide whether it is a hamadryad or not. The arrangement seen in a racer, and most other snakes as well, is that shown at Figs. 60, 61, that of the Hamadryad at Fig. 62. In the former there is only one pair of large shields, in contact with each other, behind the three shields lying between the eyes; in the Hamadryad there is an additional pair called the occipital shields. The young Hamadryad is quite differently coloured, black banded with yellow, but the occipital shields are always present and are a sure guide to its identity.

The King Cobra feeds on other reptiles, mainly snakes and monitors. Its bite is usually rapidly fatal to man and there is no doubt that it is a very dangerous animal, but the belief that it is habitually aggressive and attacks on sight has no foundation. If this were so cases would frequently be reported of deaths from its bite, for it is not rare in Malaya, but one very seldom hears of such cases. Occasionally unusually bold or savage individuals may be met with, but most hamadryads are just as anxious to avoid people as other snakes are. The breeding habits are interesting and unusual. A kind of nest consisting of a heap of leaves is made and the eggs laid at the bottom of it. Above them and separated by a layer of leaves, but still within the heap, the mother lies coiled, guarding them.

The **Common Cobra** (*Naja naja*). The form of this snake found in Malaya is generally black with some irregular white markings under the throat, but brown or yellow specimens are found in the northern states. It grows to about six feet in length and is not easy to distinguish, at a glance, from several species of blackish harmless snakes, but if brought to bay its erect posture and spread hood are unmistakeable. The hood is formed by the loose skin of the neck being pushed out by the ribs, which are elongated in that part of the body; the mechanism is very like that which spreads the parachute of the flying lizards. Like the Hamadryad the Cobra also has distinguishing scale characters. Examine the scales bordering the lower lip, and between the fourth and fifth from the front will be found a small triangular scale whose presence is definite evidence that the snake is a cobra (Fig. 63); the enlarged third upper lip shield is a feature shared by both cobras and the coral snakes, and so is good evidence of a poisonous snake (Fig. 63).

Cobras feed on rats and mice and frogs; they certainly do good service by destroying the former, entering their holes and swallowing whole broods of the young at a time. The bite is dangerously poisonous, though cases of people recovering from it without treatment are not infrequent. The Cobra also has the

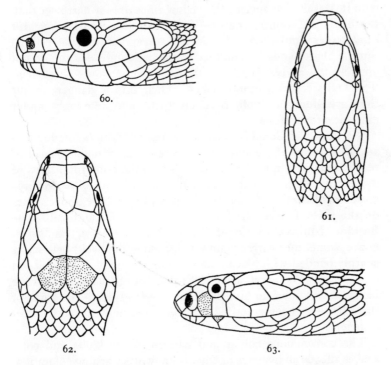

Figs. 60 to 63. Diagrams of the head-shields of: 60, 61. Common Malayan Racer; 62. Hamadryad; 63. Common Cobra. In 62 the occipital shields, and in 63 the third upper lip-shield and the triangular cuneate shield are stippled.

habit of spitting its venom, when angry or frightened, to a distance of six feet or more. If it enters one's eyes it may cause serious injury; never closely inspect a cobra imprisoned behind wire netting unless your eyes are protected. The Cobra does not make a nest like the Hamadryad, but both male and female are believed to stay near the eggs and guard them until they hatch.

Two of the three kinds of **Kraits** known in this country

are not uncommon. The **Banded Krait** (*Bungarus fasciatus*) is the largest and perhaps the commonest. It is very conspicuously marked with alternate black and pale yellow rings or bars, which are about equal in width and encircle the body. The Mangrove Snake (*Boiga dendrophila*) is sometimes confused with it, but in that species the yellow rings are far narrower than the black intervening spaces. The **Malayan Krait** (*Bungarus candidus*) is similarly banded with black and white (not yellow) but the black bands are confined to the back and sides and do not encircle the body. It seldom grows to much over three feet. The kraits feed on other snakes. Their bite is dangerous but they are sluggish, inoffensive creatures and bite only under extreme provocation.

Two kinds of **Coral Snakes** are common, both belonging to a genus in which the gland which secretes the venom, instead of being contained in the head, extends into the body for a third of its length. Both are conspicuously coloured, the **Blue Malaysian Coral Snake** (*Maticora bivirgata*) being blue above, paler on the sides and red beneath and on the head and tail. The **Banded Malaysian Coral Snake** (*M. intestinalis*) is brown above, sometimes with a yellow stripe along the back; below it is sharply banded with black and white on the body, black and red on the tail. The coral snakes also feed on other snakes and are hardly ever known to bite people; no case of death from one of them has ever been recorded. *M. bivirgata* may exceed five feet in length.

The conspicuous colour and pattern of the kraits and coral snakes affords an instance of what is known as warning coloration. The action of snake venom is never so rapid that a relatively large animal, when bitten, has not plenty of time to deal with the snake before it loses the power to do so. Hence it is to the advantage of a poisonous snake to make known its venomous nature and so dissuade predatory animals from attacking it (we are not concerned here with the relations between snakes and humanity). Nothing could be more conspicuous than the sharply contrasted banding of the kraits or the pillar-box red of the coral snakes, and there is little doubt that they are designed to serve as a warning.

The **Vipers** are a very distinct group of snakes, all poisonous.

They include such well-known snakes as the American rattle-snakes and the very dangerous Russell's Viper, which occurs in Thailand and in Java and South Sumatra, but, fortunately, not in Malaya. Most of them are stout snakes of no great size and have the head broad and sharply marked off from the neck. The poison fangs are very long and when the mouth is closed they lie flat with their points directed backwards and are enclosed in a fleshy sheath. The upper jaw and certain bones of the skull are arranged as a system of levers, and when the snake opens its mouth to bite the fangs automatically spring erect and the sheath slips back.

All the Malayan species of viper belong to the group known as **Pit-vipers,** which are distinguished by the presence of a deep pit on each side of the head, between eye and nostril. This is a thermo-sensitive organ, designed to detect heat in very small amount; it enables the snake to find warm-blooded prey (small mammals and birds) in complete darkness. The bite of these snakes is not dangerous to human life and usually results in more or less acute pain and swelling around the part that is bitten. The commonest species is **Wagler's Pit-viper** (*Trimere-surus wagleri*, Plate 11). This is a snake in which young and adult are very different in appearance. The young is green with two rows of red and white spots; the adult is black speckled with green and barred with yellow. It lives in trees and bushes and when found is usually very sluggish and disinclined to move. Wagler's Pit-viper is the species which is kept in the snake temple at Penang. Several other species of *Trimeresurus* are found in Malaya; they are all distinguished by the broad, flat head with the pit in the side of the face, and by the fact that the scales on the top of the head are small and irregularly arranged, instead of being symmetrically arranged shields as in all the snakes we have considered hitherto.

Sea Snakes. This is a well-defined group of snakes, entirely marine, and distinguished by having the tail flattened like the blade of an oar for swimming. Most of them never come to land, but live in the surface waters of the sea, feeding on fish and bearing their young alive in such an advanced stage of develop-ment that they are able to swim away and take care of themselves as soon as they are born. All the sea snakes are venomous and their bite is dangerous to human life. Fortunately they never attack bathers and the only people who get bitten occasionally are fishermen who accidentally hook them or catch them in their nets. The **Common Sea Snake** (*Enhydrina schistosa*) is the most abundant species. It grows to between three and four feet and is grey, the young with black rings.

The **Amphibious Sea Snake** (*Laticauda colubrina*) comes ashore to lay its eggs, being one of the few sea snakes which reproduce in this way, and is often found under stones on the shore on small islands. Nothing seems to be known about its venom, for although these snakes are often handled by inquisitive people they have never been known to bite anyone. The colour is bluish grey with regular black bands on the body, and the head is marked with black and yellow. Some of the sea snakes attain quite a large size, up to nine feet in length, and one, the black and orange banded *Astrotia stokesi*, has been described as being as thick as a man's leg above the knee.

Amphibians. This group of animals, which includes frogs, toads, caecilians and the newts and salamanders of temperate countries, is truly intermediate between the fish and reptiles. In all of them the early stages are passed as strictly aquatic water-breathing creatures called tadpoles, while the adult is an air-breathing animal. An amphibian, in fact, spends the earlier part of its life as a fish and the later as a reptile.

Frogs and Toads. A great variety of these animals is found in Malaya. A few are familiar, but the majority are forest dwellers, which are seldom seen, though they can be heard croaking at night by people who live or camp in the jungle.

The **Common Asiatic Toad** (*Bufo melanostictus*) is abundant almost everywhere and can be found any evening by simply walking around the garden with an electric torch. Like the European frog it has become a martyr to science and provides the introduction to anatomy for medical and zoological students in Asian countries. It is a typical toad with dry, warty skin, brown in colour, the ridges and warts of the skin black. The eggs are laid in long jelly-like strings twined about water weeds in ponds. They can be hatched and the tadpoles reared in an aquarium without any difficulty.

The true frogs (*Rana*) differ from toads in having a smooth, slimy skin and in spending a great part of their adult lives in water. The **Green-backed Frog** (*Rana erythraea*) is one of the commonest and is beautifully coloured, bright green above with a dark brown stripe along each side of the head and body, and pure white below. It is abundant everywhere in swamps and rice fields. The **Giant Frog** (*Rana macrodon*) is one of the largest frogs known and may exceed nine inches from nose to "tail". While most batrachians (as frogs and toads are collectively called) live almost entirely on insects, the Giant Frog eats crabs, snails, scorpions and has even been caught tackling a snake. Its colour varies from olive to bronze brown with a paler stripe down the middle of the back.

The **Bullfrog** (*Kaloula pulchra*) is the author of the tremendous bellowing chorus that rises from swamps on rainy nights. It may be native to the northern states, but is said to have been introduced into Singapore shortly before the beginning of the present century, and has probably spread thence to other localities in southern Malaya. Anyone who has heard it croaking will be surprised at its small size when confronted with it, for it is no larger than the Common Toad. It is prettily coloured, rich brown with a broad, dark-edged yellow or pink stripe along each side. As in all frogs it is the males that croak, and those of *Kaloula* do so floating, partly blown up with air, on the surface of the water.

A large number of frogs are inhabitants of the trees and have disc-shaped suckers at the tips of the toes to enable them to hold on to the smooth surfaces of leaves and branches. The commonest of these is the **Malayan Tree-frog** (*Rhacophorus leucomystax*). It is very variable in colour, grey, green or yellowish brown spotted or striped with black. **Wallace's Flying Frog** (*R. nigropalmatus*) is also a member of this genus. It is rather rare but deserves mention as it is yet another case of a "glider." The fingers and toes are very long and broadly webbed with skin, and they serve as a parachute to enable the animal to make gliding leaps from tree to tree. Unlike other frogs and toads tree frogs do not enter the water to breed, but lay their eggs in frothy masses on plants growing in or overhanging pools of water. These slip off, or are washed off by rain, into the water below and float until they break up and release the tadpoles, which have already hatched and begun developing.

The **Toad-frogs** are, as their name implies, somewhat intermediate between toads and frogs; they look like toads but have a moist, slimy skin. The **Nose-horned Frog** (*Megophrys nasuta*) is the commonest of them and is a quaint looking creature with a horn-like projection of skin over each eye and another on the snout. It is fairly common in wooded country, but its irregular outline and brown colour make it very difficult to see against a background of dead leaves. The tadpoles, which are found in hill streams, are remarkable in having the mouth turned outwards in the form of a funnel, wider than the head, with which minute particles of food are collected from the surface of the water.

Caecilians. No one but a zoologist would take these curious creatures for amphibians; they look more like snakes or eels. The adults burrow in the soft soil beside streams and are seldom seen, but the immature ones, which are aquatic, are common in small hill streams and can be found by turning over stones. They are very like small snakes, but have no scales and the tip of the tail is compressed as if it had been pinched between finger and thumb. There are two species in Malaya, the **Sticky Caecilian** (*Ichthyophis glutinosa*) and the **Black Caecilian** (*I. monochrous*); the former has a yellow band along each side, the latter is uniform black. The adults have a pair of tentacles on the head, which are lacking in the aquatic young.

Apart from caecilians all the Malayan amphibians are frogs and toads. The newts and salamanders are confined in Asia to the temperate regions.

CHAPTER EIGHT

FISH OF THE SEA

THERE is a greater variety of fishes in the shallow seas of the tropics than in any other environment. Malaya, standing as it does on the great Sunda Shelf, which also supports Borneo, Sumatra and Java, and which in geologically recent times was dry land, is surrounded by warm, shallow seas. The study of the fish fauna of these seas would be more than enough to occupy the time and energy of a zoologist to the exclusion of any other serious activity.

Moreover our fish are not only of the greatest interest, they are of first-class economic importance as well. It has been said that a plentiful supply of fish is a necessity to a rice-eating population, and there is no doubt that the development of sea fisheries is a most important factor in promoting the well-being of the people of this country.

The fishes are the lowest and most primitive of the vertebrate or backboned animals, and are distinguished from the rest of them by the fact that instead of limbs they have two pairs of fins, which never bear true fingers or toes, and that normally they pass the whole of their lives in the water, breathing by extracting oxygen from it by means of gills.

They are classified into two main groups, the primitive **Cartilaginous Fishes** or **Elasmobranchi** and the **Bony Fishes** or **Teleostei**; the former comprise the sharks and rays and the latter, with a few exceptions, with which we need not concern ourselves, the whole of the rest of the living fishes and, of course, the vast majority of species. The chief difference between them is clearly indicated by their names; sharks and rays have no bones, their skeletons being formed of soft cartilage. Another feature distinguishing them at a glance is the appearance of the external gill openings; these are multiple (5 to 7 on each side) in the Elasmobranchs, while in the Teleosts the gill slits are covered on each side by a bony flap or operculum, so that there appears to be but a single pair of openings.

Sharks and Rays. The best way to appreciate this sub-division of the Elasmobranch fishes is to regard the rays simply as flattened-out sharks; some sharks, like the Sawfish, show the process in an early stage, and in the guitar-rays (*Rhinobatos*) it may be said to be in a half-way condition. Generally speaking the flattening is an adaptation to living on the bottom.

The commonest sharks of any size are the **Ground-Sharks** (*Carcharinus*) which may reach ten or twelve feet but are generally smaller. The **Tiger Shark** (*Galeocerdo*) is a good deal larger, often fifteen feet and possibly reaching thirty in length; small ones have the spots or vertical stripes which give the species its name, but the markings are lost as the fish grows to full size. Many kinds of sharks (*Scyllium*, etc.), never grow beyond two or three feet in length. They are collectively called **Dogfish** and are often very abundant.

The **Hammerhead Sharks** (*Sphyrna*) are quite common and are among the strangest looking of all fish, having the head flattened and widely expanded from side to side, the eyes being placed at the ends of the lateral expansions (Fig. 64); the purpose served by this curious development of the head is quite unknown. Hardly less strange are the **Sawfishes** (*Pristis*), sharks with the upper jaw produced into a long beak beset on each side with sharp teeth (Fig. 66). This is used mainly for raking about in sand and mud for molluscs and the like on which the sawfish feeds, and perhaps also for disabling small fishes swimming in dense shoals, which it eats after the more fortunate members of the shoal have dispersed. Sawfishes can live in fresh water and are frequently found far up rivers.

Though it is a rarity in Malayan waters the great **Whale Shark** (*Rhinodon typicus*) is worthy of mention as it is the largest living fish, reaching fifty feet or more in length. It is dark in colour above, conspicuously spotted with white, and is a plankton eater, feeding just as the whales do. It follows from this that it is perfectly harmless, though, of course, if harpooned or otherwise molested its strength is enormous. A big one, 35 feet in length, was landed at Pangkor in the Malacca Strait in 1940; it is said that its captors cut it up and started to weigh it

piece by piece, but became discouraged and gave it up after they
had weighed a hundred piculs (1 picul = 133 pounds).

Records of swimmers being attacked by sharks in the seas
around Malaya are extremely rare, and cases of people swimming
for hours in the warm water and being rescued unscathed are
not infrequent. Nevertheless accidents have occurred and it

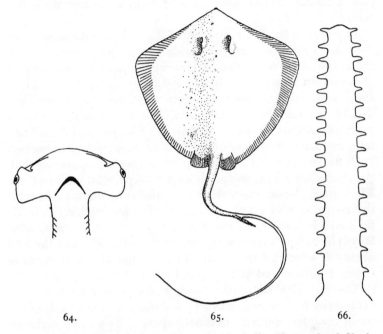

Figs. 64 to 66.   Elasmobranch fishes: 64. Head of a Hammerhead Shark;
65. A Sting-Ray (*Trygon*); 66. The snout of a Sawfish (*Pristis microdon*).

would be foolish to ignore the danger. They are probably due,
together with the great majority of shark fatalities, to the
occasional occurrence of the **Great White Shark** (*Carcharodon
carcharias*).

The typical **Rays,** in which the flattening already described is
fully developed, have the pectoral fins expanded into a wide
"wing" on each side and the tail whip-like. The mouth and
gill-slits are on the under-side of the head. Most rays live on the
bottom and glide over the surface of the sand or mud by rippling

movements of the pectoral fins. They feed largely on molluscs, and many have massive mill-like teeth for crushing the shells. The **Sting-Rays,** of which *Trygon* (Fig. 65) is the commonest genus, have a barbed spine near the base of the tail. This carries a potent poison and by lashing and writhing the tail a ray can inflict a terribly painful and often dangerous wound. Some sting-rays can, like sawfishes, live in fresh water and are found far inland.

The largest rays are the **Devil-Fishes** or **Mantas.** The "wings" are pointed and very wide, spanning much more than the length of the body, the tail is short, and on the head is a pair of large fin-like lobes which are used for sweeping the food into the mouth. Unlike other rays they are surface swimmers and fish of the open sea. They feed, like the Whale Shark, on plankton and are equally harmless. The biggest ones (*Ceratoptera*) may span twenty feet, but the commoner *Mobula* is smaller.

Of the two subdivisions the rays are of greater importance than the sharks as food fishes, the big expanded pectoral fins being the edible part. An ornamental leather called shagreen is made from the rough skin of certain rays. The Chinese delicacy, shark's fin soup, is made from the fins of various sharks; the **Guitar Rays** (*Rhinobatos*) are also an important source of it, and the best quality of all is said to be made from the fins of one of the saw-fishes, *Pristis microdon*.

The classification of the Bony Fishes is a matter of such complexity that no two ichthyological text books will be found to be in complete agreement concerning it. Two main divisions are recognised, based on a point of internal anatomy and on the condition of the anterior rays, or supporting rods, of the dorsal and anal fins, which are soft and flexible in one group and have the form of sharp spines in the other. Typical marine members of the soft fin-rayed group or Physostomi are the herrings, catfishes and eels, and the characters of the spiny-finned group or Physoclysti are best displayed by sea-perches like the snappers and groupers. Of the groups of fish described below all those after the eels are regarded as belonging to the spiny-finned division; some of them have no spines in their fins and are classified by consideration of their anatomy and early development, and are presumed to have lost the spines in the course of their evolution. The Physostomi is considered to be the more primitive of the two groups.

Herrings. None of our herrings occurs in enormous shoals like those which form the basis of the European herring fisheries, probably because plankton is less dense in tropical than in temperate and polar seas. Shoaling herrings, including our own **Tamban**[1] (*Harengula*) are plankton feeders. In this method of feeding the respiratory stream of water that passes in at the mouth and out through the gill openings, as the fish breathes, is strained through a number of comb-like structures called gill-rakers, and the plankton is extracted from it. This practice of capturing plankton by combining the action of feeding and breathing is very general among marine animals. The **Anchovies** or **Bilis** (*Stolephorus*) are related to herrings; they are little silvery fish, slender in shape, with a very long and underhung mouth. Both Tamban and Bilis are caught in great numbers and are important food fish.

The **Dorab** or **Parang-parang** (*Chirocentrus*, Fig. 67), is a large predatory herring shaped like the blade of a broad, straight sword and with formidable teeth. It can be caught on a trolled hook baited with white feathers, and is fair eating but bony. The **Shad** or **Tĕrubok** (*Alosa*) is a large herring which ascends rivers to spawn. On their way up they are well worth taking, as both flesh and roe are good eating, but after they have spawned they are tasteless and are said to be unwholesome.

The **Catfishes** are a well defined group characterised by the smooth, scaleless skin and the presence, usually, of a set of feelers or barbels round the mouth. Most of them have a bony spike at the front of the dorsal and each of the pectoral fins; this is not a fin-ray and does not disqualify them for inclusion in the Physostomi. In the notorious **Sĕmbilang** (*Plotosus*, Fig. 74), these spikes are barbed and poisonous and inflict a very painful wound if the fish is trodden on or handled. The Plotosids are elongate fish with the tail fin pointed, not forked, and continuous with the anal and hinder dorsal fins, and an array of tentacles round the mouth. They occur in shallow water on coral reefs or sandy or muddy bottoms, and are a real hazard to

---

[1] The Malay names of fishes will be used in the text as they are common currency among both English and Malay speaking people.

bathers. Although agonizing and liable to cause some constitutional disturbance the sting is never dangerous. The chance similarity of the Malay name to sěmbilan (nine) is rather confusing; it is not descriptive of any feature of the fish.

Catfishes of the genus *Arius* (**Ikan Duri**) are abundant in coastal waters and river mouths and are of some importance as low-priced food fishes; the flesh is rather oily. They are unattractive looking creatures with flat, armoured heads and the usual spike in the dorsal and anal fins; the tail is forked. A variety of catfishes live in fresh water and will be dealt with in another chapter.

The only eels likely to be met with are the **Moray Eels** (*Muraenidae*), which are particularly common living in holes on coral reefs; some grow to a large size and are most aggressive, formidable creatures, and will bite savagely if cornered. The bite is reputed to be poisonous, but there is some doubt of this and it is certainly not to be compared with that of the sea snakes, with which these eels are sometimes confused. The eel is immediately distinguished by its smooth, slimy, scaleless skin and by the presence of gill-openings on each side of its head.

The garfishes, halfbeaks and flying fishes form a natural group of surface swimming fishes which have the lower lobe of the tail longer than the upper, a feature associated with their habit of leaving the water and skittering over its surface when alarmed.

The **Garfishes** or **Todak** (*Tylosurus*) are elongate fish with the jaws greatly elongated to form a toothed beak (Fig. 68). When alarmed they leave the water and go for long distances over the surface by short jumps, driven by strokes of the tail. Sometimes, purely by accident, a man in a small boat may be in the path of a jumping todak and be wounded just as if a spear had been hurled at him. They are very shy and difficult to catch, but can be taken by a most ingenious device of a baited noose hanging by a long line from a flying kite. The fact that their bones are green puts fastidious people off eating them, but they are excellent fish and perfectly wholesome.

Allied to the garfish are the **Halfbeaks, Puput** or **Jolong-jolong** (*Hemirhamphus*). They are also elongate, smaller than

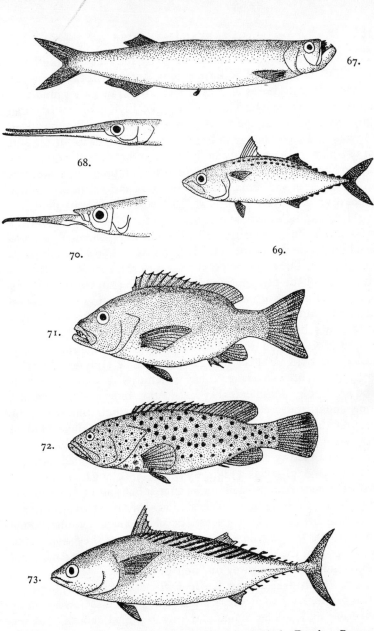

Figs. 67 to 73. Some sea fishes which are used for food: 67. Dorab or Parang-parang; 68. Garfish or Todak (head); 69. Kembong; 70. Halfbeak or Puput (head); 71. Snapper or Ikan Merah; 72. Grouper or Kĕrapu; 73. Tongkol or Tunny.

Todak, and immediately recognisable by the fact that the lower
jaw alone is produced to form a long, toothless beak (Fig. 70).

The **Flying Fishes** live in the open sea and are familiar to
every ocean traveller. The Two-winged Flying Fishes (*Exocoe-
tus*) have only the pectoral fins enlarged, the Four-winged
(*Cypsilurus*) have the ventral fins enlarged as well to form a sort
of tail-plane. Their ability to fly through the air is thought to be
an evolutionary development of the jumping and surface-
skittering habits of their relatives the gars and halfbeaks. When
it leaves the water a flying fish goes some little way along the
surface, gaining speed for flight by rapid side-to-side movements
with the lower lobe of the tail. During this process *Cypsilurus*
has only the pectoral fins extended, the ventral ones are spread to
give it extra buoyancy when it rises into the air. When it loses
flying speed the fish can come down and regain it by skittering
along the surface with its tail in the water, and so make a succession
of flights, but drying of its fin-membranes and gills soon compel
it to remember that it is a fish and not a bird.

Sea-Horses and **Pipe-Fishes** belong to the same family,
called the Syngnathidae, and have the whole body encased in a
bony, segmented covering. They generally live among seaweeds
and are feeble swimmers; they have a tiny mouth at the end of a
long snout and feed on small creatures which they catch by
suction, like a very small-scale vacuum cleaner. One kind of
sea-horse, *Hippocampus kuda* (Fig. 79), is very common and is
taken in quantity when seine nets (pukat) are pulled through
sea-grass. A pipe-fish (Fig. 78) is like an elongated sea-horse
with the neck straightened out so that snout and body lie in one
direction. Both groups have similar and most extraordinary
breeding habits. The *male* fish develops an abdominal pouch
into which the female lays the eggs. There they hatch and
develop until the young are ready to leave their father's maternal
protection and swim away on their own.

The **Shrimp-Fishes** or **Knife-Fishes** (*Centriscidae*) are even
stranger looking than the sea-horses. They also have a bony
covering and a long snout and tiny terminal mouth, but are
flattened like the blade of a knife and almost transparent. The
hinder part of the back extends beyond the tail, which is underneath and directed almost at right angles to the body. Apart

from their strange appearance the oddest thing about them is their habit of swimming slowly in small shoals in a vertical, head-downwards position.

The **Groupers** or **Kĕrapu** (*Epinephelus*) and the **Snappers,** which include the **Ikan Merah** (*Lutjanus*) are often classified together as sea perches; with their numerous allies they form the dominant group of fishes in present day seas. They are heavily built, strongly scaled fish with a big mouth and the dorsal and anal fin consisting of an anterior spined part continuous with a posterior part with soft, flexible rays. They are predatory, living near the bottom and eating any living thing they can catch; they readily take a baited hook and are also caught in large cage-like fish-traps, which are lowered to the sea floor and marked by buoys. One of the commonest of the groupers, *Epinephelus corallicola*, is a greenish brown fish with darker spots (Fig. 72); certain others (*E. tauvina* and *lanceolata*) grow to an enormous size and may exceed six feet in length and weigh between 500 and 1,000 pounds. These big groupers are called **Kĕrtang** by the Malays.

The snappers are among the most highly priced fish sold in the local markets. The common **Red Snapper** or **Ikan Merah** (*Lutjanus argentimaculatus*, Fig. 71), is a good example of them, but there are many others with various colours and patterns, and the same is true of the groupers.

The **Butterfly Fishes** (*Chaetodontidae*) are mostly found in the shallow water of coral reefs, and many of them rank with birds and butterflies as the most colourful and beautiful of living creatures. They are all deep-bodied fish, compressed from side to side, with the height of the body about equal to the length. They feed on small animals and many of them have the mouth at the end of a long snout with which they pry into the holes and crevices in the coral. One of the commonest and loveliest of them is the **Beaked Butterfly-Fish** (*Chelmo rostratus*, Fig. 75). It has a long snout and is silvery with four bright orange, dark-bordered vertical bands, the front one of which crosses the eye, and a dark band at the base of the tail; in the basal hind part of the dorsal fin is a conspicuous white-bordered black spot.

The presence of a posteriorly situated eye-like spot, often together with a band or other marking concealing the true eye, is a rather common feature in these fish. It has been suggested that it is useful to them in the following way; a predatory fish, making a grab at its prey, will allow for its victim's dash for safety by aiming a little in front, just as a gunner aims a little ahead of a moving target. If the eye is concealed or inconspicuous and a glaring false eye is placed near the rear end of the body, the enemy may be deceived into aiming behind instead of ahead, so that the instinctive forward start of the fish takes it out of instead of into the predator's jaws. This kind of "back-to-front" camouflage is not confined to fishes but occurs among insects as well.

The **Butterfish** or **Kitang** (*Scatophagus argus*) is a rather plebeian member of this aristocratic group. It is greenish with round black spots on the upper half of the flanks, inhabits coastal waters and river mouths and is quite frequently used for food.

The **Eight-striped Butterfly-Fish** (*Chaetodon octofasciatus*) is a small species, yellowish white with six to eight vertical black stripes. The beautiful **King-Fish** (*Acanthochaetodon annularis*) is a large chaetodont, brown with a pattern of brilliant blue stripes and rings and a pale yellow tail. The **Moorish Idol** (*Zanclus*, Fig. 76), is vertically banded black and yellowish white; it has a produced beak-like mouth and from the forward edge of the dorsal fin a long filament of skin trails back in the water.

Many other species are common and there is little to choose between them in point of elegance. The butterfly-fishes are the supreme ornaments of the tropical marine aquarium. They can also be seen to excellent advantage by diving in the water over those parts of coral reefs which are never uncovered by the tide. A diving helmet is a safe and simple piece of apparatus and can be used for leisured observation, but a diving mask or goggles, fitting tightly over the face to keep out the water, gives more freedom of movement to a confident swimmer. The fish are usually abundant and surprisingly tame; some will actually approach the observer, apparently out of curiosity. Viewed against the brightly coloured and weirdly shaped masses of coral they afford a spectacle that seems to belong to quite a different world from the familiar one which we inhabit.

The **Demoiselles** or **Damsel-Fishes** (Pomacentridae) are also small, colourful reef fishes. They are rather deep-bodied but more elongate and normally fish-like than the Chaetodonts. A familiar member of this family is the little **Clown-Fish** (*Amphiprion percula*), which is often kept in small aquariums. It is only two inches or so in length, bright orange with three dark-bordered vertical white bands and narrow black and white borders on the fins and tail. Under natural conditions it is always found together with a large sea-anemone, among whose tentacles it retreats when threatened with danger, but in captivity it seems to thrive well enough without this association.

The **Wrasses** (Labridae) and **Parrot-Fishes** (Scaridae) are yet other conspicuous and beautiful inhabitants of the reefs. They are fairly large fish, often brilliantly coloured and patterned with green and blue; their scales are large and they have strong, usually projecting teeth, which in the parrot-fishes are fused together to form a powerful beak. The latter feed by rasping off algae and other forms of growth that encrust the rocks, and on the living coral; the wrasses hunt crabs and molluscs, whose shells they are able to crush with their strong teeth.

The only economically important fish of the coral reefs are the **Sea-Breams** or **Dĕlah** (*Caesio*). They are taken by an exciting operation involving the positioning of a net by the reef and the driving of the fish into it by a team of swimming men, each holding a long string weighted at the bottom and flagged at intervals in its length with pieces of white cloth. These strings are jerked up and down and the moving flags scare the fish and drive them into the net. This strenuous mode of fishing is of Japanese origin and is still called by its Japanese name 'muro ami'. Local fishermen have now adopted it quite successfully.

The **Scorpion-Fishes** (Scorpaenidae) are notorious for the poison which they secrete in the spines supporting their fins. Two other groups of fishes having poisonous spines have been mentioned, the sting-rays and the Plotosid catfishes (Sĕmbilang). Some of the scorpion-fishes are more dangerous than either of these, the worst being the **Poison-Fish** or **Lĕpu** (*Synanceia verrucosa*). This is an ugly toad-like fish, irregularly shaped, coloured dirty brown and looking just like a lump of dead coral (Fig. 77). Along its back is a row of hollow spines which inject a virulent poison if they pierce one's flesh, causing very severe pain and systemic disorder, and sometimes even death. Failing proper treatment gangrene may set in resulting in the loss of a hand or foot. These fish are very dangerous and their possible presence is a warning never to venture on to coral reefs without adequate protection for your feet. The **Lion-Fish** (*Pterois volitans*) is a most spectacular creature, as conspicuous as the Poison-Fish is the reverse. It has greatly elongated fin-rays carrying curious tassels of skin, and is handsomely striped with red and black. When approached it spreads its fins and faces the intruder, plainly exhibiting the type of warning coloration and behaviour described for the poisonous snakes. Its spines are very poisonous, but its habit of self-advertisement renders it much less dangerous than the abominable lurking Poison-Fish. A number of other kinds of scorpion-fish are found around our coasts, some are quite small, but equipped with formidable if not actually dangerous spines. It is never safe to handle any very spiny-looking fish while it is still struggling.

The **Gobies** are a very numerous tribe of small fish, various species of which inhabit shallow water and rock-pools, brackish water swamps and fresh water. Most of them are obscure little creatures, but the **Mud-Skippers** (*Periophthalmus*) are familiar to almost everyone. They are the queer little fish that are to be seen hopping about at low tide in mangrove swamps and among rocks along the shore. They spend most of their time out of the water, and to enable them to breathe on land their gills are supplemented by air-breathing organs, and respiration also takes place through the skin, just as it does in a frog. They have large protruding eyes on the top of the head and are very vigilant and difficult to approach. The pectoral fins are no longer swimming organs but have become quite efficient limbs with which the fish hitches itself along; when alarmed it makes rapid jumps with its tail, and in the water swims with the head and eyes above the surface. These are the most truly amphibious of all fish, and serve to remind us of the way in which the ancestors of the higher vertebrates are believed to have colonised the land from the sea many millions of years ago.

The threadfins, barracudas and grey mullets form a natural

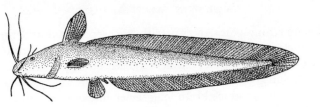

74.

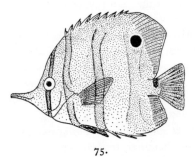

75.

76.

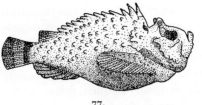

77.

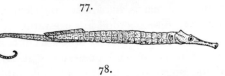

78.

79.

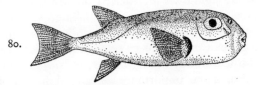

80.

Figs. 74 to 80.   Sea fishes: 74. Plotosid Catfish or Sĕmbilang; 75. Butterfly-fish (*Chelmo rostratus*); 76. Moorish Idol (*Zanclus*); 77. Poison-fish or Lĕpu; 78. Pipe-fish; 79. Sea-horse; 80. Silvery Puffer.

group of strongly scaled fish with two separate dorsal fins, an anterior spiny and a posterior soft-rayed one. **Threadfins, Kurau** and **Sĕnangin** (*Polynemus*), are heavily built fish with an underhung mouth and the lower rays of the pectoral fins separated and produced into long feeler-like organs. Some grow to a large size and are the biggest fish generally to be seen in the markets. They are bottom feeders in muddy coastal and estuarine waters, living on small creatures like shrimps and little crabs and fish, and are caught in fishing stakes and by means of drift-nets. They furnish a very important supply of both fresh and salted fish.

The **Barracudas** or **Alu-alu** (*Sphyraena*) are elongate powerful fishes, ferocious predators, with wide jaws and strong sharp teeth. They grow to about six feet and are said occasionally to attack swimmers, and to be responsible for accidents of the type generally attributed to sharks; I have never heard of anyone being attacked by a barracuda in Malayan waters.

The **Grey Mullets** or **Bĕlanak** (*Mugil*) are moderate-sized fish with large scales and a most peculiar mouth which, seen from the front, is horizontal and as broad as the head, but is of very small extent in side view. They are fish of coastal waters and river mouths, and live by swallowing mud rich in organic matter and extracting nourishment from it. They are taken in fishing stakes and nets of various kinds and are excellent eating.

The **Horse-Mackerels** (Carangidae) occur in great variety. Typically they are smooth-skinned, streamlined fishes with a series of keeled scales forming a sharp, hard ridge on each side of the hinder part of the body. The pectoral fins are rather long and curved like a sickle, and both the dorsal and anal fins are divided into separate anterior spiny and posterior soft-rayed parts. They are fish of the open sea and clear coastal waters, and are especially abundant and varied off Malaya's east coast in the waters of the South China Sea. They are predatory, chasing and catching other fishes. A number of small species belong to the genus *Caranx* and go under the name of **Crevally** or **Sĕlar**. The **Chĕncharu** (*Megalaspis cordyla*) is a moderate-sized Carangid of some importance as a food fish; it has the characters of the family and in addition a row of little detached finlets behind the dorsal and anal fins. Among the larger

Carangids is the **Talang-talang** (*Chorinemus*) which may exceed a yard in length. It lacks the lateral keeled scales borne by the more typical members of the family, and the anterior part of the dorsal fin is represented by a row of small separate spines. The horse-mackerels are excellent eating if quite fresh, but they do not keep well.

The **Pomfrets** or **Bawal** (*Stromateus*) are flattened, deep-bodied fish. The White Pomfret or Bawal Puteh (*S. cinereus*) is largely silvery white, darker on the back, and has the front edges of the dorsal and anal fins prolonged. It is good eating and always commands a high price. The Dark Pomfret or Bawal Hitam (*S. niger*) is dark brown in colour and the fins are less prolonged; it has a hard ridge on each side of the base of the tail like that of the horse-mackerels, to which it is probably related.

The true **Mackerels** (Scombridae) have much in common with the horse-mackerels. They are also swiftly swimming, predatory fish, and always possess the feature (found in some Carangids, e.g. Chĕncharu) of a row of detached finlets behind the dorsal and anal fins; on the other hand the hard ridges on each side of the hind part of the body, seen in *Caranx* and many other horse-mackerels, are never present in the Scombrids. Three kinds of mackerel are both common and economically important.

The **Kĕmbong** (*Scomber kanagurta*, Fig. 69), is a fairly small, neatly streamlined fish, six to eight inches long, which swims in large shoals and is a plankton feeder. It is an excellent food fish and is taken in great quantities in the Malacca Strait by a method known as purse seining. This is done at night when the presence of a shoal can be detected by the "phosphorescence" it causes in the water[1], and whole shoals are surrounded by a very large net.

The **Spanish Mackerel** or **Tĕnggiri** (*Scomberomorus*) is a large, slenderly built mackerel, a powerful swimmer and an inhabitant of clear coastal waters. It can be taken by trolling with a fish as bait and gives very fine sport, and is also extremely good eating.

---

[1] This well-known phenomenon is caused by small animals of the plankton, which become luminous when the water surrounding them is agitated. It has nothing whatever to do with phosphorus and is better called luminescence.

Our third common mackerel is the **Tongkol** (*Euthynnus alleteratus*, Fig. 73), which is a member of the group of large oceanic fishes known variously as tunny, bonito and albacore. They are the most powerful and speedy of all fishes, as their heavily muscled, perfectly streamlined bodies show; they are mainly inhabitants of the open sea, the Tongkol being the only one that often comes into coastal waters. Its flesh is dark red and strong-tasting, but excellent food and delicious if properly prepared. It can be fished for in the same way as Těnggiri and also gives good sport when feeding freely, but Tongkol will not by any means always bite. The **Bonito** (*Euthynnus pelamys*) is also found in Malayan waters but is more an inhabitant of the open ocean; it is paler in colour than the Tongkol, with horizontal stripes low down on the flanks.

The **Sailfish** (*Histiophorus*) is related to the mackerels and more closely to the great Swordfish (*Xiphias*) of cooler waters than ours. The Sailfish may reach eight feet in length and takes its name from the long and very high dorsal fin; the snout is prolonged to form a beak, rather shorter than that of the Swordfish. It is esteemed as a game fish in the eastern Pacific, but I have never heard of any successful attempts to take it by angling in our waters.

The **Flatfishes, Halibut, Soles** and the like, are one of the most distinct of all groups of fish. Soles have the fins middle, dorsal, tail and anal, continuous all round the body, and are best represented in our waters by the elongate **Tongue-Soles** or **Lidah** (*Cynoglossus*), though true soles (*Brachirus*) are found as well. Flatfish of the halibut type have a separate tail-fin, and the commonest of these is *Psettodes erumei* which is distinguished from all other local flatfishes by its mouthful of long sharp teeth. Species of the genus *Pseudorhombus* are of the same form, but the mouth is small and the teeth inconspicuous. All flatfishes that are large enough to be worth taking are used for food; they are bottom feeders in shallow coastal waters and can be taken on lines and by trawling or seining.

The body of a flatfish is not depressed from above like that of a ray, but from side to side, and the fish swims lying on its side. When newly hatched the young swim in an upright position and have an eye on each side of the head. Later the fish lies down on one side which, with the one exception of *Psettodes erumei*, is always the same, either right or left, in any one species. As soon as this happens the underneath eye begins to move very slowly round the head until it lies beside the upper one. In the soles both eyes in the adult are close together and wholly on the upper side of the head; in *P. erumei*, however, the moving eye does not get beyond the edge of the head. This, and the fact that alone among flatfishes it lies down on either side, suggests that it is a rather primitive member of the group.

The Plectognath fishes are an easily recognised group with protruding, nipper-like teeth and the skin leathery, spiny or covered with horny plates, never with detachable scales. Trigger-fishes, file-fishes and coffer-fishes are the main families included under this head.

The **Trigger-Fishes** (Balistidae) and **File-Fishes** (Monacanthidae) are closely related to each other and both have the body rather deep and compressed. Trigger-fishes live around coral reefs and are often brightly coloured. They owe their name to the peculiar arrangement of spines which takes the place of the front part of the dorsal fin; there is a strong, high spine with one or two smaller ones behind it, and if the hinder or hindmost one is held erect a locking mechanism holds the spine or spines in front of it erect as well. The file-fishes or leatherjackets are dull-coloured, sluggish fish, often very abundant in shallow coastal waters. They have the body much flattened, often lozenge-shaped, and with a single high, curved dorsal spine; the skin is rough and leathery and the jaws project in the form of a snout.

The **Globe-Fishes** or **Puffers** and **Porcupine-Fishes** (Tetrodontidae) possess two upper and two lower teeth forming a kind of beak, and they have the strange habit of blowing themselves up with water or air when molested. A puffer taken off a hook and returned to the water floats away looking like a little balloon; as it recovers confidence it slowly expels the air and returns to its normal shape. Most of them have the skin covered with numerous fine spines; in the Porcupine-Fish these are strong and sharp so that when the fish blows itself up it looks like a prickly football. The internal organs of these fish contain a dangerous poison, and unless they are removed immediately after death this permeates the flesh and anyone eating it is likely to die most painfully. Although immediate cleaning is said to render them safe it is advisable never to eat a tetrodont fish. The people of Malaya know them well and accidents are rare among them, and their unpleasant appearance is usually enough to stop newcomers from eating them. One, however, the **Silvery Puffer** or **Buntal Pisang** (*Sphoeroides lunaris*) is less ugly and balloon-like than most of them and just as deadly; take good heed of its appearance (Fig. 80).

The other group of Plectognath fishes is the **Trunk-** or **Coffer-Fishes** (*Ostracion*). They are small, only a few inches long, and have the head and body covered by hard, inflexible bony plates, so that movement is confined to the fins and tail, and their powers of swimming are very inefficient. They all have prominent ridges on the body and some have pairs of long, sharp horns. These are perhaps the strangest-looking of any fish one is likely to encounter in Malayan seas and are not at all rare.

Do not expect that this chapter will enable you to recognise every fish that you see. At the time of writing the standard work on Indo-Australian fishes has reached its ninth bulky volume, and it is still far from complete. What is presented here is no more than a bare introduction to the subject.

CHAPTER NINE

FRESH-WATER FISHES

THE number of species of fish that inhabit our rivers, streams and swamps is probably rather less than two hundred. This is far less, of course, than the sea fish, but the fresh-water ones are not without economic importance and are of great interest to the naturalist and zoologist for a variety of reasons.

More than one-third of the total belong to the family Cyprinidae or **Carps,** of which the Goldfish is a familiar example, though not a native of Malaya. The carps are always distinctly scaled and are peculiar in never having teeth in the jaws; instead there is a set of so-called pharyngeal teeth in the throat which, in some of the large species, can exert a very powerful crushing action. The Cyprinids are of interest in being the largest and most important group of fishes that is wholly confined to fresh water; no carp lives or can live for any part of its life in the sea. In size they range widely from the little "Barbs" and Rasboras, beloved of aquarium keepers, to fishes over a yard in length, like the Kĕlah and Tĕmĕlian of the big rivers. Only a few can be mentioned specifically.

Two of the commonest species are the **Bagoh** (*Puntius lateristriga*), which is distinctively marked with one horizontal and two vertical black bars on each side, and which often swarms in lakes and reservoirs, and *Puntius binotatus*, which is silvery with a dark patch below the dorsal fin. Both are fairly small, rarely exceeding six inches. The **Sĕbarau** (*Hampala macrolepidota*, Fig. 83), is a common river fish and grows to a fair size; it is silvery with big scales and a vertical black bar on each side. The species of *Tor*, known locally as **Kĕlah** and related to the Indian Mahseer, are larger and give fine sport to anglers. Largest of all our Cyprinids is *Probarbus jullieni*, a heavily built fish, silvery with parallel dark bands along the sides; under the name **Tĕmĕlian** it is very highly esteemed as food. The **Lampam** (*Puntius schwanefeldi*) is a common and very beautiful carp with the fins and tail bright red, and the tail marked in addition with a black streak along the upper and lower margins.

Of the small species, suitable for aquariums, the best known is *Rasbora heteromorpha* (Fig. 88), a pretty little fish, silvery and orange with a black triangle on each side. Although the most familiar of the Rasboras it is not a typical member of the genus, most of which are much more slender in shape; *R. taeniata* (Fig. 90) is a normally shaped Rasbora. There are over a dozen species of this genus found in Malaya, none of which much exceeds six inches in length. The smallest, the elegant little black-spotted red *R. maculata,* is fully grown at an inch. The species of *Puntius* (or *Barbus,* hence the popular name "Barb") are even more numerous and include quite big fish as well as little ones, such as the Lampam, mentioned above. The handsomely striped **Tiger Barb** (*P. partipentazona,* Fig. 86), and the **Six-striped Barb** (*P. hexazona,* Fig. 87) are among the commonest and most popular of the aquarium-sized species of *Puntius.*

Before leaving the Cyprinids mention must be made of the several kinds of carp which are reared for the market in specially constructed ponds by the Chinese. These are not Malayan species and, although they flourish and grow here, will not breed under natural conditions in our climate. Formerly the young fry were imported by ship from China, but in recent years have been conveyed by air, the extra cost being offset by the far lower mortality of a journey of only a few hours. Research is being carried out into artificial breeding in Malaya and promising results have already been obtained.

The fresh-water **Catfishes** are very numerous and varied. Like the marine ones they have the skin smooth and scaleless and often possess long whiskers or barbels round the mouth. The largest of our fresh-water fishes are catfishes of the genus *Wallago,* known locally as **Tapah** (Fig. 85), which grow to over five feet in length and may weigh a hundred pounds. They have bands of formidable, short, backwardly curved teeth in the jaws and feed mainly on other fish. They are known to pull under swimming dogs, and the belief that they will attack a man in the water should not be disregarded, though I know of no actual case of it. Tapah live in the big rivers and haunt especially the

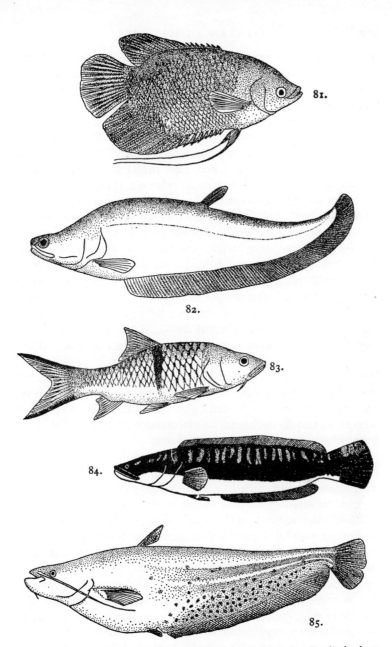

Figs. 81 to 85. Fresh-water fishes: 81. Goramy or Kalui; 82. Featherback or Bělida; 83. Sěbarau; 84. Snake-head or Toman; 85. Giant Catfish or Tapah.

deep pools. Our most abundant catfish is the **Kĕli** (*Clarias batrachus*) which swarms in ditches and rice-fields all over the country. It is caught in large numbers in fish-traps and on lines and taken to market alive. This is possible because the Kĕli has an air-breathing organ in addition to its gills, so that large numbers can be confined in very little water, conditions in which ordinary fish would quickly suffocate. Other common catfishes are **Baung** (*Mystus*), **Patin** and **Lawang** (*Pangasius*), and **Lais** (*Kryptopterus*). The last are small relatives of the Tapah; some kinds are small enough for the domestic aquarium and are called "Glass Catfish" from the extreme transparency of the body.

The **Goramy** family (Anabantidae) includes some of the most interesting of the Malayan fish, and the larger species, Sĕpat and Kalui, are important food fishes as well. All of them have an accessory air-breathing organ and can live in what would be for most fish very adverse conditions, provided they can come to the surface for air. If they are kept below the surface, even in well oxygenated water, they will drown, as the gills alone are not sufficient to provide for respiration. The most celebrated of this tribe is the so-called **Climbing Perch** (*Anabas testudineus*). This fish lives in ponds and swamps and, in rainy weather, will leave the water and make its way across country, so that newly dug ponds are soon colonised by it. Early travellers to the East told exaggerated stories of it, maintaining that it could climb trees, hence its rather unsuitable name.

Even more familiar to people living in Malaya is the little **Fighting Fish,** especially the Siamese species *Betta splendens.* This beautiful little fish has been domesticated in Thailand for over a hundred years for the sake of matching one against another and wagering on the result of the fight. Special fighting strains are maintained and a strange mosquito-breeding industry exists to supply larvae to feed fighting fish kept by numerous amateur and professional fanciers. It is only the male fish which fight, and they have the urge to combat so strongly developed that not only can two males never be kept in the same receptacle, but two tanks, each containing a male must not be put side by side without an intervening screen, or they will wear themselves out trying to get at each other. A male fighting fish is even aroused to bellicose fury by the sight of his own reflection in a mirror. A most attractive feature of the sport is afforded by the display of the rival fish before the fight begins; the fins and gills are spread out and waves of brilliant red and blue pass over the body. The fight is never to the death, and ends simply by one fish becoming exhausted and deciding that it does not want to fight any more, and even the vanquished fish very rarely receives fatal injuries.

The breeding habits are remarkable and can easily be observed in an aquarium. When the urge comes upon him to found a family the male fish makes a floating nest of sticky bubbles, which he blows with his mouth. He seeks a mate and several hundred eggs are laid, which are then placed in the nest. After the eggs are laid the female swims away and forgets about the whole business. The father fish stays with the nest until the little fish are hatched and grown large enough to take care of themselves. He constantly renews its structure by blowing new bubbles, carefully replaces any eggs or babies which may fall out and valiantly drives away intruders, including his mate, who will eat her offspring if given the chance.

The Siamese Fighting Fish is found in a wild state here and there in Malaya, probably as a result of aquarium keepers releasing unwanted fish of Siamese origin, though it may be indigenous in the northern states. There is a very common native Malayan species, *Betta pugnax* (Fig. 91) which is larger, more stockily built and less brightly coloured.

The **Goramy** or **Kalui** (*Osphromenos goramy*, Fig. 81), is the largest of the Anabantids and reaches over ten pounds in weight. It is fairly common in the wild state and can very easily be kept in ponds and fattened for eating. Small ones, two or three inches long, can be used to stock a pond. As they are air-breathers they travel well, and when released in the pond can be fed on leaves, those of hibiscus, kangkong and kĕladi are particularly suitable. On this diet they increase in weight by about one and a half pounds a year, and are ready to eat after a year or two, but can be grown to a much larger size if desired. The flesh is excellent, ranking with the best of the sea fish. The Goramy makes a nest of grass and twigs to contain its eggs.

Three species of **Sĕpat** (*Trichogaster*) are found in Malaya. The two smaller ones are pretty and esteemed by aquarium keepers (Fig. 89); the largest, the **Sĕpat Siam** (*T. pectoralis*) has been introduced from Thailand and is now an important source of food for the rice-growing people in the north of Malaya. During the months when the rice-fields are flooded the fish spread all over them, feeding on the minute water plants called algae. They make a bubble nest like that of the Fighting Fish and are very prolific, and take only four months to come to maturity. At the end of the growing season, when the fields are drained for the harvest, many of the fish take refuge in ponds specially constructed to trap them, and the rice-planters gain a supplementary "harvest" with the expenditure of very little extra effort. Enough fish always escape into ditches and irrigation canals to provide for the next year's generation.

The **Snake-Heads** (Genus *Channa* or *Ophicephalus*) are allied to the Anabantids and also have an air-breathing organ. They are elongate fishes with long dorsal and anal fins, and are all predatory, feeding on other fishes, frogs or anything else they can catch. The biggest of them, the **Toman** (*Channa micropeltes*, Fig. 84), reaches nearly a yard in length and when fully grown is a beautiful fish. The back is black and the throat and belly white, a sharp line dividing the colours; within the black part are a number of vertical violet and green bars. When young, the Toman is longitudinally striped with black and white, wholly unlike the adult. Several of the smaller species are common in swamps and streams, and one, the **Aruan** (*Channa striata*), is abundant enough in rice-field country to be of some importance as a food fish.

Two species of **Featherbacks** (*Notopterus*), both known locally as **Bĕlida,** are found, and are the largest of our swamp-dwelling fishes; the larger, *N. chitala* (Fig. 82), sometimes reaches a yard in length. They are useful food fishes but hardly abundant enough to be economically important; the flesh is said to be good but full of small bones. The eggs are laid on submerged timber and posts standing in swampy water, and the male fish guards them and keeps them clean and free of sediment. He attacks all intruders, including even human ones, and is very easily caught when guarding his eggs. Fishermen who take advantage of this are both cruel and improvident, for the eggs are bound to perish without the father's care.

The term **Eel** has come to be applied to any elongate, snake-like fish with a smooth slippery skin. None of the Malayan eels are related to the Migratory Eel, so often described in European and American natural history books, nor do they go to the sea to lay their eggs. The **Bĕlut** or **Swamp-Eel** (*Fluta alba*) is common in swampy waters, and the quite unrelated **Spiny Eels** or **Tilan** (*Mastacembelus*) are represented in Malaya by a number of species. They are easily recognised by the curious overhanging snout or short trunk and by the row of needle-sharp spines along the back.

The **Loaches,** which are related to the carps, in spite of their very different appearance, are present in some variety. Nearly all are little fish, and some are so elongated as to be almost eel-like. One very interesting genus, *Homaloptera*, is found in swiftly flowing streams and rivers. These loaches have the body much flattened from above, and the under surface forms a kind of sucker which enables the fish to cling to stones and sub-merged timber in the rapid current. Some of the loaches are prettily marked, and the black-barred, pinkish-yellow *Acanthoph-thalmus semicinctus* (Fig. 92) is a great favourite with aquarium keepers. Most loaches have a number of short barbels round the mouth, which look like a little bristly moustache.

The little **White-Spot** (*Aplochilus panchax*), is one of our most abundant fish. It does not exceed two inches in length, and can be seen anywhere in swampy water, swimming near the grassy margin at the top of the water; it can be recognised immediately by the shining white spot on the top of its head.

Most of the fresh-water **Gobies** are little fish, but one, *Oxyeleotris marmorata*, grows big enough to be suitable for eating; it is an elongate fish, black handsomely marbled with grey or brown. *Brachygobius sua* is a small goby, hardly more than an inch long, which is often seen in aquariums. It is a dumpy little fish with a large head, and banded black and yellow; aquarium keepers call it the Bumble-Bee Fish.

The last of our fresh-water fish to be mentioned is the **Kĕlĕsa** (*Scleropages formosus*), a dark brown fish with very large, hard scales and the dorsal and anal fins far back near the tail. It grows to between one and two feet and is not very common, but is worthy of notice as it belongs to a primitive group of fishes, most of which have long ago become extinct. Of all the Asiatic groups of true fresh-water fishes this is the only one which is also present in Australia and New Guinea, and is a relic of the very remote period when the continents were joined together.

This brings us to a very interesting aspect of the study of fresh-water fish; its application to zoogeography. This is a branch of the science of zoology which uses the present day distribution of animals to provide evidence of changes, in the remote past, in sea level and in the relations to each other of land areas. For instance, the close similarity of the faunas of the Malay Peninsula, Borneo, Sumatra and Java to each other and to that of the south-east Asiatic mainland, and their great contrast with those of New Guinea and Australia, is taken as evidence that those three great islands have been joined to Malaya, and so to Asia, in comparatively recent times, geologically speaking; but that they have been severed from Australia and New Guinea for a vastly longer period. This is borne out by soundings, which show that the seas between Malaya and the three islands are shallow, but those beyond very deep. The shallow area on which Malaya and these islands stand is called the Sunda Shelf, and the former land which it represents, and which jutted out from south-east Asia in the Pleistocene Period or Ice Age, has been named Sundaland.

Now the capacity of land animals to preserve evidence of such changes in the distribution of land and sea clearly depends on their inability to cross barriers of sea once these are formed. Winged animals like birds and bats are able to fly across such barriers;[1] air-breathing animals without the power of flight sometimes float across, clinging to great rafts of trees and other vegetation which are washed out of river mouths in times of flood. But animals which can only live in fresh water have practically no natural means of crossing the sea, and so they afford the very best evidence to the zoogeographer. The fresh-water fish are among the most easily studied of these, and often give remarkably conclusive evidence; for example, the carps or Cyprinidae scarcely extend at all beyond the boundaries of Sundaland, though they are abundant in Asia and on all the islands standing on the Sunda Shelf.

---

[1] They do so to a less extent than one would expect; zoogeographical boundaries are often quite well defined by the distribution of birds.

Mention has been made several times of aquarium keeping. This is a very popular hobby in Europe and America, and Malaya is the source of many of the pretty little tropical fish which are imported into these countries, sold at high prices and kept in artificially warmed water. Here no such elaborate arrangements are needed and, since no hazardous and costly journey is involved, the fish can be bought cheaply; better still they can be caught by the aquarist himself.

There is no space in a book like this for elaborate instructions on aquarium keeping, and numbers of books exist which are devoted entirely to the subject. The short account which follows is intended only to encourage readers to try this fascinating hobby, and to save beginners from making the more obvious mistakes. It applies only to the fresh-water aquarium; keeping a marine aquarium is a much more difficult and complicated business.

The best kind of tank to use is the rectangular type with glass sides, which is sold by aquarium dealers. It should be well washed out, and then a couple of inches of clean, fairly coarse sand should be put in it after which it can be filled with water. Both from the point of view of its appearance and of the health of the fish, water plants should be planted in the sand; these are best obtained from dealers as it is not easy, unless you are a botanist, to select suitable kinds found growing wild. Clean sand is all they need to grow in, on no account should soil be put in the tank. After the plants have been put in, let the tank stand for a few days before obtaining the fish. When you get them, content yourself with a few; overcrowding is one of the chief causes of failure. If the fish spend all their time with their noses at the surface of the water, it means that they have insufficient oxygen to breathe, and this is probably because there are too many in the tank. Remember that the number of fish you can keep depends not on the volume of water but on its surface area, as it is through the surface that the oxygen diffuses into the water from the air. The plants assist by giving out oxygen, under the influence of light, and absorbing carbon dioxide, an excess of which poisons the fish.

It is sufficient to feed the fish once a day, and they should never be given more food than they will eat immediately. The reason for this is that uneaten food in an aquarium will soon go bad and poison the water, and the fish will die. Excess of food and overcrowding are the two most frequent causes of failure. Prepared fish foods in the form of a sort of powder are sold, and most fish will eat them, but they should be given live food as well. Tangled masses of a small red worm called *Tubifex* are sold, and are very good food for all except the smallest fish, but best of all are mosquito larvae. These can easily be obtained by putting out bowls of water with a few dead leaves in each. Mosquitoes will soon find them and lay their eggs, and larvae will appear after a few days. They can be taken out with a glass syringe or pipette. Of course these bowls must on no account be forgotten about or left long unattended, so that mosquitoes come to maturity in them.

The aquarium should be put in a fairly well lighted place, but never where direct sunlight will reach it. The plants need light to perform their health-giving function of absorbing carbon dioxide and giving out oxygen, but too much light will encourage the growth of microscopic plants called algae, which float in the water and, if unchecked, will turn it into a sort of green soup. The fish do not seem to suffer, but your aquarium ceases to be a thing of beauty. So long as the fish and plants appear to be thriving there is no need to change the water, but it is well, once a week, to siphon out a few inches of water with a four foot length of rubber tubing and then top up with clean water. When siphoning pass the end of the tube over the surface of the sand so as to pick up accumulated dirt, on the vacuum cleaner principle.

If you choose to catch your fish rather than to buy them from a dealer, use an ordinary dip-net with a mesh of mosquito-net size, and do your hunting in weedy ditches and ponds; places where road-bridges cross streams are often very productive. A wonderful variety of little fish can be taken in such places, a few of which are shown at Figs. 86 to 92.

There is good sport for the angler in the larger Malayan rivers, especially those far from settled human habitation, not polluted by mining silt nor over-fished by riverine folk. An artificial lure of the "spoon" type is the best bait for the larger sporting fish like Kĕlah, Sĕbarau and Toman. The big Tapah are usually

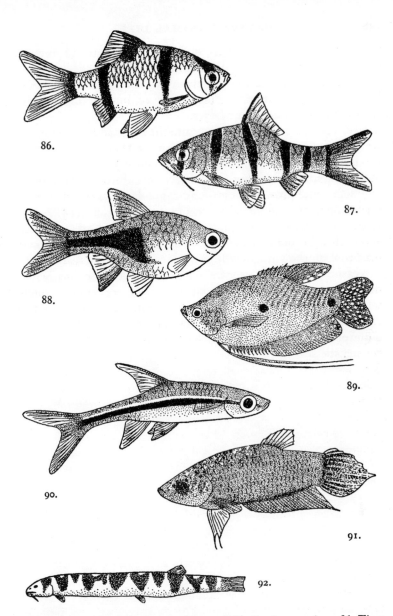

Figs. 86 to 92. Small fresh-water fishes suitable for the aquarium: 86. Tiger
Barb (*Puntius partipentazona*); 87. *Puntius hexazona*; 88. *Rasbora hetero-
morpha*; 89. Sěpat (*Trichogaster trichopterus*); 90. *Rasbora taeniata*; 91. Malayan
Fighting Fish (*Betta pugnax*); 92. A Loach (*Acanthophthalmus semicinctus*).

caught with live bait, a carp, such as a Lampam, of about a pound being used on a small shark-hook. Most of the small and moderate-sized fish can be caught by float-fishing, and some of the smaller Cyprinids can be taken on a fly, but not much of this type of fishing is done in Malaya.

Very few of our fish extend up into the cold mountain streams. I know of only two, Tĕngas and Kĕjau or Daun (species of the genus *Acrossocheilus*) which are found above 3,500 feet, though there are quite big streams well above this altitude. To remedy this defect and provide recreation for holiday-makers an attempt was made in 1935 to introduce trout into the streams at Cameron Highlands. Both Brown and Rainbow Trout were tried, the eggs being brought in batches of about 20,000 from England, kept cool on the voyage with iced water. Fish were reared quite successfully from these eggs and released in the streams, where they throve and grew fairly well, but failed to maintain themselves and have now completely died out. From one point of view this is fortunate, for if they had thriven and multiplied it is quite possible that they would have exterminated the two indigenous species.

CHAPTER TEN

INSECTS

THE Malayan members of the groups of animals we have considered hitherto can be numbered by scores or at most by hundreds. The insect species are in thousands and no attempt can be made here to give even the briefest summary of the fauna as a whole. Rather this and the next chapter will give some account of insects as such, illustrated by Malayan examples.

First the term **insect** must be defined, for it is not always correctly understood. There is a very large group of animals called the **Arthropods,** a word which means "jointed legs". It includes such familiar creatures as crabs, spiders, centipedes, beetles, flies, etc., all of which have jointed limbs and a hard external covering. The insects are a subdivision of the arthropods characterised by usually having wings in the adult and never more than three pairs of legs. Centipedes, spiders and crustaceans like crabs and prawns, are therefore not insects, but cockroaches, flies, bees, beetles and butterflies are.

Insects (and other arthropods as well) do not grow continuously as we do; at intervals they shed the hard outer covering of the body and limbs, rapid growth taking place immediately after each such shedding or moult. It is characteristic of insects that the wings are not fully developed until after the last moult. It follows from this that a winged insect can never grow; a small fly cannot be the young of a large species, but must be the adult of a small one.

This leads us to consideration of the life histories of insects, which are of two kinds. When a cockroach hatches from the egg it is already recognisably a cockroach, not much more different from its parents than a baby is from an adult human. As it grows it increases in size and the wings develop by stages corresponding with the successive moults. When a butterfly's egg hatches, however, the offspring is a worm-like creature, no more like a butterfly than a snake is like a bird. This is the larva or caterpillar, which feeds on leaves and grows rapidly, changing its skin at intervals. When it is fully grown the larva slips its skin off for the last time and reveals the third stage in development, the pupa or chrysalis. This is variously shaped in different species, covered by a hard shell and without any means of feeding or locomotion. After an interval of several days or weeks the shell splits open and the butterfly crawls out, bedraggled at first, with its wings looking like little shapeless bags. But amazingly quickly they expand, flatten and harden and in an hour or two the insect can fly. The classification of insects depends to a large extent upon which of these two types of life history they undergo.

There are various reasons for choosing the **Butterflies and Moths** as a group to consider first. They are familiar to everyone, many kinds are abundant and their life histories are easily studied by finding the eggs and larvae and rearing them in captivity.

The eggs of butterflies are generally laid singly on the young juicy shoots of the plant which affords food for the larva. It is important to remember that each species feeds on one, or at most on several related kinds of plants. The mother butterfly, although she herself feeds on the nectar of flowers, is guided by an infallible instinct to the leaves which will correctly nourish her caterpillar offspring. Butterfly eggs are of course very small, pin's head size or less, and one is more likely to find the larvae. To rear these take them home with some sprigs of the food plant, which should be put in water in a small bottle and the whole enclosed in some kind of cage with gauze or perforated zinc sides to let in the air. Plug the mouth of the bottle with cotton wool, or the larvae are almost sure to creep into the water and drown themselves. Give them fresh sprigs of food every day, of the same plant that you found them on, but do not forcibly transfer them from old to new food, in fact never handle them. Put the new food in the bottle with the old and allow them to crawl on to the new themselves. Sooner or later (if they are butterfly larvae) they will hang themselves up on the food plant, or on the side of the cage, and remain for a day or so before changing into pupae. The suspended larvae are in a very

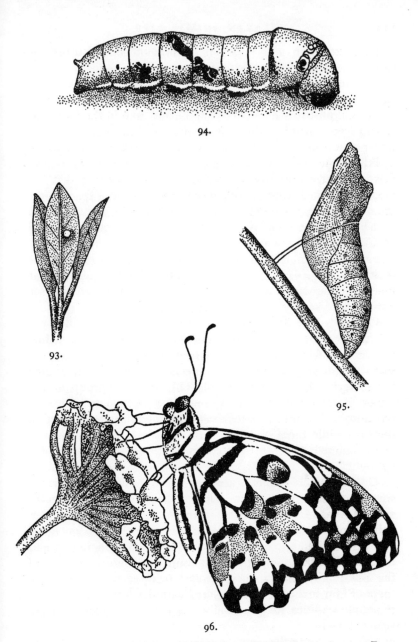

Figs. 93 to 96. Life history of the Lime Butterfly, *Papilio demoleus*: 93. Egg; 94. Fully grown larva; 95. Pupa; 96. Butterfly or Imago.

delicate condition and must on no account be disturbed or handled; the pupae are best left where they are too.

After ten days or so you will notice one morning that the pupa has darkened in colour. This means that it is about to hatch, and it will probably do so between 8.0 and 10.0 in the morning. If you have leisure to do so it is well worth keeping the pupa under observation in the hope of witnessing the actual hatching and the miraculous expanding of the wings. Even when you have just watched a butterfly emerge it is hard to believe that the broad, patterned wings were packed into so small a space a few minutes before. Among the easiest caterpillars to find are those of the several species of swallow-tail butterflies whose larvae feed on Citrus trees (Lime or Limau). They are green and brown in colour and resemble each other so closely that the Lime Butter-fly's larva (Fig. 94) will serve as a pattern to recognise any of them. Cinnamon (Kayu Manis) is also well worth searching for butterfly larvae.

The butterflies and moths together form a group called the Lepidoptera or scale-winged insects. The loosely attached powder on their wings consists of innumerable tiny overlapping scales, whose varying colours and precise arrangement determine the pattern. The butterflies are really but one group of the Lepidoptera of which the moths form by far the more numerous remainder. In butterflies the feelers or antennae are clubbed at the tips, while those of moths are variously formed but almost never clubbed; nearly all butterflies fly by day and most moths by night.

The caterpillars of moths are very varied in form and some are smooth, others more or less hairy. Those of the hawk-moths and the Atlas Moth are worth looking for and are described later. When breeding moth larvae remember that they do not hang themselves up to pupate like butterfly ones. Many spin a case or cocoon to contain the pupa (silk is obtained from the cocoon of the Silk-moth); others bury themselves in earth. A box with three or four inches of earth covered with dry leaves will provide pupating facilities for practically any caterpillar that does not suspend itself.

Malaya's butterflies and moths number several thousand species, many of them most magnificent insects; mention can be made of only a few of them. One of the commonest is the little **Grass Yellow** (*Eurema hecabe*), bright yellow with black borders to the wings; its green larvae feed on Madras Thorn, *Albizzia* and other leguminous trees. The stages of the **Lime Butterfly** (*Papilio demoleus*) are illustrated (Fig. 93-96), and the **Great Mormon** (*Papilio memnon*) is also a lime feeder. This is the largest butterfly that is commonly seen outside jungle; the male is black with a dusting of blue scales, the females always have some white and red on the wings and occur in several quite distinct forms. The beautiful orange- and white-marked butterfly shown on Plate 13 is the **Malay Lacewing** (*Cethosia hypsea*).

To see butterflies at their best you must go into the jungle, along paths and beside rivers. Sometimes they congregate in scores on patches of wet sand or mud to drink. The **Whites** and **Yellows** of the family Pieridae are always conspicuous at these gatherings, and often the beautiful **Kite Swallow-tails** (*Graphium sarpedon, doson,* etc.), black, banded or spotted with bright blue-green, are present in crowds. The males of **Rajah Brooke's Birdwing** (*Troides brookiana*) may sometimes be seen too. This is our most magnificent butterfly, black with brilliant green feather-shaped marks on the fore wings; the female is marked with white and is seldom seen. It is a curious fact that only male butterflies are found at these gatherings, which have been compared to clubs where the men foregather while the ladies are seriously employed in laying eggs among the trees and bushes.

Some butterflies are attracted by the fermenting juice of fruit, and collectors take advantage of this by putting down baits of rotting pineapple. The so-called **Viscounts** and **Barons** (genus *Euthalia*) can be taken in this way, and it is the only satisfactory way to get specimens of the Amathusiids, big mysterious butterflies, most of which inhabit deep jungle and have the wings dark brown often variously marked with blue.

The family **Danaidae** is well represented by fairly large butterflies, dark coloured, often shot with iridescent blue (*Euploea*) or conspicuously spotted and striped (*Danaus*). They are of particular interest because it has been shown that they are not generally eaten by insectivorous animals, like birds and lizards, on account of their nasty taste. The really remarkable thing is that certain butterflies of other groups, which are edible, have come in the course of evolution to resemble Danaids so closely that they are hard to distinguish from them, at least when they are flying. This protective mimicry is believed to be effective in discouraging attack by animals which are familiar with the appearance of Danaids and are wise enough to leave them alone. Of course to the entomologist the true affinities of these mimics are made clear by their anatomy, and their larvae and pupae always have the characters of the group to which they really belong.

There are also butterflies that gain protection by resemblance to inanimate objects. The most notable of these are the **Leaf Butterflies** (*Kallima* and *Doleschallia*) which, when sitting with closed wings are indistinguishable from a dead leaf.

The Lycaenidae or "**Blues**" are exceedingly numerous in Malaya and it is sometimes difficult to distinguish between the different species. Most of them are small and many have brilliant metallic colours, often, but by no means always, in various shades of blue. The larvae of many of them live in company with ants, which either attend them on their food plants for the sake of a sweet liquid which the little caterpillars secrete, or even bring them up in their nests; in this case the guests ungratefully feed on the ant larvae. There is one small group of Lycaenids, the Gerydinae, whose larvae are predatory, feeding on aphids or greenfly. The butterflies are dull little brown or brown and white insects often seen in hedges on roadsides.

There are two good books on Malayan butterflies. The one for beginners is *Common Malayan Butterflies* by R. Morrell (Longmans), while the serious collector will need *Butterflies of the Malay Peninsula* by A. S. Corbet and H. M. Pendlebury (Oliver and Boyd).

Over nine hundred species of butterflies are known from Malaya, but the **Moths** must number several thousands. The finest of them, and one of the largest moths in the world, is the **Atlas Moth** (*Attacus atlas*), whose wings are patterned in shades of rich brown, with a transparent "window" in each, and may span as much as ten inches. It is by no means rare and often flies into lighted rooms at night. The enormous caterpillars reach four and a half inches in length and are pale green with spikes on the back and a dusting of white waxy powder. They

feed on an unusually wide variety of bushes and trees and the
cocoon is spun among the leaves of the food plant. Mention has
been made of the **Hawk-moths.** They are stout-bodied,
narrow-winged insects with exceedingly powerful flight. Many
of them are large and handsome, though they are not as a rule
brightly coloured. The majority are night fliers, though one
group, the **Humming-bird Hawk-moths,** fly by day or at dusk.

98.

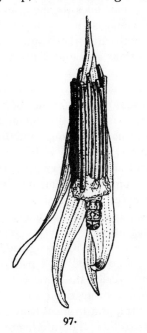

97.

Figs. 97 and 98. Bag-worm Moths:
97. Larva of *Clania crameri*; 98. Imago
of *Clania variegata*, natural size.

The larvae of hawk-moths are often very striking; they are
smooth and hairless and most of them have an erect horn at the
tail end. Some are marked on each side of the fore part of the
body with spots that look exactly like eyes; when disturbed the
larva strikes an attitude which, in conjunction with the staring
"eyes," gives it an alarmingly snake-like appearance and may well
discourage attack by birds and lizards, which have good reason
to fear snakes. Another large and striking moth that is often seen
sitting on trees and buildings is the **Swallow-tailed Moth**
(*Nyctalemon patroclus*). Its attitude of rest is very much like
that of a specimen set and pinned in a collection, and its

colour is dark chocolate brown with an oblique white stripe across both wings and the hind wings tailed and tipped with white.

A group of moths whose larvae constantly attract attention (though the adults are seldom seen) are the **Bag-worm Moths** (Psychidae, Figs. 97, 98). The larvae construct silk-lined cases of tiny twigs, scraps of leaves or other materials, each species making a case of a particular pattern. The caterpillar never leaves the case but drags it about as a snail does its shell, and when it pupates does so in the case, which is then suspended among the food plant. Only the male moths are winged and they seek out the females, which remain, lay their eggs and die in the cases which they inhabited as larvae.

Beetles. As insects are to other animals in point of numbers, so are beetles to the rest of the insects. About a quarter of a million species have been described and named throughout the world and very many more await discovery, especially in tropical countries like Malaya. They are found almost everywhere, in the tops of trees or flying high above them, in soil and mould, in wood, living or dead, in the darkest caves, in all fresh waters, but never in the sea. They range in size from that of a mouse to specks requiring a microscope for recognition. They are very variable in appearance, but most beetles are easily recognised: the body, behind the head and thorax, is covered by a pair of horny sheaths called elytra, which are really the fore wings transformed from organs of flight to form a protective covering; the hind wings are folded under the elytra, and in most (but by no means all) beetles enable the insects to fly. The life history includes larva and pupa stages like that of the butterfly.

Beetles are among the most formidable of our insect enemies; both as destroyers of crops and of stored food certain species do immense damage. Only a few of the most familiar or notable of the Malayan beetles can be mentioned.

The largest and some of the handsomest beetles belong to the **Scarab** family (Scarabaeidae). Among these is the **Rhinoceros Beetle** (*Oryctes rhinoceros*) which attains a length of nearly two inches and is a pest of coconut palms, boring into the young shoots to feed on the sweet sap. The larvae, big white maggot-like creatures, are harmless and live in decaying vegetable matter. Even larger are the members of the genus *Xylotrupes* (Fig. 99), which have similar habits but are seldom common enough to constitute a pest. Both these beetles are black in colour. The **Chafers** also belong to this family; many of them are agricultural pests, but here the damage is done mainly by the larvae, which feed on the roots of plants. Some of the Green Chafers (*Anomala*) are common and often fly into lighted rooms. They are stout, hard-shelled beetles, rather less than an inch in length, and handsomely coloured, metallic green above and burnished copper below.

The **Metallic Wood-boring Beetles** (Buprestidae) include the most beautiful of all beetles. They are often fairly large and

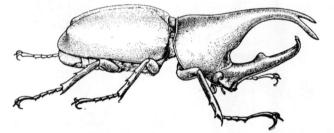

Fig. 99. Scarabeid Beetle (*Xylotrupes gideon*), natural size.

may display brilliant metallic colours. The **Jewel Beetle** (*Chrysochroa fulminans*, Fig. 100), is of such an intense metallic green that it is valued for making articles of jewellery. The larvae of the Buprestids are borers in living wood and may be objects of concern to foresters.

Rather similar to the Buprestids in appearance are the **Skip-jacks** or **Click-beetles** (Elateridae). When disturbed they sham dead, dropping from their hold to the ground, there hoping to escape notice. As often as not they land on their backs and, as their legs are short, appear as helpless as an inverted turtle. They are adapted, however, to cope with this situation by means of a peculiar mechanism a little like that of a mousetrap, which, with a distinct click, throws the beetle into the air; this per-formance is repeated until the insect is lucky enough to land right way up. The larvae of the Elaterids feed underground on the roots of plants and are known as **Wireworms.**

The **Leaf Beetles** (Chrysomelidae) include a very large number of sun-loving insects found mainly on foliage and feeding on leaves, both as larvae and adults. Some of them, including that notorious potato pest, the Colorado Beetle of temperate countries, are agricultural pests. Many leaf beetles are attractively coloured, none more so than the curious **Tortoise Beetles** (Cassidinae, Fig. 101). These are round with the

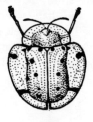

101.

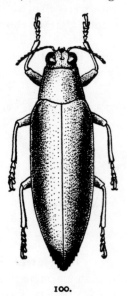

100.

Figs. 100 and 101. 100. Jewel Beetle (*Chrysochroa fulminans*); 101. Tortoise Beetle (*Aspidomorpha miliaris*), × 1¼.

margins of the elytra expanded, giving them a shield-like appearance. They are small, seldom exceeding half an inch; some are yellow boldly spotted with black, others brightly metallic, looking like drops of burnished gold. Unlike those of the Buprestids these beautiful colours quickly disappear after death.

The **Long-horned Beetles** (Cerambycidae) are easily recognised by their very long antennae. Some of them are large, handsome insects, and one of these, *Batocera albofasciata* (Fig. 102), is quite common. It is greyish in colour with yellow spots on the elytra and a pair of red marks on the thorax, which has a spine on each side. When handled it moves its thorax up and down, making a curious creaking noise. The larvae of these beetles are borers in wood like those of the Buprestidae.

The **Weevils** (Curculionidae) are the most numerous of all the beetles and over 40,000 species have received names. Their distinguishing mark is the long snout, which has the jaws at the end of it and is used for boring holes in the seeds, fruits, buds, etc., in which the weevils lay their eggs. Most of them are small, many minute, but one unusually large species is common in this country. This is the **Palm Weevil** (*Rhynchophorus ferrugineus*, Fig. 103), which varies in length between one and two inches and is black with a broad red streak on the middle of the thorax.

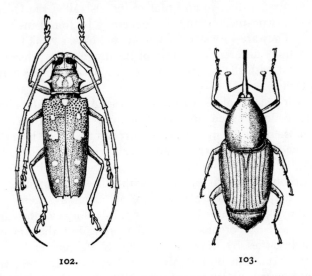

102.   103.

Figs. 102 and 103.   102. Long-horned Beetle (*Batocera albofasciata*);
103. Palm Weevil (*Rhynchophorus ferrugineus*), natural size.

The eggs are laid on palm trees of various kinds, usually in wounds or cuts made in the bark, such as the steps cut in the trees for climbing. The larva tunnels in the trunk and crown of the palm and often kills the tree.

Among the members of the group not readily recognisable as beetles are the **Fireflies** (Lampyridae), which fly slowly about at night, flashing their tiny lamps. They are usually seen singly, but occasionally they congregate on trees or bushes, usually near water, and by some means not clearly understood their flashing is synchronised, so that the whole bush is alternately lit up and darkened, affording a really remarkable spectacle. The larvae of fireflies are predatory and feed largely on snails.

Dragon-flies and **Damsel-flies.** The former of these are almost as conspicuous as butterflies, big gauzy-winged insects seen everywhere flying in the sunshine, but always more numerous and in greater variety near water. They fly with remarkable speed and power and always rest with the wings extended on each side in the attitude in which specimens are set in a collection. The Damsel-flies, which are classed by entomologists together with the dragon-flies in an order of insects called the Odonata, are far less conspicuous but can generally be found in swampy places. They are very slender-bodied and have a weak fluttering flight, wholly different from that of the dragon-flies; they nearly always rest with the wings held over the back, like the majority of butterflies.

The early stages of both groups are passed in the water, and the aquatic young, which are called nymphs rather than larvae, because there is no pupa stage, are predatory. The lower lip is hinged and greatly enlarged, and when at rest covers the face like a mask, but it can be shot out with great speed to seize the prey, for which purpose it is provided with pincer-like spines; other insects, tadpoles and little fish are all eaten by them. Both types of nymphs breathe by means of gills. Those of the damsel-flies are leaf-like organs outside the body, but the dragon-fly nymph breathes by drawing in water at its rear end; if it is frightened this can be forcibly ejected and the creature shoots rapidly forwards by jet propulsion. When its time comes to leave the water the nymph climbs up a reed and, after a short interval, its skin splits and the adult dragon-fly or damsel-fly emerges.

Our commonest dragon-fly is the red-bodied *Crocothemis servilia*, which is often to be seen in gardens and by the roadside. Its wings are colourless as is the case in the majority of dragon-flies, but by no means all of them. Along jungle paths a small species with reddish brown wings is often seen; this is the male of *Neurothemis fluctuans*, the female of which has the wings clear, usually with brown tips. The genus *Rhyothemis* includes some of our prettiest dragon-flies; *R. phyllis* is a fairly large one and is easily recognized by the conspicuous yellow and black patch at the base of the hind wings, which are otherwise colourless. In reedy

(M.W.F. Tweedie)

Plate 13. Malay Lacewing Butterfly

Plate 14.　Leaf Insect

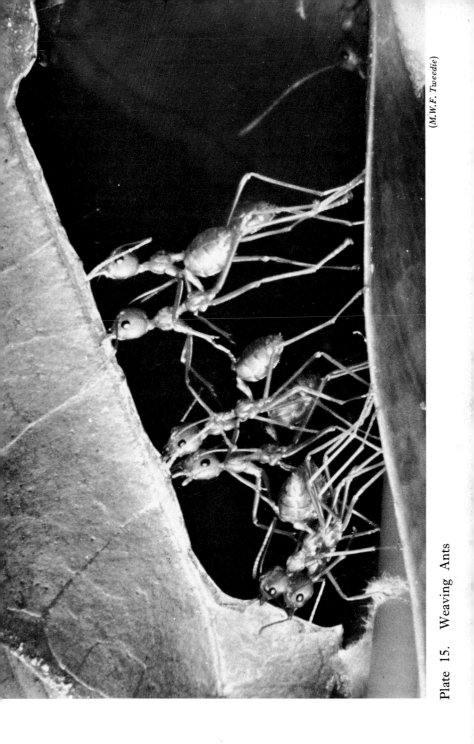

(M.W.F. Tweedie)

Plate 15.   Weaving Ants

Plate 16.   Cicada   (M.W.F. Tweedie)

(M.W.F. Tweedie)

swamps our smallest dragon-fly, *Nannophya pygmaea*, may be found. It sits with the tip of its brilliant red body cocked up in the air, and the span of its slightly yellowish wings is about one inch.

Although less conspicuous than dragon-flies, damsel-flies are common in swamps and around ponds and streams. Most of them have the wings clear, but in some of the less common kinds they have beautiful blue or green iridescent tints. A species of *Pseudagrion* is shown at Fig. 104.

The true **Flies** are a very distinct group of insects, having only a single pair of wings. These are the fore-wings, the hind ones being represented by a pair of little knobs which act as balancers. If these are removed the fly is unable to steer a course, but flies wildly in circles. They include forms like the familiar and disgusting House-fly, the mosquitoes and midges, the blow-flies, whose maggots consume decaying carcasses, the long-legged crane-flies, the attractive and some-times useful hover-flies and many others, mostly tiny, obscure insects known only to learned entomological specialists. In the development, egg, larva and pupa form distinct stages, but the details of their life histories show a great range of variation. Many of the

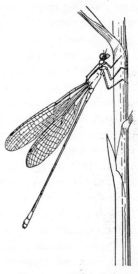

Fig. 104. Damsel-fly (*Pseudagrion*), × 1⅓.

larvae are maggot-like and feed on decaying matter; among these are the House-fly and blow-flies. The larvae and pupae of the mosquitoes are aquatic, the latter unusual in being active though, like other pupae, unable to feed. Other fly larvae feed on living vegetable matter, both above and below ground, are parasites in the bodies of other insects or higher animals or, like those of some of the hover-flies, are predatory.

Flies probably constitute a more serious threat to our comfort and security than any other insects, owing to the fact that the feeding habits of the adult insects so frequently provide a means for the spread of the micro-organisms, or germs, which cause disease.   This comes about in two ways.   Firstly the females of many of the flies feed on animal, including human, blood, by piercing the skin with their needle-like mouth-parts, injecting some saliva to prevent the blood from clotting, and then sucking the mixture in again.   If the insect is infected with the disease germs, some of these are injected with the saliva and, since it is not all sucked up again, the victim of the bite becomes infected. The saliva is also an irritant poison, and this causes the itching and swelling in the region of the bite.   The mosquitoes are the most notorious of the flies of this kind and are considered the most important of the insect enemies of mankind.

The other way in which flies spread disease is by feeding on infected filth and then visiting our food.   The common House-fly is one of the worst offenders.   It breeds in any kind of rubbish containing animal or vegetable matter, especially household garbage, and the adult flies seem to find crude sewage and a bowl of sugar equally attractive.   They have the unpleasing habit of regurgitating part of their last meal on to their next one in order to liquefy it, and it is all too easy to imagine what will happen in a community whose garbage is not regularly disposed of, whose sanitation is unhygienic and who take no trouble to protect their food from flies.   Diseases like dysentery, typhoid and cholera spread rapidly under such conditions.

Typical flies like the **House-fly** are less common in Malaya than in most tropical countries, and it is supposed that the absence of any marked dry season prevents their increase in some way; it is certainly true that flies are most numerous in dry climates.   In our large towns, however, man can create conditions which will lead to house-flies becoming a pest.   The disorder that prevailed during the Japanese occupation of Singapore had this result and the **Malayan House-fly** (*Musca vicina*) was swarming at the time of the liberation.   Their relative scarcity is a tribute to the efficient disposal of garbage and sanitation measures under the present administration.   Flies of various kinds are often numerous in fishing villages, due to untidy methods of drying fish and failure to dispose properly of the inedible parts of them.

Mosquitoes are too familiar to need description.   All of them breed in water, usually laying their eggs so that they float on the surface. The larvae swim actively by a wriggling motion and have no gills, but must come up to the surface of the water to breathe air. Control of the harmful species is effected by spreading on the water a film of light oil, which the larvae encounter when they come up to breathe. The pupae of mosquitoes are rounder in shape than the larvae, but also swim actively; they also have to come to the surface to breathe but they do not feed.

Of the numerous kinds of mosquitoes which inhabit this country three genera are worthy of mention. The commonest mosquitoes are species of *Culex*, *C. fatigans* being the most abundant. Its larvae breed in dirty water and the adults are more of a nuisance than a danger, as they are not important conveyors of disease. *Culex* mosquitoes fly mostly after dark. The species of *Aedes* are the so-called **Tiger Mosquitoes.** They fly during the day, their attack is insistent and their bite intensely irritating. They owe their English name to the black and white stripes on their bodies and legs, but it would still be appropriate if they were not so marked. They are carriers of dengue fever and, in countries where the disease occurs, of the deadly yellow fever. The common *A. aegypti* breeds in small accumulations of water such as collect in half coconut shells, tin cans and defective gutters. Their control is largely a domestic matter; if you and your neighbour keep your surroundings tidy you will probably not be much troubled with them. The eggs are laid, not in the water, but on the sides of the container just above the surface, where they remain without hatching until rain (or filling up of e.g. a flower vase) submerges them. This enables the mosquitoes to survive periods of dry weather in a form other than the adult.

The **carriers of malaria** all belong to the genus *Anopheles*. The adults can be recognised by their attitude when at rest, the body being held not parallel (as in *Culex* and *Aedes*) but obliquely to the surface on which the insect is standing. When an *Anopheles* bites you it looks like a tiny needle stuck slantwise into your skin. The larvae are also very distinct; those of most mosquitoes, when they come to the surface to breathe, hang head-downwards, taking in air through a tube on the tail. *Anopheles* larvae lie horizontally with their backs touching the surface film of the water. The habits and biology of these mosquitoes have been very closely studied. It has been shown that the minute parasite which causes malaria undergoes a complicated life cycle, certain stages of which are passed in the mosquito and the rest in man. The mosquito's habit, already referred to, of injecting its saliva and sucking up the blood ensures that the disease is transmitted both from a person suffering from malaria to a healthy mosquito and from an infected mosquito to a healthy person. It has also been discovered that only certain species of *Anopheles* transmit malaria, others being from our point of view harmless, either through immunity to the disease or through a preference for biting animals other than man. Further, each of the carrier species has its own special breeding habits, knowledge of which makes it possible to destroy the larvae and so to control the disease.

The **Spotted Anopheles** (*A. maculatus*) is generally regarded as the worst carrier of malaria in this country. It breeds in slowly flowing or oozing water of the kind known as seepage water, especially when this is exposed to the sun. Any disturbance of the soil or underlying rock, such as quarrying, road-making or building, is likely to make artificial breeding places for it. Weekly spraying of likely breeding places with oil is effective against this mosquito, but in inhabited areas the occurrence of breeding places suited to it can be prevented by rather elaborate methods of drainage. While *A. maculatus* is the carrier species of hilly country, *A. letifer* (formerly known as *A. umbrosus*) takes its place on the flat coastal plains. The adults live in shady jungle and bite during the day as well as by night; the larvae are found in streams and swamp-water and prefer their surroundings shaded. Oiling, removal of vegetation both in and overhanging the water, and drainage are measures employed against it. The third important carrier, *A. sundaicus*, inhabits the coast and breeds in brackish water. If the sea water is kept out by earth-works, breeding is prevented, and free admission of tidal water along open channels greatly reduces it. The effect of these two methods is to make the available water either wholly fresh or wholly salt, neither of which is liked by the larvae. A number of other species of *Anopheles* are carriers of malaria in Malaya, but these three are the most important.

The **Biting Midges** (Ceratopogonidae) are minute flies with a bite that causes discomfort out of all proportion to their size.

It varies in its effect and some people suffer more severely than others. The flies pass freely through the mesh of an ordinary mosquito net and where they are numerous one faces the alternative of submitting to their attacks or using a sand fly

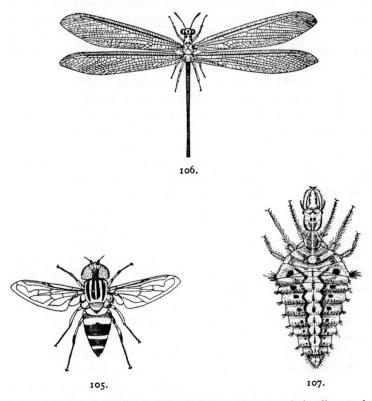

106.

105.   107.

Figs. 105 to 107. 105. Hover-fly (*Eristalis acervorum*). × 2; 106. Ant-lion, × 1⅓;
107. Ant-lion larva, greatly enlarged.

net, which keeps them out but largely excludes the air as well. Fortunately they do not, so far as is known, carry disease. They are not the same as Sand Flies, which do carry disease but belong to a different family of flies, the Psychodidae. Biting midges are often very bad in mangrove swamp and occasionally in inland secondary jungle. Not much is known about their breeding, but the larvae are generally aquatic or semi-aquatic.

It is a relief to turn at last to a group of flies which offer us neither danger nor discomfort nor offence. The **Hover-flies** (Syrphidae, Fig. 105), are pretty creatures, often brightly marked like wasps, but quite harmless, lovers of flowers and the sun. They have the remarkable habit of hovering motionless with vibrating wings, but are alert and amazingly quick if a stroke is made at them with a net. They seldom occur together in large numbers and in Malaya are commoner in the hills than in the lowlands. The larvae of many of them are highly beneficial as they feed on aphids or green-fly, which suck the juices of plants. These Syrphid larvae are slug-like and taper towards the head. They live on the plants on which their prey is to be found and pupate on the branches or twigs. Other Syrphid larvae are aquatic and others again live in the nests of ants and termites.

The **Neuroptera** or **Nerve-winged Insects** are a group of four-winged insects, mostly with weak powers of flight. They include the **Lacewing Flies,** whose larvae feed on aphids, as do those of some of the Syrphids, and the Myrmeleontidae or **Ant-lions** (Figs. 106, 107). All observant people must have noticed in dry dust, in places sheltered from the rain, especially under raised houses, funnel-shaped pits an inch or so in diameter. Watch these pits and you may see an ant or other small insect wander into one. It will probably lose its footing on the loose, dusty slope, and as it tries to scramble out you will see little jets of dust thrown up from the bottom of the pit, directed at the unfortunate insect. The effect of these is to prevent it escaping, and sooner or later it will roll to the bottom and be seized in the jaws of the maker and occupant of the deadly little trap. This is the larva of one of the ant-lions, whose name is taken from the larval and not the adult mode of life. It lives in a cavity in the dust under the bottom of its pit and uses its flattened head and large, curved jaws to throw dust up at any wingless insects, especially ants, which fall into its trap. The adults are not often seen; they fly at night and somewhat resemble dragon-flies, having two pairs of gauzy wings, but the antennae are longer than those of dragon-flies and clubbed at the tips, and their flight is weak and uncertain.

CHAPTER ELEVEN

INSECTS (*Continued*)

Bugs. This word is used by most people to describe any unattractive insect, but it should be applied only to two orders of insects, the true bugs (Hemiptera) and the clear-winged bugs (Homoptera). The most obvious character all the bugs have in common is the form of the mouth-parts, which are designed for piercing and sucking; this is not, of course, confined to them, being found among the blood-sucking flies and others, but it is not uniformly characteristic of any other large group of insects. While some bugs are blood-suckers, like the notorious Bed-bug, the great majority feed on the sap of plants.

The **True Bugs** are flattish insects and each of the fore-wings, when they are present, is divided into two parts, a thick, horny portion in front and a thin, membranous one behind. They somewhat resemble beetles, but the division of the fore-wings and their beak-like mouth-parts are generally obvious enough to distinguish them. The most typical of them are the Shield-bugs (Pentatomidae, Fig. 108), shield-shaped insects, unpleasant because of the horrible smell they give out when molested. The **Assassin-bugs** (Reduviidae) are rather similar in appearance but are predatory, feeding on other insects. They should be handled with care as their bite is poisonous and painful. Some of the Hemiptera are aquatic; of these the **Water Striders** (Gerridae, Fig. 109), are to be seen on almost any pool or stream. They rest on the surface film of the water on the tips of their four long hinder legs, the front pair being short and used for grasping their prey. The **Giant Water-bugs** (Belostomatidae), which prey on creatures as large as frogs and small fish, may reach a length of four or five inches. They are winged and are sometimes attracted to light.

The Homoptera or **Clear-winged Bugs** have more the appearance of flies, but possess two pairs of wings, which are of the same thickness and texture throughout. The **Aphids** or **Green-fly** are among the most familiar of them. They occur all over the world and do immense harm to agriculture both by draining the sap of plants and by spreading plant diseases, in just the same way as mosquitoes do among ourselves. All other insects which prey upon aphids are to be accounted our friends.

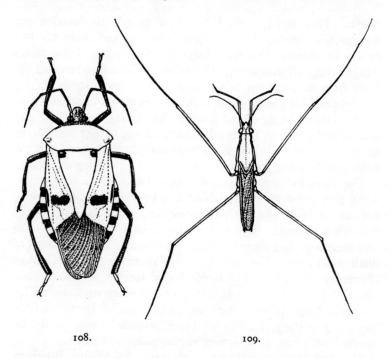

108.   109.

Figs. 108 and 109.   108. Shield-bug (*Catacanthus incarnatus*);
109. Water Strider (*Gerridae*), × 1½.

Characteristic of the tropics are the large Homopterous insects called **Cicadas** (Plate 16). The largest Malayan species is the **Empress Cicada** (*Pomponia imperatoria*), a really magnificent insect whose wings span eight inches. More frequently seen are the green-bodied species of the genus *Dundubia* (Figs. 110, 111), which span three to four inches. Most cicadas have transparent wings, but in some they are coloured, as in *Tacua speciosa*, whose forewings are black with red veins and the hind wings black with a clear border; the dark coloured body is crossed by a green band on the thorax and the wings span six inches. This beautiful cicada is found in mountainous and hilly country, but is not common. The cicadas with coloured wings look rather like moths, but the colour is in the wing membrane, not in the form of easily detached scales. Even more remarkable than the impressive size and appearance of the cicadas are their voices.

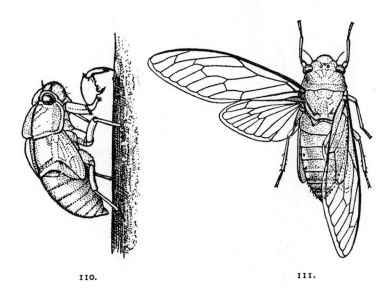

110.   III.

Figs. 110 and 111. Cicadas: 110. Empty skin of a nymph; 111. Imago of *Dundubia mannifera*, natural size.

Many insects can make a noise, and they usually do it by rubbing one surface against another (stridulating). The extraordinarily powerful sustained note of the male cicada is produced in quite a different way: a pair of membranes or tymbals, contained in a cavity in the body, is vibrated and the resulting sound is amplified by the cavity, which acts as a sounding box. They are among the most difficult insects to catch, for they fly very fast and settle on the trunks of trees, usually out of reach. Some collectors hunt them with a small gun and dust-shot, contenting themselves with the rather damaged specimens that they so obtain.

Another group of rather conspicuous Homoptera is the **Fulguroidea.** They are very varied in appearance; some have strange prolongations of the head and are called lantern-flies, a name given to them by the early students of insects in the mistaken belief that they were luminous. Others, belonging to the

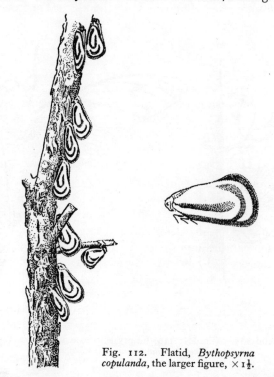

Fig. 112. Flatid, *Bythopsyrna copulanda*, the larger figure, × 1½.

family Flatidae, look rather like small moths. One of these, *Bythopsyrna copulanda* (Fig. 112), is very common; sometimes a roadside bush is seen to be covered with a white woolly deposit among which numbers of this little black and white Flatid are sitting and flying about. The white wool consists of fine threads of wax produced by the young or nymphs of the insect.

All the bugs develop by gradual stages, without definite larva and pupa, the wings developing completely at the last moult.

Usually the young live in the same surroundings as the adults, but the cicadas are exceptional. The eggs are laid on the twigs of trees and the newly hatched young descend to the ground and burrow, passing their lives sucking sap from roots. When the time comes for their final moult they crawl a little way up the trunk of a tree and the perfect insect emerges, leaving behind the empty skin of the nymph clinging to the tree (Fig. 110). These empty skins are often abundant at a height of two or three feet on tree trunks in jungle. Nothing is known about the length of time spent underground by the tropical cicadas, but a North American species is known to spend the astonishing period of seventeen years in developing.

The **Orthoptera** (grasshoppers and crickets), the **Phasmida** (leaf- and stick-insects) and the **Dictyoptera** (cockroaches and mantises) are three orders that can be considered together, in fact the latter two were formerly included in the Orthoptera. They have biting mouthparts and no definite metamorphosis, the wings appearing gradually with successive moults, but being functional only after the last.

The **Short-horned Grasshoppers** and **Locusts** (Acridiidae) are eaters of vegetation and when they occur in great numbers may be catastrophically destructive. Many of the smaller kinds are common and the large yellow and black locust *Valanga nigricornis* is often seen in gardens and reaches a length of three inches. The notorious **Migratory Locust** (*Locusta migratoria*) does not appear to be established in Malaya, but outbreaks have been recorded and are thought to be invasions, probably from Borneo.

The **Bush Crickets** (Tettigoniidae, Fig. 113), have the hind pair of legs greatly enlarged for jumping like the Acridiidae, but their antennae, instead of being short, are long and thread-like. The large **Leaf-Locust**, *Pseudophyllus prasinus*, is typical of the group, and attains a length of five inches. Its fore wings are green and are held together in the form of a steeply sloping eave, enclosing the body. Other members of the family are brown and resemble a dead leaf instead of a living one. The ovipositors or egg-laying organs of the females are conspicuous sickle-shaped appendages at the rear end of the body. They may be used for boring holes in the ground or for cutting slits in twigs, the various species disposing of their eggs in different ways.

Most Tettigoniids live among the foliage of trees and some are predatory, feeding on other insects. They are nocturnal and the males maintain a shrill sustained stridulation which is sometimes a source of discontent to bad sleepers. In the long-horned grasshoppers the noise is made by rubbing the fore wings together; the Acridiidae produce a rather less penetrating note by rubbing the hind legs over the large veins of the wings. In both special structures are developed to produce the sound, the

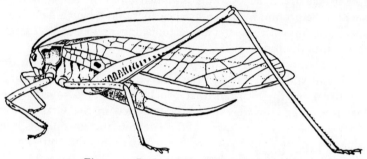

Fig. 113.   Bush Cricket, *Mecopoda elongata.*

usual principle being very like that of drawing a finger nail along the teeth of a comb. In practically all vocal insects it is only the male which sings and it is presumed that he is serenading the female, who is provided with special ears on some part of her body to receive and appreciate his song, and to distinguish it from that of any other species.

The **Crickets** (Gryllidae, Fig. 114), look rather like stoutly built short-horned grasshoppers, but have long antennae like the Tettigoniids. They are attractive little insects, often tolerated in houses and sometimes even kept as pets for the sake of their song or for the purpose of promoting combats between the pugnacious males, on which, of course, wagers are laid.

Among the **Leaf-** and **Stick-Insects** (Phasmida) we meet some of the most extraordinary adaptations for concealment that are known. The resemblance of the Leaf-Insect (*Phyllium*, Plate 14) to a leaf is so exact in every detail that it can never fail to arouse astonishment. The stick-insects (Fig. 115), with their long legs and strangely elongated bodies are hardly less remarkable, whether they are considered as camouflage devices or simply as oddities. All the Phasmids are vegetable feeders but never occur in sufficient numbers to do any damage.

In some winged stick-insects the wings, which are folded like a fan when not in use and wholly concealed, are brightly coloured, so that when it takes to flight the creature is momentarily conspicuous, but instantly merges into its background again when it settles. This phenomenon of "flash coloration" is quite often encountered among insects. Grasshoppers display it in the same way as the stick-insects, and another example is afforded by leaf butterflies, whose wings are brightly coloured above and resemble dead leaves below, the upper surface being concealed when the insect is at rest. It is supposed to be protective on the principle that when a resting insect, concealed by resemblance to its surroundings, is forced by a searching predator to take to flight, its sudden flash of bright colour startles and confuses the enemy and prevents it marking accurately the place where the intended victim comes to rest again.

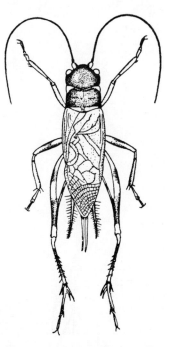

Fig. 114. Cricket, *Gymnogryllus elegans*, × 1½.

The cockroaches and mantises comprise the Dictyoptera or "net-winged insects". The common **Cockroach** of our houses is *Periplaneta americana*, which is almost centainly North African in origin and has travelled all over the world in ships. It is a tropical insect but is found in temperate countries in artificially warmed premises like bakeries. The eggs of cockroaches are deposited in a very peculiar way; they are laid in a leathery egg-case (called an ootheca), which is gradually pushed out of the body of the female as it is filled with eggs. When it is full she carries it about for a time and then deposits it in a crevice, and the young hatch out in due course.

In addition to the 'American' Cockroach there are numerous Malayan species, mostly smaller, a few larger, which live in the open. Small ones often fly into light and are sometimes taken

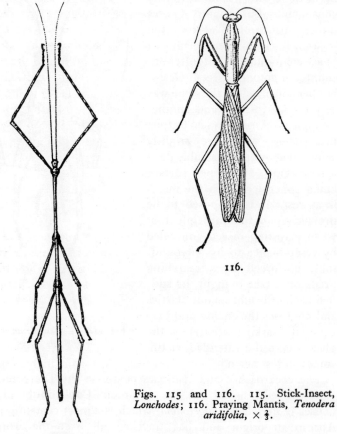

116.

Figs. 115 and 116. 115. Stick-Insect, *Lonchodes*; 116. Praying Mantis, *Tenodera aridifolia*, × ⅔.

115.

for young domestic cockroaches, which, of course, they cannot be as they are already winged. Many of the "wild" kinds can be found by stripping the bark off dead trees and logs.

The **Praying Mantises** (Mantidae, Fig. 116), are among the most interesting and attractive insects of our fauna. Their habit of walking on four legs using the front pair as hands, and their curiously expressive "faces", give them an appearance of intelligence far beyond anything they really possess, but it is a general rule that predatory animals are more enterprising and aware of their surroundings than are herbivores, and the mantises are ferocious predators. They owe their name to the deceptively devotional appearance of their characteristic pose, with the fore legs held up as if in prayer. In reality the mantis is, of course, waiting for some unwary insect to stray within reach; if it does the deadly spined fore limbs will strike and grasp and the mantis will eat its victim alive, daintily, as a lady eats a sandwich.

The most commonly encountered mantises belong to the genus *Heirodula*. They are fairly large insects and, apart from their green or brown colour, have no special resemblance to vegetable structures. They feed mainly on other insects but are prepared to eat practically any animal that they can capture and overpower. The **Dead Leaf Mantis** (*Deroplatys desiccata*) has outgrowths of the thorax and modifications of the wings which cause it to resemble a withered leaf almost as closely as the Phasmid *Phyllium* resembles a living one.

The most extraordinary of our mantises, perhaps the most remarkable of Malayan insects, is the **Flower Mantis,** *Hymenopus coronatus*. In its adult, winged condition this is an ordinary fairly large mantis, nearly white in colour, unusual only in having a petal-like expansion on each of the thigh-joints of its four walking legs. But in the later stages of its unwinged existence, right up to the last moult, its appearance and habits are truly spectacular. In the first place it is coloured, except for a green bar on the thorax, entirely bright pink; the hind part of the body is carried arched over the back and the four expanded thighs are disposed round it, so that the insect becomes, so long as it remains motionless, a large four-petalled pink flower with a rather complex centre, recalling that of some of the more highly modified orchids. The resemblance to a flower and the total dissimilarity to any kind of insect are so strong that one may notice and admire the creature and still remain deceived. The purpose of this extraordinary adaptation may be two-fold. It certainly must protect the insect against predators which hunt by sight, such as birds and lizards, and it seems likely that it also attracts to it and enables it to capture insects such as bees and butterflies, which visit flowers for their nectar and are guided to them by their bright colours. The Flower Mantis seems to be fairly common in the northern states but I have never heard of its occurring in the south or in Singapore.

The **Hymenoptera** is the name given to the order of insects which includes wasps, hornets, bees and ants. They undergo complete metamorphosis, with egg, larva and pupa stages, and in complexity and versatility of habits they may be said to occupy the same position of leadership among the insects as do the mammals, with man at their head, among the vertebrates. This is particularly true of the social forms, but the ingenuity displayed by some of the solitary wasps is also worthy of great admiration. The females of most bees and wasps and of many ants carry a sting at the hinder end of the body, with which a painful wound can be inflicted.

The **Solitary Wasps** are so named to distinguish them from those which live in large colonies or nests. They occur in far greater variety than do the social wasps though individuals of the latter are often more numerous, especially near a nest.

Almost all the insects we have considered hitherto make no special provision for the next generation beyond laying their eggs in an environment suitable for the young. Such insects as butterflies do, indeed, carefully select the correct species of plant to nourish their larvae, but many of the solitary wasps carry parental solicitude a good deal further.

They are easily observed as they constantly enter our houses; they construct nests, usually made of mud, in a variety of situations, in keyholes and crevices of all kinds, in the folds of curtains, sometimes in the open. They are not always welcomed by the housewife, but if the wasp can be detected making its nest it is well worth watching the process of building and stocking it, even if it must be destroyed afterwards. First, for a day or so, she brings pellets of mud and builds a small receptacle, varying in form with the species. When it is finished she starts bringing small creatures, usually spiders or caterpillars, which are stored away in the nest until it is full. It is then sealed up and the wasp is seen no more; she is probably making another one elsewhere.

If the nest is opened a day or two later the stored victims are found to be still there, but are not dried up or decomposed; inspected closely they will be seen to make small flinching movements, for they are not dead. They have been put in the nest by the wasp as food for her young and are accompanied by eggs, whose number is such that the larvae which hatch from

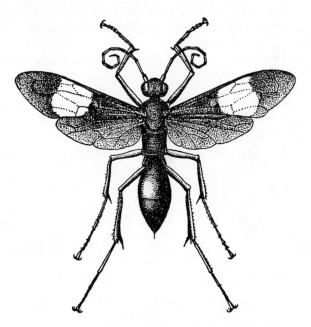

Fig. 117.   Psammocharid Wasp, *Hemipepsis speculifer*,
natural size.

them will have enough, but not too much, provision for their development. If the spiders or caterpillars were killed they would decompose and be unfit for food, but the sting of the mother wasp has the effect of paralysing them without immediately putting an end to their lives. Guided by an instinct as infallible as that which instructed its mother, the tiny maggot which is to become a wasp starts its meal with care to avoid its victim's vital organs, and thus preserves it alive until the last possible moment. This elaborate pattern of behaviour is entirely instinctive; there can be no question of instruction of one generation by the last, for the mother wasp never sees her offspring except as an egg.

Foremost among the spider-hunters are the **Psammochari-dae**. These are large, long-legged wasps which identify themselves by their peculiar nervous, twitching movements as they hunt for their prey, construct their nests or dig the burrows in which some of them store provision for their young. Many of the Psammocharids are handsome insects; *Macromeris violaceus* is shining black with deep iridescent purple wings, others, such as *Hemipepsis* (Fig. 117), have the wings variously coloured.

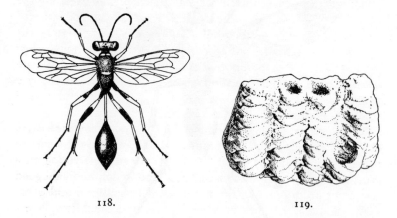

118.   119.

Figs. 118 and 119.   118. Thread-waisted Wasp, *Sceliphron madraspatanum*, × 2.
119. Its mud nest.

The **Thread-waisted Wasps** or Sphecidae (Figs. 118, 119), are solitary wasps which have the thorax and hind part of the body connected by a fine thread-like stalk. They make mud nests, sometimes in cavities, sometimes on open surfaces, in which a variety of prey is stored to provide food for the larvae, insects of various kinds, spiders and caterpillars. But any one species of solitary wasp will confine itself to a single type, or even a single species, of insect or spider.

The **Eumenidae** prey for the most part on caterpillars. They are small narrow-waisted wasps, often black and red or black and yellow, and are the chief builders of mud nests in our houses. One genus, *Eumenes*, the **Potter Wasps**, make most elegant nests like little urn-shaped pots of clay, each with a neat funnel-shaped opening.

The well-known **Social Wasps** and **Hornets** carry the practice of looking after their young to its logical conclusion, for they do not merely provide for them and leave them, but build large communal nests in which the young are actually fed and attended by the adult wasps. We meet here for the first time with so-called caste differentiation, whereby certain individuals, normally the great majority of the population of a nest, have no power of reproduction but are concerned solely with the work of building and maintaining the nest and guarding and feeding the young and the (usually solitary) functional female or "queen" who is the mother of them all. Among the Hymenoptera the sexless or worker class are always sterile females. Though they can lay no eggs they retain their sting; the fact that the males are stingless is of little consolation to anyone who is attacked by a swarm of wasps, as they are very few in number and play a wholly subordinate part in the economy of the nest.

Most social wasps make their nest hanging in a tree or the eaves of a house, a few below the ground, and construct it of a sort of paper made of chewed wood-pulp. They feed their young on a great variety of insects and insect larvae and undoubtedly do good service in keeping down the numbers of agricultural and other pests. Some species are very savage and will attack trespassers near their nests; the larger of these, which are known as hornets, are to be accounted dangerous.

Our two largest species are the **Banded Hornet** (*Vespa tropica*, Fig. 120), and the **Lesser Banded Hornet** (*Vespa affinis*), which are very similar in appearance, large wasps, black with an orange band on the abdomen. The former makes its nest in hollow trees or in the roofs of houses, the latter places it in the open, hanging from the boughs of trees and bushes. Both are common insects and often fly into houses. Their sting is severe, but they seldom use it unless they are molested or their nest is threatened. The **Slender Banded Hornet** (*Polistes sagittarius*) is similar in colour to the two species of *Vespa* just described but more slender, and the legs are long and hang down conspicuously in flight. It makes a paper nest consisting of a mass of cells opening downwards, and hanging by a short stalk.

These wasps are more aggressive than the other banded hornets and will attack anyone who approaches their nest. The sting is painful and multiple stings may be dangerous.

The **Golden Wasp** (*Vespa auraria*) is a mountain species which nests in the ground and is named from the golden-yellow colour of the body. It is common in the hill stations and is a most vicious creature, always attacking trespassers near its nest and stinging savagely. A variety of little wasps belong to the genus

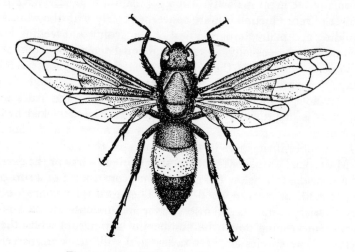

Fig. 120.   Banded Hornet, *Vespa tropica*, × 1⅓.

Ropalidia and make their nests in trees and bushes. They will attack readily, especially if one brushes against their home bush. They are all too common and the effect of a large number of stings may be quite unpleasant. The **Night Wasp** (*Provespa anomala*) is a long-bodied, rusty brown coloured wasp which flies at night and is attracted by artificial light. They often enter houses and will sting if they fall on to one's skin as a result of being bewildered by the light; the sting is extremely painful. They nest in low bushes.

Bees. These insects are not always easy to distinguish from wasps, though most of them are stouter and visibly hairy. They differ radically, however, in their habits, for all bees feed themselves and their young on pollen and honey made from the nectar of flowers. It is not correct to say that they gather honey; this and nectar are two quite distinct substances, the change from one to the other taking place in the body of the bee. Bees can also be divided into solitary and social forms; the social ones do not make their nests of paper, as wasps do, but of wax, which they secrete in their bodies.

Our only conspicuous solitary bees are the **Carpenter Bees** (Xylocopidae). Two species of these are among the most familiar of Malayan insects and do considerable damage by boring large holes in the timbers of houses. The very large black one is *Xylocopa latipes*; the smaller *Koptorthosoma confusa* (Fig. 121), has the abdomen black and the thorax yellow in the female, the male being wholly yellow. Both have dark coloured wings and the females have quite formidable stings.

The **Giant Honey Bee** (*Megapis dorsata*, Fig. 122), is common and is the biggest of our social bees. It is dark coloured with a yellow patch on the fore part of the abdomen and makes enormous hanging combs on branches of trees, buildings and overhanging cliffs; water towers which consist of a tank supported on a central pillar almost always have combs hanging from them. This is a very dangerous insect and cases are known of people being killed by multiple stings from them. A bird of prey, the Honey Buzzard, sometimes attacks the nests to eat the honey and larvae; it seems to be protected against the bees' stings, but they are, naturally, roused to fury and will vent it on any living thing near their nest. If you see a honey buzzard attacking a nest, do not approach in order to obtain a better view of the proceedings.

In some parts of its range the local people raid these great nests for their honey, usually at night and with the aid of a smoky torch to rout the bees. They are brave men who accomplish this feat, for the nest is usually accessible only to a bold climber, and, torch or no, the bees are formidable creatures. It has never been found possible to domesticate *dorsata* and in any case its honey is not of good quality. These bees fly by night as well as by day and are sometimes attracted by light, when they behave rather as the Night Wasp does.

The **Small Indian Bee** (*Apis indica*) closely resembles the European Honey Bee. It produces honey of fair quality and can

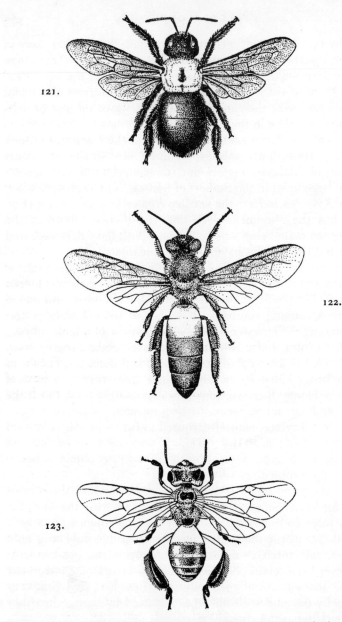

Figs. 121 to 123. Bees: 121. Carpenter Bee (*Koptorthosoma confusa*), × 1½;
122. Giant Honey Bee (*Megapis dorsata*), × 3½; 123. Stingless Bee (*Trigona
thoracica*), × 3½.

be kept under domestication. It sometimes nests in the roofs of houses but is no more than a nuisance, being far less aggressive than *dorsata* and its sting much less severe.

The little black stingless bees of the genus *Trigona* (Fig. 123) are our most abundant social bees. They are harmless but can be a tickling nuisance as they are partial to human perspiration and often crawl in numbers over the exposed parts of one's person. They nest in cavities in trees and old houses and the entrance to the nest may be marked by a funnel-shaped tube of wax. Sometimes this is white and looks almost like a flower; presumably it acts as a visual guide to the door of the nest.

Ants. While among the bees and wasps only a minority of the species are social insects, all ants are so, in the sense that they live in larger or smaller communities in which the larvae are fed and attended by the adults. In complexity of organisation the communities of the more advanced of them are far beyond those of the other Hymenoptera, in fact they excel all other social insects. Many books have been written about these extraordinary communities, often hundreds of thousands strong, practising such quasi-human activities as the keeping of other insects as domestic animals, and of other species of ants as slaves, and as the growing and harvesting of fungi by a form of agriculture more intensive and precise than any we can boast ourselves.

Specialisation of the worker caste is commonly carried beyond the condition seen among bees and wasps, and sub-castes are developed so that we find "soldiers" with enormous heads and jaws, and workers of different sizes specialised for different tasks. As in other social Hymenoptera, all of these are females which lack the power of reproduction, but they differ from the bee and wasp workers in being invariably wingless. The only winged ants are the males and queens, and the latter are winged only during the initial phase of their adult life, which is concerned with mating; after this they deliberately break their wings off. Male ants usually survive only a short time after they leave the nest on the nuptial or marriage flight.

Ants' nests, like those of social bees and wasps, are normally founded by a single fecundated queen, who personally rears a small brood of workers and then lapses into the passive role of an egg-layer, fed and tended by her own offspring. From time to time winged males and females are produced from her eggs and fare forth into the world to found nests of their own. Ordinarily the duration of the nest is determined by the life of the queen, who may live for a number of years, but in the enormous "cities" of the more advanced species new queens are constantly recruited to the service of the nest (both from outside and from within it) and there is no definite limit to the nest's endurance.

Because of their usually small size ants are not easy to identify, and a microscope is needed for systematic study of them. Some, however, are immediately recognisable.

The **Weaving Ant** or **Kĕrĕngga** (*Oecophylla smaragdina*, Plate 15) is known to everyone who at all frequently strays off the path in his walks in Malaya. It is a rusty-red, long-legged, fairly large ant that makes nests by joining living leaves together with silk in trees and bushes. They savagely attack anyone who touches or brushes against the branches bearing the nest, generally making the removal of at least part of one's clothing a positive necessity; they have no sting but bite with their jaws and eject an acrid fluid over the wound. Only the workers are red, the queens being bright green (a most unusual colour among ants) and the males black. These can usually be found by anyone who has the courage to pull a nest to pieces.

The making of the nest involves a most extraordinary procedure. The ants themselves have no means of producing silk, but the larvae have silk-glands, designed originally, no doubt, to enable them to make cocoons when they pupate, as do the larvae of some other kinds of ants; but no Kĕrengga larva ever makes a cocoon. When a leaf is to be added to the nest, or a rent repaired, a number of workers seize the edges to be joined and hold them in the required position, others enter the nest and bring out living larvae. These are passed to and fro between the edges in such a way that a web of silk is spun across the space, the larva playing a part combining that of the shuttle of a loom and a tube of glue.

Another unmistakable species is the **Giant Ant** (*Camponotus gigas*, Fig. 124), which is often seen wandering on jungle paths. It is dark reddish brown and the workers are formidable-looking creatures an inch in length. The nests are made in large stumps and dead trunks of trees and the ants, though they are abroad by day, are much more active at night.

The common house ant that invades the sugar bowl and swarms into carelessly disposed boxes of sweets is the **Pharaoh's Ant** (*Monomorium pharaonis*). It is a tiny insect, a twelfth of an inch long, yellow with a dark tail-tip. It always occurs associated with human dwellings and nests in any sheltered (and usually inaccessible) cranny. Like the domestic cockroach it has been carried all over the world by ships and, although a tropical species, establishes itself in artificially warmed places in temperate countries.

Fig. 124. Giant Ant, *Camponotus gigas*, ×2.

Some species of ants carry a sting like that of a wasp. The worst of these is the **Fire-Ant** (*Tetraponera rufonigra*), which lives in hollow stems and branches and is often common in gardens. It is about the size of a Kĕrengga, elongate and reddish with the head and tail-tip black. It stings readily and very severely.

Often under logs and stones small communities of rather long-legged, active shining black ants may be found. These are members of the most primitive group of ants, the so-called *Ponerines*. Their nests are slight impermanent affairs, like jungle kampongs when compared with the teeming cities of the higher ants. They are, indeed, small hunting communities closely comparable with those of primitive man, and all the Ponerine ants carry a formidable sting, just as the Sakai goes armed with his blow-pipe and poisoned darts.

Termites. These insects are often referred to as "white ants". The term is an unfortunate one and its use should be discontinued; they are not, generally speaking, white and they are not related to the ants, but comprise an order of their own, the *Isoptera*, whose nearest relatives are probably cockroaches. They resemble the ants in one respect only, that of living in organised communities; here the resemblance is, indeed, remarkable and affords perhaps the most impressive instance of convergent evolution known.

In both groups large "nests", consisting of a complex system of intercommunicating chambers and galleries, are made. Differentiation into castes, wingless soldiers and workers of different grades as well as initially winged males and queens, has occurred, and the reproductive role is confined to one or a few queens and males, the workers being sterile and playing a utilitarian part in the economy of the nest wholly similar to that of worker ants. Both exhibit a variety of quasi-human activities such as cultivating fungi for food, and the extreme subordination of the individual to the interests of the community that prevails among ants is equally developed by the termites. This is really the sum of the resemblances between them and it is true that they produce two superficially very similar pictures.

One fundamental difference between ant and termite communities is that the workers and soldiers in the latter are sterile individuals of both sexes. Another of equal importance lies in their life histories, for termites are primitive insects with no defined metamorphosis, and their young, instead of being helpless grubs or even more helpless pupae, are active little creatures, able to run about and forage for themselves when only a few days old. Again, in a termites' nest there are established kings as well as queens, and the "royal pair" live together in a specially enlarged chamber deep down in the nest. In their anatomy ants and termites differ in much the same degree as do the wasps and cockroaches to which they are respectively allied.

The nests are built by the workers, usually of finely masticated wood or earthy material cemented together by the insects' saliva. Most termites make their nests underground but some, belonging to the genus *Lacessititermes*, make globular nests covered with a blackish crust among the branches of trees, while others build curiously shaped pillars, which may often be seen in jungle.

The "king" termite, who started life with wings, looks much like an adult worker except that the stumps of the wings remain after he sheds them. The queen, after fertilisation, undergoes an extraordinary change, and is unique among insects in that she grows enormously after her last moult. It is only the abdomen that enlarges and results in the well-known relatively huge sausage-like queen termite. The growth is, of course, correlated with her egg-laying function, in which she surpasses even the queen ant; 4,000 eggs have been observed to be laid in twenty-four hours, and there seems to be little doubt that a single queen may produce millions of offspring in the course of her life of several years. The nests of the more primitive termites contain a number of queens, but only one is present in those of the higher forms, although these latter nests are by far the more populous.

The workers and soldiers are distinguished, as in ants, by the larger heads and jaws of the latter, and both castes are produced in different sizes. The role of the workers is to build and maintain the nest and tend and feed the royal pair and young; that of the soldiers to protect the nest, especially against ants, which are the termites' most implacable enemies. The soldiers of *Lacessititermes* have the head produced into a tapering snout from which a sticky fluid can be ejected. It is used normally to cement the nest, but can be discharged at intruders and will completely gum up and immobilise an insect the size of an ant; a most effective form of chemical warfare.

As well as the castes mentioned above there exist curious wingless, potentially reproductive forms which, by suitable feeding, can be turned into producers of eggs, in the event of an accident befalling the queen. It follows that her destruction, even if she is the sole queen in the nest, does not necessarily put an end to its activities.

The founding of new colonies follows the ant pattern closely, except that the king and queen co-operate. The "swarming" of

termites, when the winged forms leave the parent nest, is a
familiar phenomenon and many nests may swarm simultaneously
so that clouds of "flying ants" appear round our lamps. They
flutter feebly and break off their four gauzy wings when they
land on the table, and the softness of their bodies under ones
finger identifies them immediately as termites. Basins of water
placed under hanging lamps will trap them in hundreds, as they
fly as readily to the reflection as to the light itself. When the
swarming is by day it is a signal for all the insectivorous birds in
the vicinity to gather for a feast, and, day or night, an enormous
toll is taken by frogs, toads, lizards and predatory insects,
especially ants; an inconsiderable fraction of one per cent of the
total survive to found new colonies.

They live almost entirely on vegetable food, very largely on
wood, to aid the digestion of which they harbour a fauna of
minute animals called Protozoa in their intestines. It is those
species which feed on dead wood that set such a very serious
problem to constructional engineers in the tropics, for they make
no distinction between the timbers of a house and the substance
of dead trees in the jungle, which it is their natural and useful
mission to destroy. As they burrow into the wood, avoiding the
surface because they hate and fear the light, their activities may
pass unnoticed until a catastrophic collapse of riddled beams or
rafters takes place. Their dislike of the light often leads to their
detection, however, for if they do have to venture into the open
they build tubular tunnels of chewed wood, which immediately
betray their presence. The cellulose of paper is an equally
welcome article of diet, and termites can create costly havoc
among stored books in a very short time. Protection of timber
from their ravages is effected by making access to it mechanically
impossible and by treating it with chemical preservatives, which
must be done before and not after construction.

Some termites attack living wood and are one of the more
serious pests of rubber. Another rather unexpected harmful
activity of some of the subterranean species is biting through the
lead casing of electric cables laid under the ground, and so
causing failure of insulation. They do this, of course, simply
because the cable lies in their path as they burrow.

The cultivation of fungi for food is much more general among the termites than the ants, but the keeping of "livestock", such as aphids, for the sake of their secretions, is more particularly a feature of ant communities, though the nests of both groups support a varied fauna of parasites, scavengers and "guests".

The commonest Malayan termite is the small *Macrotermes gilvus*, which sometimes swarms in incredible numbers around lights at night. It makes mound-like nests and grows fungus in them. The shelter tubes often found running up the bark of trees usually belong to this species. A much larger species is *Macrotermes carbonarius*, which is dark in colour and comes out at night in search of vegetable debris to fertilise its fungus gardens. The soldiers of this termite can give a severe bite and hang on with their mandibles buried in one's flesh; the only way to get rid of them when they have secured a good hold is to cut the mandibles off at the base and extract them separately.

Often in the jungle one encounters dense, seemingly endless, moving columns, a couple of inches wide, of blackish termites. They are frequently mistaken for ants, but their soft squashy bodies identify them. They are members of the genus *Hospitali-termes*; their nests are made on or in old tree stumps.

The ground-living termites play a very important part in maintaining the fertility of the soil, aerating it, mixing its upper and lower layers and taking quantities of vegetable matter underground. Earthworms, generally regarded as the chief performers of this role in temperate regions, are subordinate therein to the termites in the tropics.

CHAPTER TWELVE

LIFE OF THE SEA SHORE

THE term sea shore is generally taken to mean the area between the extremes of high and low tide, and the descriptive term "littoral" is applied to it and to the faunas and floras associated with it. Its nature varies widely: if the land slopes steeply or precipitously the shore is likely to be rocky; if the land is low and level it will be sandy, and sandy shores can be further subdivided into those which slope steeply into the sea and those which shelve gently. In the latter case a much wider area is exposed by the falling tide. Near a river mouth, where suspended silt is deposited in the form of mud, mangrove swamp is developed in the tropics. Another characteristically tropical type of shore is that forming the landward edge of a coral reef, which may occur anywhere where geological conditions are right and the water clean and free from silt. The best of the coral grows below tide limits but a spring tide will uncover some of it; the true shore above it is usually clean sand. All the types of shore grade into one another, and sandy shores, especially those which shelve gently, are often more or less contaminated with mud.

As might be expected each kind of shore is inhabited by a quite distinct assemblage of animals, in most of which we can recognise adaptations for the environment in which they live. We will consider the various types in turn and include a brief account of the animals, not strictly littoral, which inhabit the shallow water below the level of the lowest tides, and which swim up over the shore itself when the tide advances and covers it.

Let us first visit a gently shelving sandy shore at low tide (the "good tide" of the naturalist and that of the bather and picnicker are diametrically opposed); a wide expanse of sand will be exposed, and if it is a little muddy so much the better, for mud is food to a host of marine animals.

Both at high tide mark and on the level sand a good many shells will be lying about. Ordinary sea shells are the hard parts of animals belonging to the great division or phylum called the **Mollusca.** They are subdivided into several groups of which two are conspicuous in the littoral fauna. These are the **Gastropods** or **Snails,** whose shell is usually formed of a coiled tube (some are shell-less and known as slugs), and the **Lamellibranchs** or **Bivalves,** cockles, mussels, oysters and the like, in which the shell consists of two saucer-like halves hinged together. Each half of the shell of a bivalve is called a valve. Shells are most attractive objects to make collections of, but whenever possible you should obtain living specimens as the empty shells found on the beach are usually worn and discoloured and often broken and incomplete. The soft part of the animal can be removed by putting the shell into boiling water for a few moments and then picking it out with a pin or piece of wire and cleaning the inside with a syringe.

Most of the molluscs of the sandy shore are burrowers, feeding by swallowing sand or mud or, when the tide is up, straining water through their gills and extracting plankton. At low tide they remain buried and must be dug for. None are so expert at recognising the signs of their presence and collecting them as the sea-side village folk, for they use them for food. If you see one of these folk wandering about the sand carrying a basket, go and ask politely to inspect the catch, and, if you are a shell collector, have some small change in your pocket.

These burrowing molluscs are mainly bivalves. The Tellinidae are always well represented, with delicate shells, white often marked or flushed with pink, when they are called **Sunset Shells** (Fig. 126). Various members of the Veneridae are found, *Paphia*, beautifully coloured and patterned and concentrically ridged, *Gafrarium* (Fig. 127) with radial as well as concentric ridging, and the smooth *Meretrix meretrix* or Kĕpah, an excellent food mollusc. The **Cockles** (*Cardium*) have only strong radial ridging and the same is true of most of the **Ark Shells** (*Arca*) in which the hinge is long and straight and consists of numerous small teeth which fit together and hold the two valves firmly in place; one species, the Edible Ark or Kĕrang (*Arca granosa*, Fig. 128), is of economic importance. The **Fan Shells** (*Pinna*, Fig. 125), are not rare; they have the shell wedge-shaped, eight inches or more in length, and live in the sand with the sharp end downward and the edges of the valves just showing above the surface. The mollusc is anchored in the sand by a tuft of strong hairs called the *byssus*, which makes it quite difficult to pull out. Of the gastropods the egg-shaped white and reddish brown **Sand Snail,**

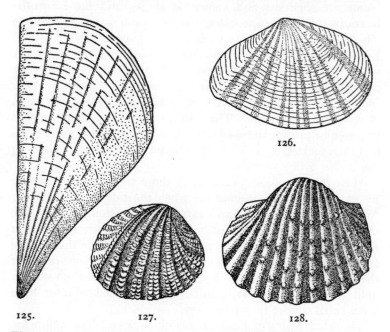

Figs. 125 to 128. Sea Shells (Bivalves): 125. Fan Shell (*Pinna atropurpurea*); 126. Sunset Shell (*Tellina virgata*); 127. *Gafrarium tumidum*; 128. Edible Ark (*Arca granosa*).

Natica mamilla, is also a burrower and preys on the bivalves, boring a neat hole in their shells into which it inserts its proboscis; the unfortunate victim's only defence is to close the valves of its shell tightly, a measure of no avail whatever in this emergency. If the sand is muddy numbers of little snails may be crawling about on its surface. The turriform (tower-shaped) *Potamides cingulatus* is one of the commonest of these and the neat and active **Dog Whelks** (*Nassarius*), with a porcelain-like thickening round the opening of the shell, may be abundant. One of the

129.

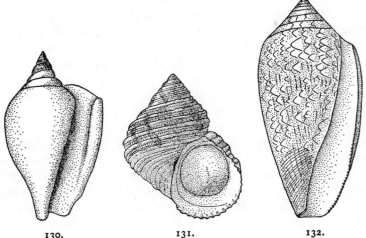

130. 131. 132.

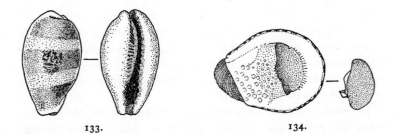

133. 134.

Figs. 129 to 134. Sea Shells (Gastropods): 129. Scorpion Shell (*Lambis lambis*); 130. *Strombus isabella*; 131. Turban Shell (*Turbo ticaonicus*); 132. Cone Shell (*Conus textile*); 133. Green Cowry (*Cypraea errones*); 134. *Nerita albicilla*, shell and operculum.

Strombs, (*Strombus isabella*, Fig. 130), is very common and is quite an important food mollusc.

The molluscs will have first claim on the attention of the naturalist whose pleasure it is to make a collection of interesting and beautiful objects. To those who would rather watch living animals I recommend the **crabs,** for many of the littoral species carry on the business of their lives when the tide is out, and largely in full view of the observer. On almost any shore of the type we are considering the **Soldier Crab** (*Dotilla mictyroides*) can be found. It is a long-legged, round-bodied, spidery looking little creature, the larger males being slate-blue with pinkish limbs. Often they occur in hordes so that, as one approaches, their retreat gives the impression that the shore itself is moving; when overtaken they either take refuge in a previously dug burrow or burrow straight down into the sand with a spiral motion. If you remain still for a minute they will come out again and resume feeding, which they do in a most peculiar manner that can easily be observed. The crab scrapes up a quantity of sand with its claws and pushes it into the lower end of its mouth, which has the form of a vertical slit. The sand is sucked or chewed in some way which extracts finely divided organic matter from it, and is then discarded from the top end of the mouth in the form of a pellet. As the tide continues to fall the sand becomes more and more thickly covered with these feeding pellets. If you watch the crabs along the edge of the rising tide you can see them burying themselves in preparation for their period of quiescence when the sea covers their feeding grounds. When they do this each crab builds over itself a dome-shaped roof of wet sand pellets, rather like an Eskimo igloo, under which it is enclosed with a quantity of air. By burrowing downwards, this pocket of air is carried down and forms an open chamber in which the crab rests in comfort. When they emerge along the edge of the falling tide each one, as it comes out, is followed by a stream of bubbles.

On coasts where only a narrow strip of more steeply shelving sand is exposed, *Dotilla* does not occur, but its place is often taken by the smaller *Scopimera*. These are very timid little crabs which never wander away from their burrows but feed only close to them, making a characteristic pattern of radiating

shallow furrows and rows of feeding pellets, which are formed
in just the same way as those of *Dotilla*.

Above high water level much larger burrows may be found
with a mass of ejected sand round their entrances. These are

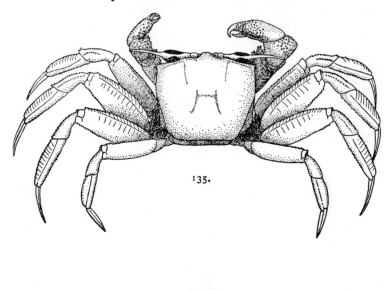

135.

136.

Figs. 135. and 136.   135. Sand Crab (*Ocypode ceratophthalma*);
136. Calling Crab (*Uca manii*).

the homes of the **Sand Crab** (*Ocypode*). *O. ceratophthalma* (Fig.
135), the commonest species, is pale horn colour and may span
more than four inches with its legs. A good deal of effort is
needed to dig one out of its burrow and the adults rarely come
out during the day, but young ones, spanning an inch or two and
living in quite small burrows, are out all day. These crabs live
partly by extracting food from the sand like *Dotilla* but are also

predatory to a limited extent, and the young are scavengers. When pursued they run with amazing swiftness, either to the refuge of their burrows or into the sea. On the inner surface of the claw is a row of small regularly spaced horny projections which can be drawn across a ridge at the base of the arm to produce a squeaking sound; the purpose of this is probably the same as the similar stridulating apparatus of a grasshopper, to enable the two sexes of the same species to find and recognise each other.

Near low water mark or in the shallow water below it the remarkable **King-Crab** (*Limulus* or *Tachypleus*) may be found, often in pairs, as the animals come into shallow water to breed and bury their eggs in the sand. It has a smooth greenish-brown dome-shaped carapace with some spines on its hinder margins and a long spike-like tail, and grows to about fifteen inches in total length. In spite of its name it is not really a crab, or even a crustacean, but belongs to the Arthropod order Arachnida and is thus more nearly related to scorpions and spiders than to crabs. It is perfectly harmless and can be handled without hesitation; the tail is not a sting and does not serve as a weapon, its only apparent use is to enable the animal to right itself if it gets turned upside-down. Its chief interest lies in the fact that it is a "living fossil," a survival from the remote geological past; remains of king-crabs, almost identical with those living now, are found in strata which were deposited nearly two hundred million years ago. Bear this, and its harmless nature, in mind when you find a king-crab, and treat it kindly and with the respect which is due to its ancient lineage.

The **Starfishes** and **Sea-Urchins** belong to the phylum **Echinodermata.** The former are usually shaped like a star and more often than not five-rayed. Their bodies are rendered nearly, but not quite, rigid by the presence of numerous calcareous ossicles or "little bones" embedded in their flesh, and some have external spines as well. They move by putting out on the under surface numerous little suckers called tube-feet by means of which they slowly glide over the sand or mud; these tube-feet can be seen very clearly if a starfish is turned over on its back under water. They are predatory and feed on molluscs, mainly bivalves, which they attack by embracing the shell and dragging the valves apart by a slow, relentless pull, applied by the tube feet. The starfish's stomach is then pushed out through its mouth, which is at the centre of the lower surface, and into the unhappy mollusc's shell and its body is digested. In places where oysters are cultured starfishes may be a serious pest.

Sea-Urchins differ from starfishes in having a rigid shell which is globular or cake- or biscuit-like in shape and always covered with spines, sometimes strong and sharp, sometimes so fine as to resemble bristles. The spines are attached by ligaments which quickly decay when the animal is dead, so that empty shells of sea-urchins found on the shore have almost always lost the spines altogether. These animals feed, like so many of the inhabitants of sandy and muddy shores, by passing silt through the alimentary canal and extracting nourishment from it. They have tube-feet like those of starfishes, but in sea-urchins they are not confined to the lower surface.

Starfishes and sea-urchins must be sought at the lowest ebb of the tide as they are animals which normally avoid exposure to the air, though the littoral species are not harmed if such exposure is only for a short time. *Archaster typicus* is a common starfish which frequents rather muddy places; it is about six inches across, usually five-rayed and has closely set spines along the edges of the rays. The much larger *Oreaster nodosus* is found in shallow water and is sometimes stranded. It may measure ten inches in diameter, is dark red in colour and the upper surface is beset with large irregular knobs and spines. Of the sea-urchins several species of *Salamacis* (Fig. 137) are common on sandy shores; they are globular with the lower surface flattened, and two or three inches in diameter. When alive the shell is thickly beset with short sharp spines which are prettily ringed with red or violet. **Cake-Urchins,** such as *Laganum* (Fig. 138), are often common; they have the shell flattened like a biscuit and are covered with fine hair-like spines, which are soon lost when the animal dies. They live partly buried in mud or sand and on the upper surface there are tube-feet specially modified as breathing organs. The fine slits through which these are pushed out are regularly arranged and form a five-rayed petal-like pattern on the surface of the shell.

Of the sub-littoral fauna, which inhabits the shallow water

below low tide level, by far the best view can be obtained by attending the pulling in of a seine net or pukat. In this method of fishing a long strip of netting, buoyed along the top, weighted along the bottom, is paid out of a boat in a large semicircle, and the two ends are then hauled in to the shore; the operation is carried out on sandy, gently shelving beaches at low tide, and its object is, of course, to catch fish. Many of the fishes described in a previous chapter are taken in this way and in addition a great

137.   138.

Figs 137 and 138.   Sea Urchins: 137. *Salamacis sphaeroides*;
138. Cake Urchin, *Laganum depressum*.

variety of crustaceans. **Swimming Crabs** of the family Portunidae are always abundant and are distinguished by having the hindmost of their four pairs of legs flattened to form paddle-like swimming organs. One of them, the **Blue Crab** (*Portunus pelagicus*), is used extensively for food; it has the whole front margin of the carapace serrated and a long spine projecting outwards on each side. Another swimming crab (*Matuta*), of a different family, is common as well. It has all the legs flattened for swimming, a long spine on each side of the carapace (but no serrations like those of *Portunus*) and is yellowish, finely speckled with red. Often large numbers of **prawns** are caught, mainly species of *Penaeus*, which are of considerable economic importance as a source of food. Among them you will often find specimens of the **Mantis-Prawns** or Stomatopods. These are distinguished by being flattened from above instead of compressed from side to side like an ordinary prawn, and by the remarkable front limbs which are adapted for a predatory mode of life. Their last joint is spined and folds back into a groove in the next to last joint, just as the blade of a penknife into its handle, forming a ruthless grasping organ. The mechanism is exactly like that of the front limb of a praying mantis, and serves just the same purpose.

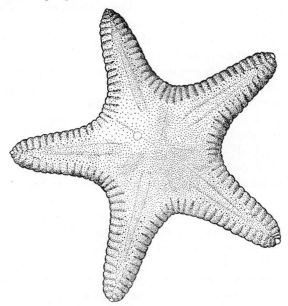

Fig. 139. Starfish, *Goniodiscaster scaber*.

Although they are not littoral animals mention must be made of **Jellyfish** as they often drift into shallow water and are stranded between tide marks. Together with the corals and sea anemones they belong to the phylum Coelenterata (see below under coral reefs). This relationship becomes apparent if the life history of a jellyfish is studied. The eggs, which are released into the water, settle on a rock and grow into what appear to be small sea-anemones. When these reach full size each of them becomes constricted at regular intervals in its length, so that it comes to look like a pile of saucers. Finally the "saucers" break away one by one and reveal themselves as baby jellyfish. Not the least interesting aspect of jellyfish is their power of stinging. Many species are harmless, but a few have long ribbon-like tentacles hanging from the umbrella-shaped body, and these are covered with hundreds of tiny stinging cells. Each of these consists of a capsule charged with virulent poison and containing a threadlike portion which is turned inwards and lies coiled inside the capsule, just as the finger of a glove may be pushed inside-out so that it lies inside the hand. Contact with any solid object, such as your arm or leg, causes the thread-like portion to be shot out with sufficient force to pierce your skin, carrying with it some of the poison. Contact with the tentacles of a stinging jellyfish results in hundreds of these cells coming into action and the effects may be serious. The pain is intense and a temporary paralysis may be caused, which is obviously very dangerous to a swimmer out of his depth. After a time weals like those following a burn develop and take a long time to heal. A bad case of jellyfish sting should always be taken straight to hospital. Stinging jellyfish seem to be more frequent in the Malacca Strait than elsewhere in Malayan waters.

Another group of off-shore animals which deserve mention are the **Squids,** which are extensively used for food and as bait for fishing, and known collectively as Sotong. They belong to the division of molluscs called Cephalopods, which also includes the octopuses. In these animals there is always a ring of tentacles on the head, which are beset with suckers, and sometimes with horny hooks as well, and are used for grasping prey. The eyes are very well developed and resemble in structure and efficiency those of vertebrate animals.

The squids have no external shell, but most have a flattened internal structure, usually chalky in texture, which is really a sort of skeleton. These are often found washed up on the shore. All our shallow water squids, such as *Sepia* and *Sepioteuthis* are quite small animals, but some of the deep sea kinds are gigantic, as much as 45 feet long including the tentacles. These are by far the largest of all the invertebrate animals.

At one end of our sandy bay there is a rocky headland; let us go and see what forms of life haunt the tumbled boulders which form the shore at its base. The fauna is not a rich one and consists mainly of animals adapted to withstand the beating of the waves. **Barnacles** are numerous; while they give purchase to the sole of a shoe on the slippery rocks, their sharp shells may cut and graze your skin severely if you fall. It comes as a surprise to many people to learn that barnacles are crustaceans. Their minute larvae are free-swimming and resemble those of more typical crustaceans, such as shrimps and prawns; after a period of drifting in the sea those which find themselves in the neighbourhood of a rock, or any other suitable resting place, settle on it and grow into the familiar barnacle. The shell really consists of a number of plates, cemented together to form a low cone, open at the top. This opening can be closed by a pair of movable plates which are opened only when the animal is covered by the water. It then puts out long feathery appendages with which it ceaselessly sweeps the water like a fisherman with a net, and feeds on the minute living creatures which it catches. Close examination of these appendages immediately reveals the animal as an arthropod.

Very often the rocks will be encrusted with small **Oysters,** which are, of course, bivalve molluscs, and a few gastropods will be found, cap-shaped **Limpets** and snails of the genera *Nerita* and *Monodonta*. Both the last have very strong shells so that even if their hold on the rock is broken by a wave they will not be injured by the subsequent battering, and *Nerita* (Fig. 134) has a hard operculum with which the opening of the shell can be closed.

If there are any rocks awash not far from the water's edge, fairly large long-legged crabs may be seen walking about on them. Wade out towards them and they will retreat actively to the far side of the rock and wait, peering over the edge of it to keep you under observation. If you try to catch them you will be surprised at their agility and sureness of foot; only when hard pressed will they run down the rock into the sea. These are probably the common **Rock Crab** (*Grapsus grapsus*). The smaller *Metopograpsus*, with square carapace and purple claws, is more likely to be found in sheltered crannies between the boulders; its favourite haunt, however, is the wooden piles of piers and fishing stakes.

Mangrove swamp is the name given to the assemblage of

plants that grows in the mud deposited at river mouths in the tropics. Deposition of mud where rivers meet the sea takes place in all parts of the world and is due to precipitation of silt, which remains very finely divided in fresh water but clots and falls to the bottom when it meets the salt water. Untouched mangrove forest is a luxuriant growth consisting largely of tall trees, but its continuous exploitation for fire-wood has reduced most of the Malayan mangrove to a low growth which would hardly maintain itself at all without the conservation and control exercised by the Department of Forestry.

The dominant littoral animals of the mangrove are amphibious crabs, which live similarly to *Dotilla* and *Scopimera* (and belong to the same group, the Grapsoidea), feeding and carrying on the business of their lives when the tide is out, and hiding in burrows when it advances. Practically all of them feed on the surface film left on the mud by the tide; as there is no lack of this material in mangrove swamps the pursuit of food, usually such an urgent business in nature, presents them with no problem and they do not seem to have many serious predatory enemies. As a result, perhaps, of such rich and secure living conditions they occur in great variety and numbers.

The most conspicuous and remarkable of them are un-doubtedly the **Calling Crabs** (*Uca*), of which a number of species frequent the mangrove and muddy foreshores. The males (Fig. 136) are extraordinary little creatures with one claw (it may be the right or the left), enormously enlarged and conspicuously coloured. Sit and watch them for a few minutes and some of them will be seen to wave their huge claws solemnly in the air. These antics have been the object of study of a number of students of animal behaviour, and it seems clear that their main purpose is to stimulate and attract the female. The big claws of the males are of very little use as weapons, but if one male ventures on another's territory they may fight a duel, inter-locking the claws and wrestling until the weaker one is tumbled over or disengages and runs away; it is only rarely that either contestant suffers any injury. They feed entirely on mud which they scrape up with the delicate spoon-shaped fingers of their smaller, unmodified, claws, both being of this type in the female. They do not have to venture far from their burrows in search of food and any sudden movement sends them scuttling to earth. Several species haunt the Malayan mangrove, one of which, *U. dussumieri*, has the body coloured bright blue.

Less conspicuous than *Uca* are the species of *Sesarma*, which have the carapace square and the claws often brightly coloured, red, yellow or blue. Some are large, spanning five or six inches with their legs, and are quite formidable. If you corner one he will face you with claws upraised; grasp him and he will nip viciously and probably gain his freedom by scuttling away leaving one claw with its sharp points buried in your flesh. All crabs are ready to part with their limbs in an emergency and can grow new ones from the stumps of the old.

One other mangrove crab must be mentioned, the **Asiatic Edible Crab** (*Scylla serrata*). This is a swimming crab allied to the Blue Crab (*Portunus*), and is not amphibious, but lives in the tidal creeks which flow through the swamps. It is the most important edible crab of South-east Asia and grows to a large size, the carapace reaching six inches in breadth. It is dark brown in colour and the carapace has a series of nine teeth on each side; the hindmost legs are paddle-shaped. It is caught in small baited nets suspended on a rod and line, which are allowed to rest on the bottom of the creek for a time and are then quickly pulled up, giving the crab no time to scramble out.

A feature of mangrove swamp and the country around it which cannot escape notice is the numerous mounds of mud, each with a hole in the top, appearing like miniature volcanoes. These are often called crab-holes in the belief that they are made by the large crabs (*Sesarma*), which often take refuge in them. In fact they are made by a lobster-like crustacean, the **Mud-Lobster** (*Thalassina anomala*), which lives in the semi-liquid mud underlying the swamp and from time to time carries up and throws out at the surface a quantity of this mud, presumably in order to keep open the chamber in which it lives. The Mud-Lobster's burrowing activities will result in the undermining and collapse of embankments in mangrove swamp unless measures are taken against the animal in their construction, and it has been accused of creating conditions favourable for the breeding of the coastal malaria carrying mosquito, *Anopheles sundaicus*.

Some of the mangrove molluscs are used for food. Among

them are a big bivalve (*Polymesoda*), whose shell may be three or four inches across, and a snail, *Cerithidea obtusa*, with the soft parts spotted black and red.

Many species of fish swim up the creeks when the tide rises and there are quite a number which live permanently in the brackish water. Among these, gobies are numerous—relatives of the Mud-Skipper which has already been described. The astonishing **Archer-Fish** (*Toxotes*) is also found in brackish water creeks. This is a deep-bodied little fish, yellowish with black bars, which swims at the surface watching the overhanging vegetation. If it sees an insect on a leaf or twig it spits at it, with remarkable force and precision, a rapid succession of drops of water which knock it off its perch into the creek, where it is seized and eaten by the fish. Machine-gun-fish would be a more appropriate name for it, for no archer can shoot at a rate of several arrows a second.

Prawns also frequent the mangrove creeks in great numbers and are sometimes enclosed and "farmed" in specially constructed ponds made by constructing embankments in the swamp.

The mangrove crabs are fascinating, but he must be an enthusiastic naturalist indeed who maintains that their surroundings are pleasant. On the other hand naturalists in the tropics enjoy a rare privilege in being able to visit **coral reefs,** for here there are no sand-flies or mosquitoes, the water is clear and clean and the marine life vivid and abundant far beyond description in the short space that we can devote to it. Try to take advantage of low spring tides to examine the reefs, for only then is much of the living coral uncovered or accessible to comfortable wading, and wear shoes with soles thick enough for protection against the spines of sea-urchins and poison-fish and sharp fragments of coral.

The **Coral** itself is, of course, a kind of animal, and belongs to the primitive phylum **Coelenterata.** A **Sea-Anemone** (of which several kinds occur on the reefs) is a simple coelenterate and consists of hollow fleshy stalk or base with a crown of tentacles, which are used for gathering food, the whole appearing rather like a flower and called in zoological language, a polyp. A piece of coral consists of many such polyps, more or less fused together and supported by a hard skeleton formed of carbonate of lime extracted from the sea water. They (or it, for it is hard to define the individual in such an organism as this) feed by sweeping the water with their tentacles and extracting the minute plankton. Everyone is familiar with the white skeletons of coral seen in museums and used as ornaments, but the living creature is usually beautifully coloured, shades of green, brown and red being most frequent. A lot can be seen at a low spring tide, but to see the coral gardens at their best one must dive over the permanently submerged parts, as described in the chapter on sea fish, or float over them in a boat with a glass window in its bottom.

The **Soft** or **Alcyonarian Corals** are so unlike the popular conception of coral that they are seldom recognised for what they are. One common reef-living species consists of lobular masses of purplish substance of the consistency of rubber. The polyps are eight-armed and tiny and appear like a short fur covering the coral when it is submerged. Out of the water the polyps are withdrawn and only a shapeless fleshy mass presents itself to justify the unpleasant popular name "Dead Men's Fingers," which has been bestowed on corals of this type.

Several kinds of **sponges** are found, but the type from which the familiar bath sponge is made only occurs in deeper water. Some of the littoral sponges are rounded, others are branching structures, often dark green in colour; they can be distinguished from Alcyonarian corals by the presence of regularly spaced round holes in their surface. Sponges are also animals, even more lowly and primitive than corals, and consist of a skeleton of interlacing horny or silicious (flinty) material supporting a system of branching tubes. Water is drawn in through minute pores all over the surface of the sponge and passed out through the larger holes already mentioned.

The reefs have a **mollusc** fauna, rich and varied, all their own, with hardly a species in common with the sandy or muddy shores. To collect them you need to turn over loose blocks of coral, and it is well to provide yourself with gloves, for the coral is rough and sharp, and its living slime irritant or even poisonous. Here the **gastropods** or **snails** are most numerous. **Turban Shells** (*Turbo*, Fig. 131), are common and are distinguished by the thick round operculum with which the shell is closed. These opercula are polished and prettily coloured and, under the name of cats' eyes or ox eyes, are sometimes used as buttons. Cone-shaped **Top Shells** (*Trochus*) are often found. Large ones, obtained by diving, are used for making pearl buttons, disc-shaped pieces being drilled out all round the larger (lower) part of the shell. These buttons are inferior to the real pearl buttons made from the shell of the pearl oyster. Various kinds of **Cowries** (*Cypraea*, Fig. 133), are to be found. The first sight of a living one will be a surprise to anyone who has only seen the shells in collections, for two flaps of skin extend out of the slit-like opening and meet over the back, entirely concealing the shell. The wonderful polish on the shell of many cowries is due to the protection thus afforded to its surface. The **Cone Shells** (*Conus*, Fig. 132), are handsome but have a sinister reputation. The animal is predatory and kills its prey by means of a pro-boscis bearing sharp, poisonous teeth. Cases are known of people carelessly handling these molluscs and being stung with quite serious results, even deaths having been recorded, though this is exceptional. The curious **Scorpion Shells** (*Lambis*, Fig. 129), with finger-like projections around the margin, are among the largest shells commonly found on the reefs. The massive **Helmet Shells** (*Cassis*) are usually only obtainable by diving over the permanently submerged areas.

The most notable of the coral reef bivalves is the **Giant Clam** (*Tridacna*). Except for the gigantic squids of the ocean depths this is the largest of the mollusca, and a shell in the Raffles Museum is more than three feet across. This was found in a semi-fossilised condition on one of the islands off the east coast. Present day specimens never reach this size in Malayan waters, though they do so on the Great Barrier Reef of Australia and other localities in the Pacific. They attach themselves to the living coral and in the course of time this grows round the shell, so that large ones are usually more or less embedded in the coral, but maintain a wide opening to the water outside, and enough space to open and close the valves. The power of the muscle of *Tridacna* which closes the shell is very great, and stories are told of divers accidentally putting a hand or foot between the valves, which close like a trap and hold the victim until he drowns.

The soft parts, seen between the undulating margins of the valves, are brilliantly coloured, blue, green or red.

Two species of **File Shells** (*Lima*) are common in reef pools. The shell is white and delicate and the animal's gills extend outside it and form a bright red fringe round its edge. Nearly all bivalves are slow moving creatures, if, indeed they can move at all, but *Lima* swims actively by rapidly opening and closing the valves of the shell. The **Scallops** (*Pecten*) are the only other bivalves which do this. Several species of *Barbatia*, a close relative of *Arca* and having the same long, finely toothed hinge, are abundant, attached to masses of dead coral. The elongate brown **Date-Mussels** (*Lithophaga*) bore into it and it takes a hammer and chisel to extract them.

The Cephalopods are represented on the reefs by small **Octopuses.** These live in holes in the coral rock, but sometimes venture out in search of their prey, which consists almost entirely of crabs. In spite of its powerful claws a crab is quite helpless in the clutch of an octopus. The strong tentacles, beset with clinging suckers, are much too tough and rubbery to be affected by pinching, and the crab is soon dragged down to the creature's mouth and killed by bites from its parrot-like beak. It is well worth watching a prowling octopus in a rock pool, for it is constantly changing colour, and may turn from almost black to pale, sandy brown within a second. If startled or pursued it retreats under cover of a "smoke-screen" of black, inky fluid, which it discharges into the water.

Crabs are abundant; those of the family Xanthidae predominate and the large pink oval *Atergatis integerrimus* (Fig. 140) is one of the commonest. *Pilumnus vespertilio*, so thickly covered with dark brown hair that it is hardly recognisable as a crab, is also very common. Many of the smaller Xanthids, such as *Actaea* and *Carpilodes*, are beautifully sculptured and coloured, some of the species of *Carpilodes* being deep crimson. Various kinds of Swimming Crabs are found, species of *Thalamita* being the most conspicuous; they are similar to *Portunus* and *Scylla* but have fewer, four or five, teeth on the sides of the carapace.

Of the other crustaceans found on the reefs the **Snapping Shrimps** (*Alpheus*) are interesting. They have one of the claws or chelae greatly enlarged and so modified that it can be closed with a sudden and quite loud snap. This produces an effect in the water almost like a miniature explosion, and may well be effective in repelling the shrimp's enemies or even in stunning small creatures, which can then be gathered up for food at its leisure. A beautiful green **Mantis-Prawn** (*Gonodactylus chiragra*) is also common. Its claws are not spined like those of *Squilla*, but it can strike a sharp and painful blow with them, and will quickly break a glass tube or thin-walled bottle if it is imprisoned in it.

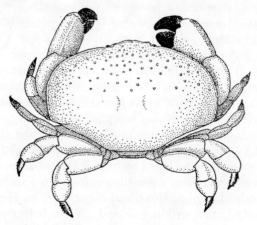

Fig. 140.   Coral Reef Crab, *Atergatis integerrimus*.

This is as good a place as any to mention the **Hermit-Crabs.** Various species occur on sandy and muddy shores, but they are nowhere so conspicuous as on the clean sandy beach that forms the landward limit of a fringing coral reef. Hermit-crabs are crustaceans which have become adapted to using empty gastropod shells as a protection for their bodies. The hind part of the body is quite soft and unprotected and is formed so as to fit the spiral twist of a gastropod shell. Like those of almost all crustaceans the newly hatched young are free-swimming animals, members of the plankton, and as different from their parents as a caterpillar is from a butterfly. At a certain stage in its development the young hermit-crab seeks a small empty shell and inserts its hind body in it. Thereafter it lives continually in a succession of shells, seeking out a larger one whenever its growth renders the present one inadequate.

Hermit-crabs are found in the depths of the sea, between tide marks and living partly or entirely out of the water on the shore. It is these land-dwelling species, belonging to the genus *Coenobita*, that we are most likely to meet, dragging their borrowed suits of armour actively about among the litter that marks high water, where they lead the life of scavengers. When alarmed the crab retreats into the shell and its larger claw is so shaped that it forms a perfectly fitting operculum and effectively secures the animal against any enemy that is likely to attack it.

Among the **Echinoderms** we meet with two new types. The **Brittle-Stars** (Fig. 141) differ from the starfishes in having the rays long and flexible and distinctly marked off from the central disc. They are quite active and crawl by writhing movements of the rays or arms, which are always five in number, and may be smooth or spiny. The spiny ones are most numerous and include such genera as *Ophiothrix*, and among the smooth ones *Ophiarachnella gorgonia*, prettily banded with dark and light green, is common. The species figured, *Ophiolepis annulosa*, is light and dark brown. Most brittle-stars break off their arms very readily when handled, and perfect specimens are quite hard to collect.

The other type is the **Holothurians** or **Sea-Cucumbers**, which are slug-like in appearance and wholly unlike sea-urchins or starfishes. One common species, *Holothuria atra*, is black and often exceeds a foot in length. This unattractive looking creature is one of the most conspicuous of the reef-dwelling animals; if handled it ejects a white fluid which hardens into sticky threads on contact with the water. Some sea-cucumbers, under the name of Trepang or Beche de Mer, are of commercial importance, as they furnish the basis of a soup that is highly esteemed by Chinese people.

Of the **Sea-urchins** the big, black, long-spined *Echinothrix diadema* is all too common. It occurs usually a little below low tide level, so that one is likely to encounter it when swimming or wading. The spines are very sharp and penetrate your foot or leg at a touch, and are so brittle that they almost always break off in your flesh. They are barbed, but the barbs are directed towards the tip so that they are fairly easy to extract if you can get hold of them. The smaller *Echinometra* is a sea-urchin which occurs in cavities in the coral; its spines are quite short, not very sharp and vary in colour from black to light greenish.

A fair number of **Starfishes** are to be found, among them the beautiful blue *Luidia* and the curious genus *Culcita*, in which the

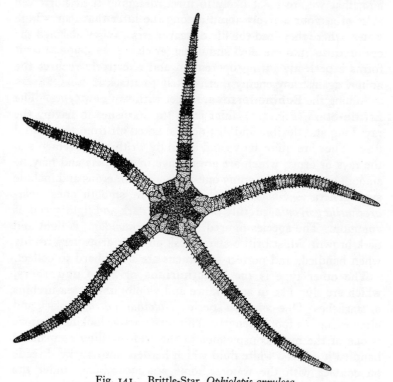

Fig. 141.   Brittle-Star, *Ophiolepis annulosa*.

arms are so shortened that the animal is not star-shaped but pentagonal and looks at first sight like a sea-urchin, from which the absence of spines immediately distinguishes it.

Space will only permit a brief mention of the numerous species of **marine worms** found on the reefs. Most of them belong to the **Segmented Worms** or **Annelida**, which are believed to be the evolutionary fore-runners of the Arthropods, and to the division of the Annelida called the Polychaets. These

Polychaet Worms are distinguished by their jointed bodies and by the presence on each joint of a pair of bristle-bearing appendages, with which the worm crawls or swims. One of them, *Eunice aphroditois*, is an impressive creature which may exceed a yard in length and approach an inch in the diameter of its body.

Wholly different in appearance and affinities are the **Planarians** or **Flat-Worms,** which appear like pieces of brightly-coloured and patterned pieces of jelly-like ribbon rippling over the surface of an upturned stone. These marine flat-worms are pretty and harmless creatures, but some of their relatives are most dangerous and disgusting, internal parasites of man and his domestic animals, tape-worms and liver-flukes.

CHAPTER THIRTEEN

OTHER INVERTEBRATES

O F the land-dwelling invertebrate animals the insects by far outnumber all the rest, and fully merit the two chapters devoted to them. However, a number of other groups include animals frequently met with in Malaya, and they will be briefly described in this final chapter.

The insects have already been defined as a group of the Arthropoda or animals with jointed limbs and a rigid external skeleton, and as being distinguished, when adult, by usually having wings and never more than three pairs of legs. Spiders, scorpions and their allies have four pairs of legs, are never winged, and belong to another division of the arthropods called the **Arachnida,** of which we have already met one member, the marine "King-Crab".

Let us first consider the **Spiders.** This is an order of animals almost as successful and ubiquitous as the insects, and including a very large number of species. All spiders are predatory, feeding almost exclusively on insects, which they kill by the bite of a pair of hollow poison fangs.

The most remarkable feature that all spiders have in common is the ability to spin silk. They do this in just the same way as many insect larvae do, by drawing out through minute orifices a sticky liquid which hardens to form a filament on contact with the air. But spiders put their silk to a variety of uses, such as lining their burrows, securing themselves when they fall, spinning cocoons to contain their eggs and constructing elaborate snares to entrap their prey. Some kinds of spiders, when newly hatched and tiny, pay out into the air long silken threads and then, clinging to them as if to a parachute, are carried great distances by the wind to new hunting grounds.

Our commonest large spider is *Nephila maculata*, whose enormous webs are often seen among trees and bushes, sometimes right across a path, and between telegraph wires. The body is black with yellow markings and, in the female, an inch and a half long, the legs spanning six inches or more. The male, as in nearly all spiders, is much smaller; it is often found in attendance on the female, beside which it looks quite tiny. Among the other web-spinners the **Spiny-bodied Spiders** (Genus *Gasteracantha*) are worthy of mention. In them the body is strangely shaped and beset with spines, and often brightly marked and coloured. The species of *Argiope* can be recognised by their webs, which have zig-zag bands of silk built into the middle.

By no means all spiders build webs. The little **Jumping Spiders** (*Salticidae*) stalk and pounce on their prey just as a cat stalks a mouse; they are very commonly seen running about with quick jerky movements on the walls of houses. The large **Huntsman Spider** (*Heteropoda venatoria*) is often found in houses; its legs may span about four inches and it is flattened and rather crab-like in appearance, an unattractive creature perhaps, but it should be treated with tolerance as it is a great destroyer of cockroaches. It is of interest as being one of the animals that has been spread all over the tropics by shipping. It is often taken to England (but cannot survive the winter there) with imported bananas, and has come to be called the Banana Spider on that account.

Biggest of all the spiders are the **Mygalomorphs**, *Lampropelma* and allied genera. They are alarming-looking creatures, usually covered with velvety black hair, their bodies very stout and sometimes more than two inches long. When molested they adopt a threatening attitude, raising the fore legs in the air, and they attack by striking downwards with the poison fangs. They prey on large insects and any other animals small enough for them to overcome; one was once found attacking a mouse. They neither make webs nor excavate burrows, but live in any hole or crevice they can find, lining it with silk.

Reports of the effect of the bite of these big spiders on man are conflicting and suggest that we do not know enough about them. Usually only local pain and swelling results, but there is a well authenticated case from Kedah of a ten years old child dying as a result of being bitten by one of them. In some parts of the world spiders whose bite is dangerous are abundant. These include the Black Widow and Red-Back Spiders (*Latrodectus*) and the Australian burrowing spider, *Atrax*. None of these is known to occur in Malaya, and there is no doubt that in this country a serious sequel to a spider bite is an exceptional occurrence.

From the zoological point of view the most interesting of the Malayan spiders are the species of the genus *Liphistius*, as they are by far the most primitive spiders known, being allied to forms found as fossils in strata of the Carboniferous Period and dating back more than 200 million years. *Liphistius malayanus* is common at Cameron Highlands and Fraser's Hill, where it makes burrows in the mossy banks beside paths. The burrow is lined with silk and has a hinged trap-door; attached to the edge of its opening, and running outwards, radially, on the surface of the moss, are a number of strands of silk, each several inches long. As the trap-door is covered with moss and so camouflaged as to be almost invisible, the spoke-like white silk threads give the only clue to the site of the burrow; if this is borne in mind they are easy to find. When found these nests should not be dug out and destroyed, but left so that other naturalists may enjoy the privilege of seeing the habitation of a rare and remarkable animal. Another species of *Liphistius*, which makes a similar nest, occurs on Penang Hill and has been found on the adjacent mainland, and a third is known from the Batu Caves near Kuala Lumpur.

Scorpions are far less numerous and varied than spiders. The little **Spotted House-Scorpion** (*Isometrus maculatus*) is the species most frequently encountered, nearly always in dwellings. It is slender and yellowish with a pattern of darker spots, and occurs in all tropical countries, probably as a result of being carried around by shipping like the American Cockroach and the spider *Heteropoda venatoria*. The **Wood-Scorpion** (*Hormurus australasiae*) is really far more abundant, but must be sought in jungle under loose bark on dead and fallen trees. It is black and much flattened so that it can creep into the narrowest crevices. *Heterometrus longimanus* (Fig. 142) is a most impressive creature, nearly six inches in length, excluding the claws, and very dark green, almost black, in colour. Like other scorpions it shuns the light of day, but is occasionally encountered walking about at night; it can usually be found by rolling over dead logs and tree-trunks in and near jungle. The very slender reddish brown *Lychas scutatus* is not rare, but the scorpions of the genus

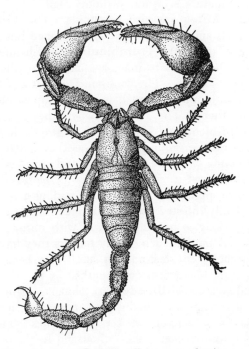

Fig. 142.   Large Scorpion, *Heterometrus longimanus*.

Chaerilus, which have a number of longitudinal ridges on the hands, are rather uncommon. Young scorpions are born alive, and in their early stages the mother carries them about clinging to her back and limbs, appearing at first sight to be infested by some kind of parasite. All scorpions carry a sting at the end of the tail; the sting is quite severe, but is not dangerous in any of the Malayan species, so far as is known.

There are a few harmless arachnids which can be mistaken for scorpions. *Thelyphonus linganus*, one of the **Whip-Scorpions,** is quite common under logs and behind loose bark. Its claws are much shorter than a scorpion's and its tail is slender and bears no sting. When disturbed it emits a liquid with a strong acrid smell. The tiny **Pseudoscorpions** may be mistaken for young scorpions, by people observant enough to notice them at all; they are seldom more than a quarter of an inch long and look just like a miniature scorpion without a tail.

Ticks and **Mites** are also arachnids. The **Mites** are all minute animals and would be left unmentioned but for the fact that certain of them, the **Trombiculids,** which infest rats and will transfer themselves to man, are carriers of the dangerous disease, Scrub Typhus. The common **Dog-Tick** (*Rhipicephalus sanguineus*) is ubiquitous, and it is almost impossible to keep a dog free of them. The females, when they are completely engorged with blood and look like small grapes, leave the host and lay eggs on the ground; as soon as they hatch the minute and active young climb on to herbage and gain access to dogs which brush against it. They moult twice before reaching the adult stage, dropping off the dog and finding a new one each time. If a badly infested dog spends much of its time indoors the house is likely to become overrun with minute and partly grown ticks. Although such greedy feeders they have an extraordinary capacity for fasting; an adult has been kept alive without food for about nineteen months.

Centipedes amd **Millipedes** are elongate arthropods with conspicuously segmented bodies and numerous legs, and are usually classified together as the Myriopoda. Their names, signifying "hundred-feet" and "thousand-feet", overstate the case; few centipedes possess a hundred legs and no millipede has as many as a thousand.

The Malayan representatives of both groups are numerous and rather inadequately known. A collection of centipedes sent from the Raffles Museum to a specialist for study in 1936 was found to contain twenty-seven species of which twenty-two belonged to previously unknown forms and required to be named. At the time of writing no comprehensive study has been made of Malayan millipedes, but, having collected both, I should say that there are more species of them than of centipedes. The two groups may be distinguished as follows:

Centipedes (*Chilopoda*)	Millipedes (*Diplopoda*)
Can inflict a poisonous bite and are predatory.	No poisonous bite, vegetarian.
Active animals that usually defend themselves vigorously if molested.	Slow-moving animals usually curling up into a spiral or ball when touched.
Each segment carries only one pair of legs, with their bases far apart (Fig. 145).	Most of the segments carry two pairs of legs, their bases close together in the middle line (Fig. 146).

The large species of *Scolopendra* (Fig. 143) are the most conspicuous **centipedes** that we have, and may reach nine or ten inches in length. They are reddish brown and have twenty-one pairs of walking legs, the last pair the longest. Attached to the first body segment and folded under the head is a pair of claws, really modified legs, which are hollow and can inflict a severe poisoned bite (Fig 144). These big centipedes have great vitality and tenacity of life and are rather horrifying animals. A redeeming feature of them is their courage in defence of their eggs and young, which are guarded for some time until they are big enough to look after themselves. A very slender centipede, two or three inches long, is sometimes encountered in houses; if touched it emits a brightly luminous liquid. This is a member of the order Geophilomorpha, and need not be feared as its poison claws are too small to pierce the human skin.

Perhaps the most remarkable of the centipedes are the long-legged ones belonging to the family **Scutigeridae,** whose appearance is so peculiar that most people do not recognise them as centipedes. The body is much shorter and stouter than in the normal forms, and is quite stiff instead of being sinuous. There are fifteen pairs of legs, which are greatly elongated, and the antennae and hindmost pair of legs are filamentous and twice or three times as long as the body. They may be found under loose bark on dead trees and sometimes come into houses. A large species is very common in dark caves in limestone hills, such as the Batu Caves near Kuala Lumpur. There they can be seen, with the aid of lamps, running about with astonishing swiftness;

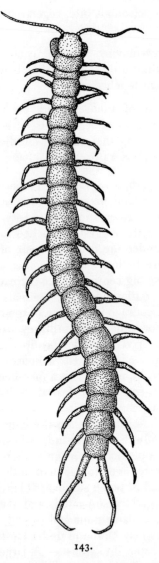

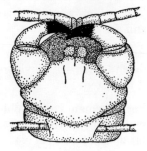

144.

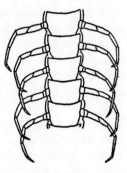

145.

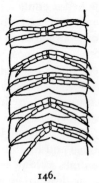

143.

146.

Figs. 143 to 146. Centipedes and Millipedes: 143. Centipede, *Scolopendra subspinipes*; 144. Underside of its head, enlarged to show the poison claws; 145 and 146. Diagrams to show the arrangement of the legs, from below, of (145) Centipede and (146) Millipede.

they feed on the swarming insect life that subsists on the bat-guano which covers the floor of the caves.

The commonest and most familiar **millipedes** belong to the order Iuloidea. They are elongate and cylindrical in shape, and the legs are short and not visible when the animal is looked at directly from above. One of these, a bright reddish brown millipede, one to two inches long, called *Trigoniulus lumbricinus*, is very common in gardens. Some Iuloids reach ten inches or so in length; a good example of these is *Thyropygus aterrimus*, which is polished black with the legs ringed with black and white, and is found in the mountains. Other giant millipedes, some black, others brown in colour, are found commonly in jungle at all altitudes.

The **Flat Millipedes** of the order Polydesmoidea are less familiar, but are very common in Malaya; some are quite large, reaching four inches in length. They have a pair of projecting plates on each segment and look, perhaps, a little like centipedes, but both their behaviour and anatomy are typically those of a millipede. The curious **Pill-Millipedes** (*Oniscomorpha*) are short and stout and look rather like beetles (but no beetle has more than three pairs of legs); when molested they roll them-selves into a hard, almost perfectly spherical ball. The larger ones are between one and two inches long and some are hand-somely coloured.

All millipedes are vegetable feeders, and their only means of defence is to emit an irritant liquid from pores opening along the sides of the body. I have often handled the giant Iuloids and can confirm that this liquid has no effect on the skin of the fingers. A case is recorded, however, of an over-zealous naturalist who put a live one into his hip pocket, and suffered injury to the skin underneath as a result.

The **Crustacea** are predominantly a marine group, but a few are found on the land and in fresh waters. The true **Land Crabs** (*Gecarcinidae*) are large crabs which inhabit jungle near the coast and on small islands. Although they live entirely on land, their early stages are passed in the sea. Another group, the **River Crabs** (*Potamonidae*) live and breed in fresh waters. A number of species inhabit hill-streams, where they can easily be found by turning over stones. Female crabs always carry their eggs outside the body, under the flap-like abdomen, for some time until they hatch. Those of marine crabs are very numerous and minute and hatch into tiny, free-swimming larvae, which are carried about by ocean currents thus securing dispersion of the species. The eggs of the river crabs are fewer and larger, and the young do not hatch until they have developed into little crabs, which even then remain for some time, clinging to the feather-like abdominal appendages of their mother. This is clearly an adaptation to their mode of life, for if the young started life as little free-swimming larvae they would be in danger of being carried down-stream into the river, and eventually to the sea, where they would perish. The familiar little **Woodlice** or **Slaters,** which are seen whenever a piece of loose bark is pulled off a dead tree, and which roll into a ball when disturbed, are also crustaceans. They are abundant in temperate as well as tropical regions, and are of interest as being the only crustaceans which are adapted for life on dry land at all stages of their existence. In appearance they are similar to the pill-millipedes, but the woodlice are usually smaller, more abundant, and have only one pair of legs to each body segment.

Before leaving the arthropods mention must be made of *Peripatus.* This is a genus of animals of wide distribution in the world, represented by a rather small number of species, most of which are rare. They are exceedingly primitive animals which have survived from remote times; their particular interest to zoologists arises from the fact that they appear to be an evolutionary link between the Annelid worms and the arthropods, and so to provide a clue to the origin of the latter. One species, *P. (Eoperipatus) sumatrensis* occurs in Malaya and is found in decaying wood in damp jungle. It is far from common and more have been found in south Johore than elsewhere. It is a caterpillar-like creature, one or two inches long, with twenty-three pairs of legs and a pair of short tentacles on the head. Its skin has a curious velvety texture and is coloured a warm dark red. It feeds on small insects and lives well in captivity if supplied with fairly frequent changes of damp rotten wood.

Although they do not approach the marine forms in diversity, the **land molluscs** of Malaya are of great interest. Two groups of Gastropods or snails are represented, the Pulmonates or lung-snails and the Cyclophorids or land operculates. Both are air breathers and the most obvious feature separating them is the possession by all the Cyclophorids of an operculum or plug with which the shell can be closed to resist drought or the intrusion of an enemy.

The most familiar of our land snails is not a Malayan species at all but an alien, introduced by a series of stages across the Indian Ocean from Africa during the last century and the early part of the present one. This is, of course, *Achatina fulica*, a pulmonate, familiarly known as the **Giant Snail.** Its large mottled brown shell is too well known to need any description, and its reputation as a garden and agricultural pest also needs no elaboration. Like the rabbit in Australia and the Colorado Beetle in Europe it is a resounding example of the danger of introducing, deliberately or accidentally, members of the fauna of one region into the territories of another.

Of the native pulmonates one of the commonest is *Hemiplecta striata*, a small pinkish brown snail often found in gardens. Some of the other species of this genus are large, handsome snails, and *H. humphreysiana*, a common lowland jungle species, is figured (Fig. 148). Finest of them all is *H. (Platymma) tweediei*, whose flattened, coal-black shell reaches nearly three inches in diameter and whose body is coloured black and brick-red. This is a mountain species and most of the recorded specimens are from Cameron Highlands. Another common pulmonate genus is *Amphidromus*, the yellow *A. perakensis* (Fig. 149), being representative. In almost all snails, if you hold the shell with the spire upward and the opening towards you, the opening will be on the right-hand side, and the shell is said to have a right-handed or dextral twist. A few species have normally a left-handed or sinistral twist to the shell, and very rarely sinistral variations of normally dextral species are found. The species of *Amphidromus* are exceptional in having as many sinistral as dextral individuals, so that any collection of half-a-dozen is like to include both. *Phaedusa* is another fairly common pulmonate genus, of which the shells are very long and attenuated; that of *P. filicostata* is illustrated at Fig. 151.

Of the Operculates or Cyclophoridae *Cyclophorus perdix* (Fig. 147), is a good example. The shell is between one and two inches in diameter, flattened, but with a small pointed spire, and with the opening thickened and turned outwards; it is found in lowland jungle. In *Rhiostoma* and *Alyeacus* there is usually a little tube which connects the inside of the shell

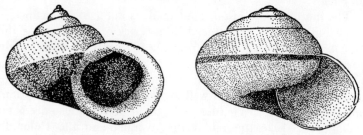

147.   148.

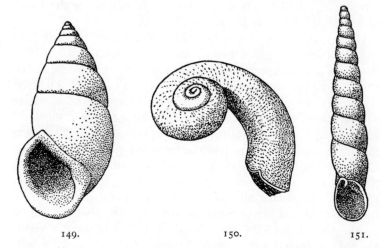

149.   150.   151.

Figs. 147 to 151.   Land Shells: 147. *Cyclophorus perdix*; 148. *Hemiplecta humphreysiana*; 149. *Amphidromus perakensis* (sinistral specimen); 150. *Rhiostoma chupingense*; 151. *Phaedusa filicostata*.

with the exterior, so that the animal can breathe when the operculum is closing it. A remarkable species of *Rhiostoma*, *R. chupingense* from Perlis, is illustrated at Fig. 150.

Both these genera, in fact most of our Cyclophorid molluscs, are almost confined to the precipitous limestone hills that form such conspicuous landmarks in central and northern Malaya, for example at Batu Caves near Kuala Lumpur and around Ipoh. Most Malayan soils are rather deficient in calcium carbonate or "chalk", and as snails have a very urgent need of this substance to make their shells of, it is no wonder that our richest land molluscan faunas are to be found on these hills, which are virtually composed of it. Snails are so abundant on these hills that their empty shells can always be found in plenty in the debris that collects at the base of the cliffs. If this is examined carefully it will be found to contain, as well as a variety of shells large enough to be readily visible, numerous tiny shells, many an eighth of an inch long or less, and beautifully twisted and sculptured (Figs 152-154). They are not young snails but adults of minute species, and some very interesting observations have been made concerning the distribution of some of them.

The more southern of the Malayan limestone hills, such as the Batu Caves hill and those in Pahang, are very isolated from each other. Every one of these hills supports a rich fauna of shelled molluscs which belong to genera never found away from limestone. As they cannot breed or grow in the country between the hills, and as their powers of locomotion are obviously inadequate to carry them across the many miles that often separate them, each community of snails on such a hill comes to occupy an island of limestone in an impassable "sea" of relatively chalk-less country.

When the land fauna of an oceanic island is examined it is always found to include animals that are endemic to the island, that is to say they occur there and nowhere else, having evolved in isolation. In just the same way every one of the isolated limestone hills in Malaya has species of snails that are endemic to it, but here the principle applies only to a section of the fauna which is dependent on limestone for its existence, not, as on a real island, to the whole of it. There is no differentiation from one hill to another among animals which can live indifferently on the hills and in the intervening country, nor is this to be expected.

The peculiarly shaped shell illustrated at Fig. 152 is almost certainly entirely confined to a hill in Pahang, Bukit Chintamani, about the size of a modern block of flats, and found nowhere else on the earth, and there are numerous cases similar to this. On the other hand some of these little snails, in spite of being (so far as we know) confined to limestone, have a wide distribution, and are found on such hills all over north and central Malaya; such are the two illustrated at Figs. 153 and 154.

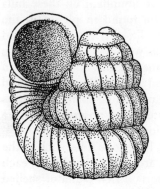

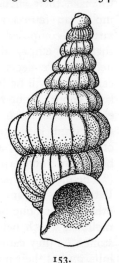

152.   153.

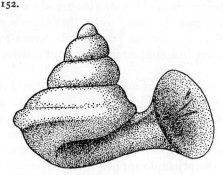

154.

Figs. 152 to 154.   Land Shells from the limestone hills, minute species greatly enlarged: 152. *Opisthostoma retrovertens*; 153. *Diplommatina canaliculata*; 154. *Gyliotrachela hungerfordiana.*

Why some species have a wide, others a restricted, distribution, is at present a complete mystery.

To find these little snails alive requires patient searching among dead leaves and on rock surfaces sheltered from the sun and wet with seeping water. Good collections of the empty shells can be made by gathering debris from the base of the cliffs, drying it and throwing it into a bucket of water. Stir it well so that as much as possible sinks, and then skim off the floating scum of vegetable fragments and shells, each of which is kept afloat by a trapped bubble of air. Dry this and pick out the shells with the help of a magnifying glass.

The only remaining invertebrate animals that claim our attention are some of the **worms. Earthworms** are abundant, but their identification and study is a matter for specialists, as it involves dissecting the animal and examining the disposition of the internal organs in relation to the numerous body segments. *Pheretima* is our commonest genus; quite a number of species are known from Malaya and doubtless many more await discovery.

Leeches are predatory blood-sucking worms, and the land leeches belonging to the genus *Haemadipsa* constitute perhaps the most unpleasant hazard of the Oriental rain-forest type of jungle. Everyone who has been in the jungle in Malaya is familiar with their appearance: elongate, active, dark-coloured creatures having an adhesive sucker at each end of the body, by means of which they progress by rapid looping movements. The body is very extensible and can be contracted to a blob or stretched until it appears like a piece of bootlace, but is so remarkably tough that pinching between the fingers is quite inadequate to injure the creature. Their fierce appetite for mammalian blood, and their energy and tenacity of purpose in obtaining it are quite horrifying. They are able to detect a victim's approach and will hurry to intercept him; on what senses they rely for this is not definitely known, but it seems likely that they are sensitive to the vibration of footfalls, and an acute sense of smell may also play a part in guiding them.

The bite is inflicted by a trifid (three-branched) set of jaws armed with minute, sharp teeth and situated in the anterior sucker. A quantity of saliva is injected into the wound to prevent coagulation of the blood, and it is this (just as in the case of the mosquito) which causes the irritation that usually follows a leech bite. The bite of the **Common Land Leech** (*Haemadipsa zeylanica*) is generally quite painless at the time of infliction, but that of certain other species, such as the brightly coloured

Haemadipsa picta, is accompanied by quite severe stinging pain. Although leeches have remarkable powers of penetration, there is no doubt that the protection of suitable clothing is to a large extent effective in keeping them off; drill trousers tucked into the tops of high canvas boots, laced as tightly as comfort permits, is the best combination. The mesh of worsted socks or stockings offers no barrier at all to leeches, and shorts are a positive invitation to them. Although the legs are most frequently attacked, leeches will climb all over one's person, and when walking through jungle periodic halts and leech inspections are advisable. Chemical deterrents such as soap or weak carbolic acid applied to the clothing are useful, but tend to become diluted and ineffective if streams and rivers are crossed by wading. Leech bites usually start irritating some time after their infliction and continue so for several days. It is difficult to refrain from scratching them and they are very liable to become infected, and may result in serious ulcers. Disinfection of bites with iodine should be a daily routine when working in jungle.

The much larger **Buffalo Leeches** (*Hirudinaria*) live in water and are particularly abundant in swamps and rice-fields frequented by water buffaloes. They are sensitive to movements in the water and will swim rapidly towards anyone wading, with a vertical undulating action. Their bite is severe and can usually be felt at the moment of infliction. They will also climb into a boat floating in such places. Workers in rice-fields are often bitten by them, and I have been attacked when wading in search of small fish for my aquarium.

The **Land Planarian Worms** or Turbellaria are not very common, but always excite interest when they are seen because of their peculiar appearance. They are flattened, ribbon-like worms, sometimes several inches long, shiny, owing to a coat of slime, and often brightly coloured and marked with transverse and longitudinal bands. The striking appearance of some is enhanced by a large crescent-shaped head. They are found in damp places and crawl actively with a characteristic rippling movement.

GLOSSARY

ADHESIVE. Having the power of clinging or sticking.

AMPHIBIA. A group of vertebrate animals, including frogs and toads, which pass the earlier part of their lives in water and the later part, when they are adult, on land.

AMPHIBIOUS. Living partly in the water, partly on land.

ANAL FIN. The central, unpaired fin of a fish situated below and in front of the tail.

ANTENNAE. The feelers on the head of an insect.

ANTERIOR. Towards the front.

AQUATIC. Living in water.

ARACHNID. A member of a group of arthropods, including spiders, scorpions, ticks and the marine king-crabs.

ARBOREAL. Living in trees.

ARTHROPOD. A member of the phylum Arthropoda, animals with jointed limbs and often a hard external skeleton; insects, crustaceans, spiders, centipedes, etc.

CALCAREOUS. Consisting of calcium carbonate or chalk.

CARAPACE. The shell which covers the back of crabs and similar animals.

COCOON. A protective case enclosing the pupa of an insect.

CONCENTRIC. Running one inside the other like circles drawn with the same centre.

CONVERGENT EVOLUTION. When two unrelated or remotely related groups or species of animals closely resemble each other because their mode of life is similar, they are said to have arrived at this similarity by convergent evolution.

CRUSTACEAN. A member of the arthropod class Crustacea, lobsters, prawns, crabs, etc.

DIGIT. Finger or toe of a vertebrate animal.

DORSAL. Relating to the back or upper surface.

ENTOMOLOGY. The scientific study of insects.

ENVIRONMENT. The surroundings and conditions in which an animal lives.

EXOTIC. Used of animals living in a country which is not their native one; not indigenous.

FAMILY. In classification a group of similar genera. See remarks on classification in the introduction.

FAUNA. The animals inhabiting a region, considered as a whole.

FILAMENT. A very fine thread.

GASTROPOD. A member of a group of molluscs, including snails and slugs.

GENERA. Plural of genus.

GENUS. A group of similar species, the plural is genera. See remarks on classification in the introduction.

GEOLOGY. The scientific study of the earth's history.

GRANULAR. Like grains and forming a rough surface.

HABITAT. The type of surroundings in which an animal lives.

HERBIVOROUS. Feeding on plants.

ICHTHYOLOGY. The scientific study of fishes.

IMAGO. The final or adult stage in the life history of an insect.

INDIGENOUS. Native to the country it inhabits.

INSECTIVOROUS. Eating insects.

INVERTEBRATE. A term comprising all animals without a backbone.

IRIDESCENT. Coloured like the rainbow.

LARVA. The first stages, after hatching from the egg, of an animal which starts life in a form completely different from that of its parents. The plural is larvae.

LATERAL. Relating to the sides.

LITTORAL. Living on the sea shore between tide marks.

LOBULAR. Consisting of rounded fleshy projections or lobes.

LONGITUDINAL. Running lengthways.

METAMORPHOSIS. The changes that take place in the life history of an animal that passes through several distinct stages in its growth, e.g. the majority of insects.

MIGRATE. To perform regular seasonal journeys from one part of the world to another, breeding in one of them. Many birds have this habit and are called migratory or migrant.

MOLLUSC. A member of the phylum Mollusca, snails, oysters, mussels, etc.

NOCTURNAL. Awake and active during the night.

NYMPH. In entomology any of the early stages of an insect which does not pass through distinct larva and pupa stages.

OPERCULUM. A plug or stopper.

ORDER. In classification a group of similar families. See remarks on classification in the introduction.

ORGANIC MATTER. Matter which is living or which is derived from the substance of living creatures.

PECTORAL FINS. The pair of fins of a fish which represent the fore limbs in the higher vertebrates.

PHYLUM. A major division of the animal kingdom, the plural is phyla. See remarks on classification in the introduction.

PLANKTON. Small and minute animal and plant life floating freely in the sea.

POSTERIOR. Towards the back.

PREDATOR. An animal which captures, kills and eats other animals.

PRIMITIVE. Displaying characters which are ancestral and so provide clues to evolutionary history.

PROBOSCIS. An elongation of the snout; any trunk-like organ.

PUPA. The third stage in the life history of insects which pass through the four stages: egg, larva, pupa, imago. The plural is pupae.

PUPATE. To turn into a pupa.

RADIAL. Running out from a point like the spokes of a wheel.

SEDIMENT. Mud or other finely divided matter which accumulates by sinking in still water.

SEGMENTED. Consisting of a number of similar regions or pieces joined to each other in a series as pipes are joined to make a drain.

SERRATED. Toothed like the edge of a saw.

SPECIES. A single kind or sort of animal or plant. The word is the same in singular and plural. See remarks on classification in the introduction.

SPECIMEN. An individual considered as representative of its kind.

STRATA (plural of stratum). Geological term for rocks deposited in layers, usually by the agency of water.

THORAX. In insects that part of the body just behind the head, to which the legs and wings are attached.

TRANSVERSE. Running crossways.

UNGULATE. A mammal whose feet have the form of hoofs.

VENTRAL FINS. The pair of fins of a fish which represent the hind limbs in the higher vertebrates.

VERTEBRATE. An animal possessing a backbone. The vertebrates comprise the fish, amphibians, reptiles, birds and mammals, and are classified as a subphylum of the phylum Chordata.

VESTIGE, VESTIGIAL. Used to describe organs or characters which, in the course of evolutionary change, have become small and without function as a result of disuse.

ZOOLOGY. The scientific study of animals.

MALAY NAMES

The list that follows is intended as a guide to enable readers to correlate Malay and English names of animals which are mentioned in the book and only the more commonly used Malay names are included. These are in alphabetical order; an English or scientific name can be referred to its Malay counterpart by looking it up in the general index, where its serial number in the list is given.

1. Agas. Biting midge.
2. Alu-alu, Ikan. Barracuda.
3. Ampai-ampai. Jellyfish.
4. Anai-anai. Termite.
5. Anjing. Any kind of dog.
6. Anjing hutan. Wild dog.
7. Angkut-angkut. Kinds of solitary wasp that make a mud nest.
8. Aruan, Ikan. A Snake-head, *Channa striata*.
9. Ayam. Fowl.
10. Ayam děnak. Jungle fowl.
11. Ayam hutan. Jungle fowl.
12. Ayam pěgar. Fire-backed Pheasant.
13. Babi. Pig.
14. Babi hutan. Wild Pig.
15. Babi janggut, Babi nangui. Bearded Pig.
16. Badak. Rhinoceros or Tapir.
17. Badak běrěndam, Badak kerbau. Two-horned Rhinoceros.
18. Badak murai. Tapir.
19. Badak raya, Badak sumbu. One-horned Rhinoceros.
20. Bagoh, Ikan. A carp, *Puntius lateristriga*.
21. Balam, Burong. Spotted-necked Dove.
22. Bambun. Mongoose.
23. Bangau, Burong. Egret.

24. Barat-barat, Ikan. Leatherjacket, genus *Monacanthus*.
25. Baung, Ikan. A fresh-water catfish, genus *Mystus*.
26. Bawal, Ikan. Pomfret.
27. Bayan, Burong. Long-tailed Parakeet.
28. Běberek. Bee-eater.
29. Bělalang. Grasshopper, Cricket, Mantis or similar insect.
30. Bělalang kachong. Praying Mantis.
31. Bělalang patong. Dragon-fly.
32. Bělalang, Ikan. Flying Fish.
33. Bělanak, Ikan. Grey Mullet.
34. Bělangkas. King-crab.
35. Bělatok. Woodpecker.
36. Belibis. Lesser Whistling Duck.
37. Bělida, Ikan. Featherback.
38. Bělontok, Ikan. A fresh-water goby, *Oxyeleotris marmorata.*
39. Bělut, Ikan. Swamp-eel.
40. Běngkarong. Skink.
41. Běngkunang. Larger Mouse-deer.
42. Běnturong. Binturong or Bear-civet.
43. Běrang-běrang. Otter.
44. Berek-Berek. Bee-eater.
45. Běrkek. Snipe.
46. Běrok. Pig-tailed Macaque.
47. Běronok. An edible sea slug or Holothurian.
48. Běruang. Bear.
49. Bětok, Ikan. Climbing Perch.
50. Bewak; Biawak. Monitor Lizard.
51. Biawak pasir. Granular-scaled Lizard, *Liolepis*.
52. Bilis, Ikan. Anchovy, genus *Stolephorus*.
53. Buaya. Crocodile.
54. Buaya jolong-jolong. Malayan Gharial, *Tomistoma*.
55. Buntal, Ikan. Globe-fish, Puffer.
56. Buntal pisang, Ikan. Silvery Puffer.
57. Burong. Bird.
58. Butbut. Coucal.
59. Chaching. Earthworm.
60. Chak padang. Richard's Pipit.
61. Chak padi. Munia.

62. Chamar, Burong. Tern.
63. Chawi-chawi. Drongo.
64. Chĕgar, Burong. Forktail.
65. Chĕketing, Burong. Red-wattled Lapwing.
66. Chĕncharu, Ikan. A Horse-mackerel, *Megalaspis cordyla*.
67. Chĕnchurut. Musk Shrew.
68. Chĕnĕkah, Chengkok, Chigak. Leaf Monkey.
69. Chĕngkadak. Praying Mantis.
70. Chĕngkiak. *See* Kiak-kiak.
71. Chenok, Burong. Malkoha.
72. Chĕriwit. Red-wattled Lapwing.
73. Chichak. House Gecko.
74. Chichak tĕrbang. Flying Lizard.
75. Chipan. Tapir.
76. Daun, Burong. Leaf Bird.
77. Daun, Ikan. A carp, genus *Acrossochilus*.
78. Dĕkan. Bamboo Rat.
79. Dĕlah, Ikan. Sea Bream, genus *Caesio*.
80. Dĕndang. Crow.
81. Dĕndang laut. Brown Booby.
82. Duri, Ikan. Catfish of the genus *Arius*.
83. Duyong. Dugong.
84. Ĕmas Burong. Mountain Minivet.
85. Ĕnggang. Rhinoceros Hornbill, and other large horn bills.
86. Gagak. Crow.
87. Gajah. Elephant.
88. Gajah, Burong. Whimbrel.
89. Gamat. Sea Slug, Holothurian.
90. Gĕlam, Burong. Bittern.
91. Gembala kerbau, Burong. Jungle Myna.
92. Gĕronggong. Stinging jellyfish.
93. Gonggok. Millipede.
94. Hamba kĕra, Burong. Racquet-tailed Drongo.
95. Hantu, Burong. Owls (large kinds).
96. Harimau, *see* Rimau.
97. Hĕring, Burong. Vulture.
98. Ikan. Fish.
99. Jampok, Burong. Collared Scops Owl.

P

100. Janek. Sea Urchin, *Echinothrix*.
101. Jĕbong, Ikan. Trigger-fish, genus *Balistes*.
102. Jĕlatek. Java Sparrow.
103. Jĕlu masak pisang. Weasel.
104. Jintek-jintek. Larva of mosquito.
105. Jolong-jolong, Ikan. Halfbeak.
106. Halipan, *see* Lipan.
107. Kaki dian, Burong. Redshank.
108. Kala. Scorpion.
109. Kala bangkang. Large scorpion, *Heterometrus*.
110. Kala jĕngking. House Scorpion, *Isometrus*.
111. Kalui, Ikan. Goramy.
112. Kambing gurun, Kambing hutan. Serow.
113. Kanchil. Lesser Mouse-deer.
114. Karang. Coral.
115. Katak. Frog, toad.
116. Katak pisang. Green-backed Frog, *Rana erythraea*.
117. Katak kuak. Bullfrog, *Kaloula pulchra*.
118. Katak puru. Toad of rough-skinned kind, like *Bufo melanostictus*.
119. Kĕdidi. Sandpipers and small plovers.
120. Kĕdidi padang. Pratincole.
121. Kĕjau, Ikan. A carp, genus *Acrossochilus*.
122. Kĕlah, Ikan. A carp, genus *Tor*.
123. Kĕlawar. The smaller kinds of bats.
124. Kĕlĕsa, Ikan. A fresh-water fish, *Scleropages formosus*.
125. Kĕli, Ikan. Fresh-water catfishes of the genus *Clarias*.
126. Kĕlichap. Sunbirds, Spider-hunters and other small birds.
127. Kĕlichap jantong. Spider-hunter.
128. Kĕlichap kunyet. White-eye.
129. Kĕlengkeng, Burong. Pied Hornbill.
130. Kĕluang. Flying Fox.
131. Kĕlulut. Stingless bees, genus *Trigona*.
132. Kĕmbong, Ikan. A small mackerel, *Scomber kanagurta*.
133. Kendi, Burong. Curlew.
134. Kĕpah. A mollusc, *Meretrix meretrix*.
135. Kĕra. Long-tailed Macaque.
136. Kĕrak, Burong. Malkoha.

137. Kĕrang. A mollusc, *Arca granosa*.
138. Kĕrapu, Ikan. Grouper, various species of *Epinephelus*.
139. Kĕrawai. Night-wasp.
140. Kĕrĕngga. Weaving Ant
141. Kĕring, Ikan. Shrimp-fish.
142. Kĕriyut, Burong. Eastern Golden Plover.
143. Kĕrtang. Very large groupers, *Epinephelus*.
144. Kĕsumba. Trogon.
145. Kĕtam. Crab.
146. Kĕtam renjong. Swimming Crab, genus *Portunus*.
147. Kiak-kiak. Biting termite, *Macrotermes carbonarius*.
148. Kijang. Barking Deer.
149. Kijing. A mollusc, genus *Tellina*.
150. Kima. Giant clam, *Tridacna*.
151. Kitang, Ikan. Butterfish.
152. Kodok. Frog, toad.
153. Kongkang. Slow Loris.
154. Kuang; Kuau. Great Argus Pheasant.
155. Kubin. Flying Lizard.
156. Kubong. Flying Lemur.
157. Kubor, Burong. Long-tailed Nightjar.
158. Kuching. Any kind of cat.
159. Kuching batu. Leopard Cat.
160. Kuching hutan. Any of the smaller wild cats.
161. Kuda laut. Sea-horse.
162. Kumbang. Carpenter Bee; any large beetle.
163. Kunyit, Burong. Black-naped Oriole; Iora.
164. Kupu-kupu. Moth.
165. Kura-kura. Tortoise.
166. Kurau, Ikan. Threadfin.
167. Labah-labah. Spider.
168. Labi-labi. Mud Turtle.
169. Lais, Ikan. A fresh-water catfish, genus *Kryptopterus*.
170. Laki padi, Burong. Warblers and Tailor Birds.
171. Lalat. Fly, especially the House Fly.
172. Lampam, Ikan. A carp, *Puntius schwanefeldi*.
173. Landak; Landak raya. Common Porcupine.
174. Landak batu. Brush-tailed Porcupine and (perhaps) Long-tailed Porcupine.

175. Lang. Birds of prey.
176. Lang bĕlalang. Falconet.
177. Lang berjambul. Crested Serpent Eagle.
178. Lang hindek. Changeable Hawk-Eagle.
179. Lang kuik. Crested Serpent Eagle.
180. Lang laut. White-bellied Sea Eagle.
181. Lang lĕbah. Honey Buzzard.
182. Lang merah. Braminy Kite.
183. Lang sewah. Japanese Sparrow Hawk.
184. Lang siput. White-bellied Sea Eagle.
185. Lang tikus. Black-winged Kite.
186. Lawang, Ikan. A fresh-water catfish, *Pangasius micro-nema*.
187. Layang, Burong. Swifts and swallows.
188. Layang bĕrjambul. Tree Swift.
189. Lĕbah. Bee.
190. Lĕpu, Ikan. Scorpion Fish.
191. Lidah, Ikan. Sole.
192. Lintah. Buffalo Leech, *Hirudinaria*.
193. Lipan. Centipede.
194. Lipas. Cockroach.
195. Lokan. A mollusc, genus *Polymesoda*.
196. Lotong. Leaf Monkey.
197. Lumba-lumba. Dolphin or porpoise.
198. Main angin, Burong. Fan-tailed Warbler.
199. Malas, Burong. Long-tailed Nightjar.
200. Malong, Ikan. Moray Eel.
201. Mata hari, Burong. Paradise Flycatcher and minivets.
202. Mata latat, Ikan. The Whitespot, *Aplocheilus panchax*.
203. Mati anak. Plaintive Cuckoo.
204. Mawas. The Orangutan (which does not occur in Malaya); sometimes used for large Siamang.
205. Mĕmĕrang, *see* bĕrang-bĕrang.
206. Merah, Ikan. Red Snapper.
207. Mĕragi, Burong. Painted Snipe.
208. Mĕrak. Peafowl.
209. Mĕrbah. Most dull coloured bulbuls, babblers and shrikes.
210. Mĕrbok. Zebra Dove.

211. Monyet. Any monkey.
212. Murai. Magpie Robin.
213. Murai batu; Murai hutan. Shama.
214. Murai gila. Fantail Flycatcher.
215. Musang. Any of the civets.
216. Musang bĕlang. Linsang.
217. Musang bulan; Musang pulut. House Musang, and other civets.
218. Musang jĕbat. Malay and Indian Civets.
219. Napoh, Napu. Larger Mouse-deer.
220. Nyamok. Mosquito.
221. Olak-olak, Burong. Brown Booby.
222. Pachat. Land leech, *Haemadipsa.*
223. Pachat, Burong. Pitta.
224. Panglin. Purple Swamphen.
225. Parang-parang, Ikan. Dorab, genus *Chirocentrus.*
226. Pari, Ikan. Ray.
227. Pasir, Ikan. Loach.
228. Patin, Ikan. A fresh-water catfish, genus *Pangasius.*
229. Paus, Ikan. Whale.
230. Pĕkaka. Any of the larger kingfishers.
231. Pĕlaga, Ikan. Fighting Fish.
232. Pĕlandok. Lesser Mouse-deer.
233. Pĕngguling, *see* Tenggiling.
234. Pĕnyĕngat. Wasp, especially small social wasps like *Ropalidia.*
235. Pĕnyu. Green Turtle.
236. Pĕnyu kambau. Leathery Turtle.
237. Pĕnyu sisek. Hawksbill Turtle.
238. Pĕrgam. Green Imperial Pigeon.
239. Pĕrgam bukit. Mountain Imperial Pigeon.
240. Perling, Burong. Philippine Glossy Starling.
241. Pikau. Blue-breasted Quail.
242. Pipit padang. Richard's Pipit.
243. Pipit padi. Munia.
244. Pipit rumah. Tree Sparrow.
245. Pipit, Ikan. Beaked Butterfly-fish, *Chelmo rostratus.*
246. Puchong. Bitterns and herons.
247. Puchong bakau. Little Green Heron.

248. Puchong batu.   Reef Egret.
249. Pulasan.   Marten, weasel.
250. Punai.   Pink-necked Green Pigeon.
251. Punggok.   Hawk Owl.
252. Puput, Ikan.   Halfbeak.
253. Puting běliong.   Fan Shell, *Pinna*.
254. Puyoh.   Common Button Quail.
255. Puyu, Ikan.   Climbing Perch.
256. Raja udang.   Kingfisher, especially the White-collared
        Kingfisher.
257. Rajawali, Burong.   Falconet.
258. Rama-rama.   Butterfly.
259. Rawa, Burong.   Pied Imperial Pigeon.
260. Reng, Burong.   Vulture.
261. Riang-riang.   Cicada.
262. Rimau.   Tiger.
263. Rimau akar.   Clouded Leopard, or any large cat.
264. Rimau bintang.   Panther, spotted form.
265. Rimau dahan.   Clouded Leopard.
266. Rimau kumbang.   Panther, black form.
267. Ruak-ruak.   White-breasted Water Hen.
268. Rusa.   Sambar.
269. Sa-bělah, Ikan.   Flatfish.
270. Sanok, Burong.   Malkoha.
271. Sěbarau, Ikan.   A carp, *Hampala macrolepidota*.
272. Sěladang.   Wild cattle, Gaur.
273. Sělar, Ikan.   Small horse-mackerel, genus *Caranx*.
274. Sělayer, Ikan.   Sail Fish.
275. Sěmbilang, Ikan.   Catfish of the genus *Plotosus*.
276. Sěmut.   Ant.
277. Sěmut api.   Fire Ant.
278. Sěmut těměnggong.   Giant Ant, *Camponotus*.
279. Sěnangin, Ikan.   Threadfin.
280. Sěněka *see* Chěněkah.
281. Sěpah putěri.   Flower Pecker.
282. Sěpat, Ikan.   A fresh-water fish, genus *Trichogaster*.
283. Sěrigala.   Wild Dog.
284. Siamang.   Siamang, the large gibbon.
285. Simbang.   Frigate Bird.

286. Sintar, Burong.   Rail.
287. Siput.   Snail.
288. Siput bĕlitong.   A mollusc, *Cerithidea obtusa.*
289. Siput bulan.   A mollusc, *Natica mamilla.*
290. Siput butang.   Cowrie.
291. Siput gewang.   A mollusc, genus *Turbo.*
292. Siput lolak.   Top shell, genus *Trochus.*
293. Siput ranga.   Scorpion shell, genus *Lambis.*
294. Siput rangkek.   Cone shell.
295. Siput timba.   A mollusc, genus *Nerita.*
296. Sumpah-sumpah.   Green Crested Lizard, *Calotes.*
297. Takau, Burong.   Barbet.
298. Talang-talang, Ikan.   A large horse-mackerel, *Chorinemus.*
299. Tamban, Ikan.   Sardine, *Harengula.*
300. Tapah, Ikan.   A large fresh-water catfish, genus *Wallago.*
301. Tapak sulaiman.   Starfish.
302. Tĕbuan.   Hornet.
303. Tekukor.   Spotted-necked Dove.
304. Tĕkukor api.   Cuckoo Dove.
305. Tĕmbakul, Ikan.   Mud-skipper.
306. Tĕmĕlian, Ikan.   A large carp, *Probarbus jullieni.*
307. Tempua, Burong.   Baya Weaver.
308. Tĕngas, Ikan.   A carp, genus *Acrossocheilus.*
309. Tĕnggalong.   Malay Civet, Tangalung.
310. Tĕnggiling.   Pangolin, Scaly Anteater.
311. Tĕnggiri, Ikan.   Spanish Mackerel.
312. Tenggulong.   Pill-millipede.
313. Tĕnok.   Tapir.
314. Tĕritip.   Barnacle; encrusting type of oyster.
315. Tĕrubok, Ikan.   Shad.
316. Tĕtirok.   Snipe.
317. Tikus.   Any rat, mouse or shrew.
318. Tikus bulan.   Moon Rat.
319. Tikus kĕsturi.   Musk Shrew.
320. Tilan, Ikan.   Spiny Eel, genus *Mastocembelus.*
321. Tiong.   Hill Myna.
322. Todak, Ikan.   Garfish.
323. Tokak, Ikan.   Wrasse or Parrot Fish.
324. Tokek.   Tokay, *Gekko gecko.*

325. Toman, Ikan. A Snake-head, *Channa micropeltes*.
326. Tongkol, Ikan. Tunny.
327. Tukang, Burong. Long-tailed Nightjar; Coppersmith Barbet.
328. Tumbok ketampi. Malay Fish Owl.
329. Tuntong. River tortoise, *Batagur baska*.
330. Tupai. Squirrel or tree-shrew.
331. Tupai kĕrawak. Giant squirrel.
332. Tupai tanah. Tree-shrew or ground squirrel.
333. Tupai tĕrbang. Flying squirrel.
334. Udang. Prawn.
335. Ular. Snake.
336. Ular chinchin ĕmas. Yellow-ringed Cat-snake.
337. Ular kapak. Viper.
338. Ular katam tĕbu. Krait, the banded species, *Bungarus fasciatus* and *B. candidus*.
339. Ular matahari. Coral snake.
340. Ular sawa. Python.
341. Ular sĕlimpat; Ular laut. Sea snake.
342. Ular tĕdong. Cobra.
343. Ular tĕdong abu; Ular tĕdong sĕlar. Hamadryad.
344. Ulat. Any kind of worm or caterpillar.
345. Ungka. Gibbon.
346. Wak-wak. White-handed Gibbon.
347. Yu, Ikan. Shark; dogfish.
348. Yu gĕrgaji, Ikan. Sawfish.

INDEX

Numbers in roman type refer to pages and text figures; those in italic to the serial numeration of the list of Malay names on pp. 213–22.